The
Waking Dream

To my Mother

The
Waking Dream

A Study of Coleridge's Poetry

PATRICIA M. ADAIR

BARNES & NOBLE, INC.
NEW YORK
PUBLISHERS & BOOKSELLERS SINCE 1873

© PATRICIA M. ADAIR

First published 1967

First published in
United States of America 1968

PRINTED IN GREAT BRITAIN
BY BUTLER & TANNER LTD, FROME AND LONDON

Preface

Though much critical scholarship has been devoted to *The Ancient Mariner*, *Kubla Khan* and *Christabel*, Coleridge's poetry has not yet been studied as a whole. This book has been written in the growing conviction that the minor poems, however bad in themselves, often throw unexpected light upon the great poems. It is possible also to see a general line of development, even though the canon of Coleridge's poetry has yet to be finally settled.

The editing of the complete edition of Coleridge's works is now far advanced and it would, no doubt, have been ideal to wait for the completion of this scholarship before attempting a full study of the poetry. This is especially true of Miss Coburn's edition of the notebooks which illuminate the poems in so many ways. But this immense task cannot be finished for a number of years and Miss Coburn has now reached 1808, a date by which all Coleridge's best poetry was already written. In a recent article[1] she has also published valuable extracts from the later notebooks which throw light upon the poems of the last years. Though I do not always agree with her critical comments, I am, like all students of Coleridge, deeply indebted to her editing.

I believe that the early notebooks, contemporaneous with his best poetry, bring us closer than anything else to an understanding of Coleridge's creative process. This is because he himself possessed not only great imaginative power but the subtlety of introspection and analysis which enabled him to understand it. His early notebook comments, however random and scattered, are far nearer to the great poetry than the *Biographia Literaria* which, brilliant as it is, was written twenty years after *The Ancient Mariner*. A pattern of imagery and ideas closely parallel to the poems gradually emerges from the notebooks. They thus serve as a corrective to the wilder theories of the symbolist

---

[1] K. Coburn, 'Reflections in a Coleridge Mirror', *From Sensibility to Romanticism*, ed. F. W. Hilles and H. Bloom, New York, OUP, 1965.

critics and the excesses of source hunting by providing a surer and more objective basis for interpretation. Though the purpose of this study is criticism rather than biography, the notebooks also bring us close to the man who wrote them. For many years they were his only refuge in loneliness and unhappiness, and they reveal the deeply personal meaning his poetry had for him.

I believe that Coleridge's unusual proneness to reverie and day-dream, in which the conscious and unconscious powers of the mind are merged, is the secret of his greatest poetry, which the notebooks reveal. As the dream faded into the light of common day the poetry gradually declined. No one understood better than Coleridge himself that the loss of joy meant also the death of his imagination.

To write about Coleridge is also, inevitably, to write about Wordsworth. I have been especially fortunate that Mr John Jones, a distinguished critic of Wordsworth, has read most of this book in manuscript. It is a great pleasure to acknowledge my debt to his always helpful, though unobtrusive, criticism. Though he is not responsible for the faults of the book, they would have been far more numerous without him.

I would also like to thank Miss Anne Elliott, Dr Helen Gardner and Dr Catherine Ing, all Fellows of St Hilda's College, for reading the book in part or for other personal kindness during my time at Oxford.

The staff of the English Faculty Library at Oxford have also been invariably helpful and courteous.

Other intellectual debts of which I am conscious are listed in the bibliography.

Contents

List of Abbreviations and Symbols

BL   = S. T. Coleridge, *Biographia Literaria*, ed. G. Watson, Everyman, 1956.

Griggs i–ii = S. T. Coleridge, *Collected Letters*, ed. E. L. Griggs, Vols. I–II (1785–1806), OUP, 1956.

iii–iv = S. T. Coleridge, *Collected Letters*, ed. E. L. Griggs, Vols. III–IV (1807–19), OUP, 1959.

N 1   = S. T. Coleridge, *Notebooks*, ed. K. Coburn, Vol. I (1794–1804), Routledge & Kegan Paul, 1957 (Text and Notes).

N 2   = S. T. Coleridge, *Notebooks*, ed. K. Coburn, Vol. II (1804–1808), Routledge & Kegan Paul, 1962 (Text and Notes).

PW   = S. T. Coleridge, *Poems* (one vol.) ed. E. H. Coleridge, OUP, 1912.

PW ii   = S. T. Coleridge, *Poetical Works*, Vol. II, ed. E. H. Coleridge, OUP, 1912.

Hanson   = L. Hanson, *The Life of S. T. Coleridge: The Early Years*, Allen & Unwin, 1938.

House   = H. House, *Coleridge*, Hart-Davis, 1953.

Lowes   = J. L. Lowes, *The Road to Xanadu*, New York, Vintage Books, 1959.

Whalley   = G. Whalley, *Coleridge, Sara Hutchinson and the Asra Poems*, Routledge & Kegan Paul, 1955.

Introduction

MANY accounts have been given of Coleridge's school days at Christ's Hospital but Lamb's description of the casual passer through the Cloisters, held entranced by his friend's philosophical discourse, is, probably, the most famous:

... to hear thee unfold, in thy deep and sweet intonations, the mysteries of Iamblichus, or Plotinus (for even in those years thou waxedst not pale at such philosophic draughts), or reciting Homer in his Greek, or Pindar – while the walls of the old Grey Friars re-echoed to the accents of the *inspired charity-boy!*[1]

The power to hold his listener spell-bound seems already to foreshadow the Ancient Mariner. But it is above all the Grecian of Christ's Hospital who lives for us in an even more revealing anecdote which Hanson tells of this remarkable school-boy:

One day, walking along the Strand, Coleridge was enacting one of his day-dreams – in this instance, he was Leander swimming the Hellespont. But the pavement was crowded and the swimmer's outstretched arms caught the pocket of a passer-by. The alarmed boy, when challenged, denied any intention of picking the stranger's pocket and explained his unusual actions with such charm and ability that he not only escaped censure but was actually presented with a free ticket to the circulating library in King Street, Cheapside.[2]

The child was indeed father of the man. Coleridge always possessed this extraordinary charm which unhappiness and ill-health were never entirely to dim. One of the most brilliant minds of his time is also already apparent in the philosopher-schoolboy. But the capacity to

[1] Lamb, 'Christ's Hospital Five and Thirty Years Ago', *The Essays of Elia,* ed. E. V. Lucas, 1912, p. 25.
[2] Hanson, p. 18. Originally recorded in Gillman's *Life of Coleridge.*

become Leander swimming the Hellespont – in the middle of the crowded Strand – is perhaps most characteristic of all. Coleridge was never able to distinguish clearly between the real and the imaginary world and often lived in a day-dream. This was the source of both his weakness and his strength, the imperfections of his life but the greatness of his poetry. He was often to take refuge in unreality to evade the harshness of truth but the vividness of his imaginative life was also to create *The Ancient Mariner* and *Kubla Khan*. We cannot in justice condemn the man and prize the poet; the two were one.

The anecdote is also a foretaste of much later critical activity concerning Coleridge. The boy who was already immersed in Greek mythology, Homer and the Neoplatonists, became a man of immense learning. That ticket to the circulating library in Cheapside was only the first of many, for Coleridge later described himself as a 'library cormorant' who had 'read almost everything'. Scholars who have painstakingly pursued his reading of travel books, science, metaphysics, economics, theology or poetry, have discovered that this was by no means an idle boast. It is rarely safe to assume that there was a book published in his life-time that Coleridge had not read. The hunt to find the sources of his poetry, especially since the publication of *The Road to Xanadu*, has become an all-absorbing and full-time scholarly activity. Yet, though this can be very fruitful and exerts a fascination from which none of us is free, I believe it has been overdone. To establish a source is not necessarily to illuminate the meaning of a poem. All the erudition on vampires and demonology brings us no nearer to the heart of *Christabel*. Too much emphasis upon sources can, I think, even obscure the deeply personal and contemporary meaning his poetry had for Coleridge. The great poems sprang from passionate feeling which transmuted his sources and made them his own. Though memories of the old voyagers' tales, the *Odyssey* and innumerable literary associations are a presence behind *The Ancient Mariner*, this does not explain its power. Coleridge himself speaks through the eternal wanderer who never found rest, either spiritual or intellectual; the poem has the intensity of a personal odyssey. He was also so deeply aware of the conflicts of his day that, perhaps unconsciously, he expressed the troubled spirit of his age. *The Ancient Mariner* became, in some ways, a myth of the modern world. Coleridge himself, when discussing the fascination and obscurity of a poem of Dante, says: 'A good instance, by the bye, of that soul of

2

universal significance in a true poet's composition in addition to the specific meaning'.[1] This could apply equally well to his own poem. Similarly, I have tried to show that the Orphic legends underlie *Kubla Khan*, not because they are evidence of Coleridge's occult erudition, but because through them he was able to suggest the mystery of creative power and the strange depths from which it springs. I feel that Coleridge's sources are only important when they provided him with images to convey a deeply felt truth. The idea and the image become fused which, he said, was the condition of imaginative life.[2] The sources remain base metal until touched to gold by the poetic alchemy.

The schoolboy who imagined himself Leander would also provide a happy hunting-ground for the symbolists. Critics have interpreted *Kubla Khan* only in terms of sexual imagery; the dome is breast-shaped, the caves are the womb and the river a fertility symbol. Coleridge's search for Hero could, no doubt, be an early symptom of erotic tendencies. The attraction of this kind of criticism is that it becomes so easy once you get the knack of it. It has also the merit of simplicity since it reduces most poetry to the expression of basic human urges. Even on a subtler level the symbolist approach has its dangers. The many and varied interpretations tend to conflict violently with one another, partly because they are too rigid and too subjective. The suggestive power of the poetry is lost if we try to pin down the meaning too definitely. Like Proteus, it slips out of our hands if we attempt to hold it. It is also deceptively easy in an age of psychology to hazard an inspired (or not so inspired) guess as to what a poem might mean, but very difficult indeed to check by scholarly methods whether this was, indeed, the meaning it had for Coleridge himself. Only the discipline of searching his life, his letters, the whole body of his poetry and, above all, his notebooks can provide the real clues. Though *The Ancient Mariner*, *Kubla Khan* and *Christabel* have received much attention, Coleridge's poetry has never been studied as a whole. Yet I believe it has a remarkable unity. Both the juvenilia and the poems of his last years, though bad in themselves, throw light upon the themes and imagery of the great poetry. Coleridge himself recognised this poetic wholeness when he told his nephew that he considered ' . . . the chronological order the best for arranging a poet's works', since the interest arose '. . . from watching the progress, maturity, and even the decay of genius'.[3]

[1] N 2, 3014 24.7 (Notes). [2] BL, p. 174. [3] *Table Talk*, OUP, 1917, p. 286.

But the early notebooks, which are closest in time to *The Ancient Mariner* and *Kubla Khan*, are most revealing of all. Whenever he had an audience in mind, even the recipient of a letter, Coleridge tended to become self-conscious or self-pitying and was prone to dramatise his situation. But through many years of loneliness and unhappiness his notebooks became his only companions and were, certainly, never intended for publication. These haphazard jottings, scribbled with whatever came to hand, even his gout-medicine, written from the back of a notebook to the front or even across one another, bring us as near as we can get to the working of a creative mind. They also have a painful honesty which is disarming; Coleridge never deceived himself. As human documents they are, by turns, touching and amusing; an agonised prayer for God's help can be followed by a detailed recipe for an Irish stew! They provide us with invaluable clues to his reading which Lowes was the first to follow, but, above all, they reveal a creative poet at the height of his powers. Coleridge had a very remarkable mind, introspective, analytic, subtle. The union of creative power with the capacity to understand it is very rare, but Coleridge possessed this gift. When an image arose in his mind he could trace the associations of feeling which linked it with other images. Long before the invention of psychology he recognised the power of the unconscious and much of the complex working of the mind. Mentally he was much better equipped than most of his critics and, therefore, his notebook comments, however random and scattered, illuminate his poetry as nothing else can. He rarely referred to his own poems directly, perhaps because they had already expressed what he had to say. Nevertheless, as we read the notebooks with the poetry and letters, a pattern gradually emerges. The imagery of the poems reappears in the notebooks and the same ideas recur. Only when the whole pattern begins to fit together can we approach, even tentatively, the meaning of the poetry or, at least, possess a more objective basis from which to essay an interpretation.

For students of his poetry there is also, I think, some danger in dwelling excessively upon Coleridge's aesthetic theory on which so much ink has been spilt. Even the *Biographia Literaria*, brilliant as it is and difficult to avoid, was written in 1817, twenty years after most of his poetry that mattered. Unhappiness and ill-health had made Coleridge grow old quickly; the feeling from which his great poems sprang was long since dead. His philosophic position had also changed. The famous and much discussed definition of the secondary or poetic imagination in the *Biographia* stresses the power of the 'conscious will' at the expense of Fancy and the law of association.[1] This was, of course, a deliberate repudiation of Hartley and Newton and the theory of passive mind which had once held Coleridge captive. It is vital to his rejection of eighteenth century materialism that he should now see the mind creative in perception as a reflection of the great Creator Himself. I believe there was also a personal reason for the different emphasis. By 1817 the nightmare horrors of opium addiction had given Coleridge every reason to dread the power of the unconscious mind. Yet the *Biographia Literaria* here, to some extent, conflicts with the evidence of the early notebooks which attach much more importance to the role of the unconscious, especially in dreams. Opium and unhappiness had not yet turned the dream to nightmare, and, I believe, the scattered hints on the poetic process in the early notebooks are more valuable than the considered statement of the *Biographia*, because they are so much closer to his great creative period.

One of Coleridge's most vital comments on poetry was made on the voyage to Malta in 1804 when *The Ancient Mariner*, as we shall see, was much in his mind. Haunted, like the Mariner, by guilt and unhappiness, the poet was now himself 'alone on a wide wide sea' and became most strangely identified with his own creation. He was writing in the midst of a dead calm which recalled the poem, as we know from other notes, and, four entries later, he watched the sailors shooting at a bird which was following the ship. As we read, we also seem to hover between dream and reality:

> Poetry a rationalized dream dealing [? about] to manifold Forms our own Feelings, that never perhaps were attached by us consciously to our own personal Selves . . . O there are Truths below the Surface in the subject of Sympathy, & how we *become* that which we understandly [sic] behold & hear, having, how much God perhaps only knows, created part even of the Form.[2]

The imaginative process which gives life to the external world from the poet's own spirit was later expressed by Coleridge in more philosophical language but never, I think, so tellingly. In the Malta notebook

[1] *BL*, p. 167.   [2] N 2, 2086 15.52, f. 40^v.

he is so close to the experience of *The Ancient Mariner* that he recognises the dream-like identity of the feeling and the form. The poet, in the creative act, *becomes* what he beholds and hears. Coleridge emphasises that this is a partly unconscious process – the 'Truths are below the Surface' – but, since the dream is 'rationalized', we must also assume that the conscious mind shapes and orders it. Even before the opium habit took hold of him, Coleridge's notebooks and letters testify to the vividness of his dreams and, as he always sought to understand his own experience, he was also accustomed to analyse them. He was deeply interested in books on the psychology of dreams, especially in distinguishing the gradations of conscious control in their different manifestations. Professor Bald, discussing this in his important essay on Coleridge, says:

> But, between the normal modes of mental *activity* and the passivity of dreaming there are various states in which the usual controls imposed by the will and the reason are relaxed in differing degrees, and to these Coleridge applied the inclusive term 'reverie'. It included not merely ordinary day-dreaming, but, as we have seen, opium reveries and 'nightmares' as well.[1]

It was not, then, accidental that Coleridge attached the term 'reverie' to his two greatest poems. In the second edition of the *Lyrical Ballads* 1800, he gave *The Ancient Mariner* the sub-title, 'A Poet's Reverie'. The original impulse of the poem was also the dream of his friend, Cruikshank, who had seen 'a skeleton ship with figures in it'. *The Ancient Mariner* has the fluid brilliance and strangeness of a dream but also the lucid order and control of the conscious mind. This mingling of the conscious and the unconscious in poetic creation, the deeper levels with the shaping spirit, is the source of its power. Coleridge was aware of this when he said that poetry was 'a rationalized dream'. The early notebooks also help us to see how he attached his own feelings to the 'manifold Forms' of the external world. Moon and stars, sun and sea, wind and bird's wings, belong to the elemental universe but become, at the same time, the images of spiritual life. The sea is the tropical ocean of the traders' voyages but also the loneliness of spiritual desolation; the bird's wings are those of the dying albatross but they also beat

[1] R. C. Bald, 'Coleridge and "The Ancient Mariner"', *Nineteenth Century Studies*, Ithaca, 1940, pp. 39–40.

in narrowing circles on the sinner's soul. As in a dream, several levels of reality become fused and the outer world becomes the inner.

The Crewe manuscript of *Kubla Khan* also says it was '. . . composed in a sort of Reverie brought on by two grains of Opium . . .' Its subtitle is 'A Vision in a Dream'. The famous preface, where Coleridge describes how '. . . all the images rose up before him as *things* . . . without any sensation or consciousness of effort', was written many years after the poem itself and scholarly opinion now tends partially to discount it. *Kubla Khan* does seem to be too intricately ordered and lucidly controlled to be so entirely a product of the unconscious as Coleridge makes out. Yet, if we grasp the meaning we have seen he attached to the term 'reverie', the poem then seems a waking dream. Its subject is the mingling of conscious and unconscious forces in creative activity of which it is itself an image. The dark caverns from which the river rises to flow through Kubla's sunlit garden suggest, again, the different levels of creative power.

But the fusion in Coleridge's greatest poetry of dream with reason, deeper impulse and shaping spirit, was not maintained for very long, nor had he always possessed it. His early poems, written before he went to Nether Stowey, were an intellectual attempt to bridge the gulf, of which he was always conscious, between the material and spiritual, mechanical and transcendental, explanations of the universe. His early enthusiasms for Pantheism and Unitarianism were both, in different ways, attempts to cross this gulf and to see God, or at least a living spirit, immanent in the natural world. But they did not satisfy Coleridge intellectually for long and their artistic fruits in *Religious Musings* and *The Destiny of Nations* were almost worthless as poetry. This was, partly, because they were too entirely rational; the dream element was not present and the deeper levels were unstirred. The schism which science had made between subject and object, man's consciousness and the surrounding world, Coleridge struggled all his life to close, both in poetry and philosophy. But he only really succeeded in his greatest imaginative poems, and, then, only for a brief period. In *The Ancient Mariner* and *Kubla Khan* the inner and the outer world become one; the idea and the image are fused in the waking dream.

Christabel was also begun at Nether Stowey and has some of the authentic Coleridge magic but it remained incomplete, partly because the balance between the external and the internal is here upset. The

7

feeling behind the poem became too involved and personal to be contained in the outward form. Coleridge himself said that the plan or story of *Christabel* became separated from the idea or inner meaning. This was the beginning of an imaginative disintegration of which the signs are present in the poem itself. Evil now enters the mind through dreams, as Christabel lies 'dreaming fearfully' in Geraldine's arms. As he tried to finish the poem through the years of opium haunted nightmares, Coleridge became bitterly aware of the presence of sin in the unconscious mind. As we shall see, the notebook entries of the time confirm an increasingly melancholy association between evil and dreams, which had certainly not been present in the Nether Stowey years. Coleridge had now every reason to dread the terrifying activity of the unconscious. To save his own sanity he was forced to lay more and more stress upon the 'conscious will', as in the *Biographia Literaria*, but this was also a denial of those deeper levels from which much of his imaginative power had come. If its roots are severed the poetic fruit withers on the tree.

In the notebook passages which parallel the Asra poems we can see very clearly the imaginative process by which perception becomes symbol and the outer world is changed into the inner. It is even possible to mark the stages by which Coleridge attached his own feelings to the 'manifold forms'. For example, he watched the transformation of caterpillar into butterfly at first with scientific detachment and accuracy; only very gradually did it become the bitter vision of life and love which reached its final form in the poem, *Psyche*. Some of these notebook entries which I have discussed in my chapter on the Asra poems show with remarkable clarity the creative process as a gradual movement towards metaphor. We are almost looking over Coleridge's shoulder and watching the genesis of a poem. Indeed, the notebooks themselves are often as imaginative and striking as the poetry, sometimes more so. By contrast, the notebooks of 1798 contain few direct references to *The Ancient Mariner* or *Kubla Khan* or even to poetry at all, though their imagery and ideas are close to the poems. In 1798 Coleridge presumably made the imaginative leap from outer to inner without the intermediate stages; at least, we have to infer them. The dream-like method of composition, a mingling, as we have seen, of conscious and unconscious processes, made this possible. During the following decade, when the Asra poems were written,

8

the dream was fading and a more conscious awareness beginning to take its place. This gives the notebooks the unsurpassed fascination of a literary workshop but it became, by slow degrees, fatal to the poetry. It is not, therefore, surprising that one of the earliest and best of the Asra poems is called *A Day-Dream*. The lines which Coleridge quoted in the 1816 preface to *Kubla Khan* to describe the vanishing of the dream come from his own poem, *The Picture*, and might, indeed, be considered a sorrowful parable of much of his later poetry:

> Then all the charm
> Is broken – all that phantom-world so fair
> Vanishes, and a thousand circlets spread,
> And each mis-shape the other.[1]

In the *Ode to Dejection* Coleridge at last recognises clearly the divorce which he had always dreaded between man's consciousness and the natural universe. The 'shaping spirit' of imagination no longer has the power to endow 'the inanimate cold world' with life. The feeling can no longer attach itself to the form:

> I may not hope from outward forms to win
> The passion and the life, whose fountains are within.[2]

The waking dream of his great poetry has faded; 'Reality's dark dream' has intervened. In a note related to the poem, *Phantom*, which arose from a vision of Sara Hutchinson, Coleridge, as usual aware of his own problem, recognises that feeling has become completely separated from form:

> – What then? Shall I dare say, the whole Dream seems to have been *Her – She* . . . Does not this establish the existence of *a Feeling* of a Person quite distinct at all times, & at certain times *perfectly separable* from, the Image of the Person?[3]

This separation of feeling from form marked the death of his imagination. The last poems of his Highgate years were composed at an entirely conscious, even self-conscious, level and the poetry is, on the whole, deplorable. Once again, in the sorrowful verse of *Phantom or Fact*, Coleridge was himself aware how 'the life of dreams' had

[1] *PW*, p. 372. [2] ibid., p. 365. [3] N 2, 2061 15.33. See p. 209.

9

changed into 'the dream of life'.[1] His last recorded words, a fortnight before his death, show him still wrestling with the problem of dream and reality. Though the dying man can hardly have remembered the schoolboy swimming an imaginary Hellespont, Coleridge was still, at heart, a Grecian:

> I am dying, but without expectation of a speedy release. Is it not strange that very recently bygone images, and scenes of early life, have stolen into my mind, like breezes blown from the spice-islands of Youth and Hope – those twin realities of this phantom world! I do not add Love – for what is Love but Youth and Hope embracing, and so seen as *one*? I say *realities*, for reality is a thing of degrees, from the *Iliad* to a dream; καὶ γάρ τ᾽ ὄναρ ἐκ Διός ἐστι. [trans.: for the dream is from God.][2]

[1] *PW*, p. 485.   [2] *Table Talk*, July 10th, 1834, OUP, 1917, p. 313.

CHAPTER I

Early Poems

MOST of his early poems which have any bearing upon Coleridge's
later development as a poet belong to the period from 1794 to 1797,
between his leaving Cambridge and his settling at Nether Stowey. One
or two charming and simple personal poems such as *Song of the Pixies*
or the sonnet *To the River Otter* were written earlier. In some ways,
as we shall see, these personal verses anticipate his great imaginative
poetry and have far more authentic literary quality than *Ode to the
Departing Year*, *The Destiny of Nations* or *Religious Musings*. His longer
and more ambitious poems are almost worthless as poetry, merely a
recording in highly pretentious, derivative and pompous verse of his
intellectual enthusiasms at the time. This was the Coleridge 'to turgid
ode and tumid stanza dear' of Byron's gibe, and the author himself
admits the justice of the criticism in his Preface to the 2nd edition of
Poems on Various Subjects in 1797:

My poems have been rightly charged with a profusion of double-
epithets, and a general turgidness. I have pruned the double-epithets
with no sparing hand; and used my best efforts to tame the swell and
glitter both of thought and diction.[1]

The effects of the pruning are not, however, very obvious. Twenty
years later, in the *Biographia Literaria*, Coleridge again acknowledged
the stylistic faults but also put his finger upon a deeper reason for the
weakness of these early poems:

My judgment was stronger than were my powers of realising its
dictates; and the faults of my language, though indeed partly owing
to a wrong choice of subjects and the desire of giving a poetic

[1] *PW*, ed. J. Dykes Campbell, 1903, p. 540.

II

colouring to abstract and metaphysical truths in which a new world then seemed to open upon me, did yet, in part likewise, originate in unfeigned diffidence of my own comparative talent.[1]

The new world of abstract truth which seemed to open upon him is, indeed, an understatement of his intellectual ferment at the time. *Religious Musings* and *The Destiny of Nations* in particular reveal his swiftly changing eager enthusiasms, political, philosophic and religious. In this he was very like most young men of university age; the difference is that few afterwards become great poets. Though these poems amount to little more than verse propaganda for the various causes and ideas he championed at the time, they reveal the mind which, a year or two later, created *The Ancient Mariner*. I believe that the passionately felt intellectual conflicts about the nature of the universe and the life of man, which resound through *Religious Musings* and *The Destiny of Nations*, are present and still unresolved in *The Ancient Mariner*. These long, pretentious, tumid poems, though bad in themselves, still repay study because they help us to understand the greater work. Since *The Road to Xanadu* too much stress upon Coleridge's literary sources has tended to obscure the pressure of contemporary ideas upon him.

These were the years of Pantisocracy, devotion to the ideals of the French Revolution, the publication of *The Watchman*, the approach to becoming a Unitarian minister. The theories of Hartley, Priestley, Darwin, Berkeley, Plato and Plotinus, to name only the more outstanding, jostle confusing and confused in the thought and verses of the young Coleridge. Yet through the strange welter we are aware of the quality of an eager searching mind, engaged in the pursuit of truth; the ruins of one system become the foundations of the next. His deeply religious temperament gave the search its impetus, though in all his tormented life he was never quite able to reconcile his profound need for faith with his brilliant and restless intellect. His passionate hatred of tyranny, slavery and oppression, man's inhumanity to man, lies behind even the absurdities of Pantisocracy and the mental contortions in which support of the French Revolution involved him. Like Milton, whom he so admired and who so deeply influenced his style, Coleridge is concerned in *Religious Musings* 'to justify the ways of God to man'. Milton too had been a revolutionary who had used his mighty pen in

[1] *BL*, p. 3.

support 'Of Science, Freedom and the Truth in Christ'.[1] These are the three great causes which dominate Coleridge's early poems.

Pantisocracy was the scheme whereby twelve gentlemen and twelve ladies were to found an ideal republic on the banks of the Susquehannah and, by the abolition of property and the equal sharing of the rewards of their labours, to redress in the New World the miseries of the Old. We hear amusing echoes of the scheme in a letter from Coleridge to Southey, its founder member, in the autumn of 1794. Coleridge was in London, passing convivial evenings with Lamb at *The Salutation and Cat*. Another young man, also an old boy of Christ's Hospital but with apparently a clear-sighted awareness of the main chance, took to joining the two friends in the smoky little room – as he said 'to benefit by conversation'. He was recently back from America to sell land, and Coleridge eagerly passes his information on to Southey:

> He says two thousand pounds will do . . . that we shall buy this Land a great deal cheaper when we arrive at America, than we could do in England – or why (adds he) am I sent over here? That twelve men can *easily* clear *three hundred* Acres in 4 or 5 months – He recommends the Susquehannah from its excessive Beauty, and its security from hostile Indians – Every possible assistance will be given us . . . That literary characters make *money* there, that etc. etc. He never saw a Byson in his life, but has heard of them. They are quite backwards.[2]

The thought of Coleridge clearing his share of the three hundred acres, with the vague threat of bisons and hostile Indians in the background, but nevertheless making money as a literary character, is very difficult to entertain with gravity. His credulous innocence in worldly affairs and his eager enthusiasm make one uncertain whether to laugh or to cry. Indeed, the whole story of Pantisocracy is very tragical mirth. Apart from a stray sonnet it left little trace upon Coleridge's poetry but it was responsible for the central tragedy of his life. Each of the twelve gentlemen, for obvious reasons, had to have his pantisocratic partner and Southey provided the unattached Coleridge with Sara Fricker to whose sister he was himself engaged. Southey's enthusiasm for Pantisocracy very quickly waned and, much to Coleridge's disillusionment,

---

[1] *PW, Reflections on Having Left a Place of Retirement*, p. 108.
[2] Quoted by Hanson, p. 52.

the scheme was gradually dropped. But Coleridge had by then become involved in a semi-engagement to Sara Fricker, though he did not really love her and was, indeed, still in love with his boyhood sweetheart, Mary Evans. Coleridge retreated to London, *The Salutation and Cat* and Charles Lamb, but Sara and Southey were determined not to let him go. Finally, after numerous entreaties had not brought him to Bristol, Southey pursued him to London and bore the reluctant bridegroom back with him. Coleridge married Sara for a theory and so sacrificed his chances of happiness either with Mary Evans or with Sara Hutchinson whom he met too late. The marriage was disastrous for both husband and wife and was the main reason for Coleridge's later unhappiness. It does, however, provide tragi-comic evidence of how deeply the whole man was involved in his intellectual theories. Even in his early poetry, we cannot underrate their importance; Coleridge's ideas and his life are one.

Religious Musings, begun on Christmas Eve 1794, opens with an orthodox, if rather pompously expressed, vision of the coming of the Prince of Peace. The Miltonic echoes are very obvious in the lines describing Nature as a reflection of God:

> Fair the vernal mead,
> Fair the high grove, the sea, the sun, the stars;
> True impress each of their creating Sire!
> Yet nor high grove, nor many-colour'd mead,
> Nor the green ocean with his thousand isles,
> Nor the starred azure, nor the sovran sun,
> E'er with such majesty of portraiture
> Imaged the supreme beauty uncreate,
> As thou, meek Saviour! . . .[1]

The mood of high endeavour and the latinised diction and syntax are clearly Miltonic, but some of the lines which follow proclaim the gospel according to Hartley and Priestley, the sages of Associationism and the Unitarian doctrine:

> God only to behold, and know and feel,
> Till by exclusive consciousness of God
> All self-annihilated it shall make

[1] *PW*, p. 109.

God its Identity: God all in all!
We and our Father one![1]

Coleridge's note informs us that Hartley had *demonstrated* this merging
of the individual in the divine consciousness. The next lines are indebted
to Priestley and the Unitarians. God is hailed as

Him Nature's essence, mind and energy!
And gazing, trembling, patiently ascend
Treading beneath their feet all visible things
As steps, that upward to their Father's throne
Lead gradual – else nor glorified nor loved.[2]

If God is of the same essence as the natural forces of the universe He
becomes a natural rather than a transcendental deity. As H. W. Piper
points out in *The Active Universe*, it is extremely difficult to distinguish
between the Unitarian and the pantheist:

The essence of Priestley's metaphysical belief was that there was
no such thing as matter. What did exist was active force, and the
apparent solidity of matter was only the resistance of this force. Thus
the whole universe was spiritual force, and all action the direct action
of God. Though such a system can only be distinguished from
pantheism by Priestley's assertions that God, as well as being everything, was also additional to the sum of things, yet Priestley was a
devout believer.[3]

Priestley and Coleridge at this time were, in fact, trying to have it both
ways. Coleridge has a similar passage in *The Destiny of Nations* which
originally formed part of Southey's *Joan of Arc* but was never completed because Lamb's criticism of it was so stringent that his friend lost
heart. When the poem was finally published in 1817, Coleridge's included the lines:

'Glory to Thee, Father of Earth and Heaven!
All-conscious Presence of the Universe!
Nature's vast ever-acting Energy![4]

[1] *PW*, p. 110.   [2] ibid., p. 111.
[3] H. W. Piper, *The Active Universe*, Athlone Press, 1962, p. 27.
[4] *PW*, p. 146.

But he added a note which showed his awareness that they might bear a pantheistic interpretation:

> Tho' these lines may bear a sane sense, yet they are easily, and more naturally interpreted with a very false and dangerous one. But I was at that time one of the *Mongrels*, the Josephidites [Josephides = the Son of Joseph], a proper name of distinction from those who believe *in*, as well as believe Christ the only begotten Son of the Living God before all Time.[1]

The 'mongrels' or 'Josephidites' were the Unitarian followers of Joseph Priestley!

If God is not different in kind from the natural forces and energy of matter, this, as H. W. Piper again points out,[2] raises in an acute form the problem of the existence of evil. Coleridge attempts to deal with it in the next section of *Religious Musings*. He who loves God

> . . . meek he beholds
> All things of terrible seeming: yea, unmoved
> Views e'en the immitigable ministers
> That shower down vengeance on these latter days.
>
> . . . .
>
> Thus from the Elect, regenerate through faith,
> Pass the dark Passions and what thirsty cares
> Drink up the spirit, and the dim regards
> Self-centre.[3]

In yet another appended note Coleridge explains:

> Our evil Passions, under the influence of Religion become innocent, and may be made to animate our virtue – in the same manner as the thick mist melted by the Sun, increases the light which it had before excluded.[4]

Precisely *how* evil becomes the instrument of good is not made clear – merely asserted. He goes on to celebrate the principle of love in the universe:

[1] *PW*, p. 147.   [2] Piper, p. 46.
[3] *PW*, p. 112.   [4] ibid., p. 112.

> There is one Mind, one omnipresent Mind,
> Omnific. His most holy name is Love.

Whoever accepts this

> Stands in the sun, and with no partial gaze
> Views all creation; and he loves it all,
> And blesses it, and calls it very good![1]

How facile this seems in relation to *The Ancient Mariner*. What of those who reject Love and commit an act of wanton cruelty against a trusting and helpless creature? Then, indeed, the sun is no longer an image of Love but becomes 'the bloody sun' above the rotting sea. Even in *Religious Musings* Coleridge is dimly aware that the problem of evil has not been completely solved! He goes on to refer to Cain, the outcast figure who is a presence behind the Ancient Mariner:

> And that in His vast family no Cain
> Injures uninjured (in her best-aimed blow
> Victorious Murder a blind Suicide)

Murder and evil exist and the God of Love becomes a God of vengeance.

Coleridge is also forced to recognise the evil of the war with France:

> But first offences needs must come! Even now
> (Black Hell laughs horrible – to hear the scoff!)
> Thee to defend, meek Galilaean! Thee
> And thy mild laws of Love unutterable,
> Mistrust and Enmity have burst the bands
> Of social peace: . . .[2]

He is torn, like Wordsworth, by the revolutionary war and castigates the unchristian conduct of the English clergy who incite their country-men to fight. This is a problem which recurs in every generation:

> Thee to defend the Moloch Priest prefers
> The prayer of hate, and bellows to the herd,
> That Deity, Accomplice Deity

[1] ibid., p. 113.   [2] ibid., p. 115.

> In the fierce jealousy of wakened wrath
> Will go forth with our armies and our fleets
> To scatter the red ruin on their foes![1]

Nevertheless Coleridge asserts:

> These, even these, in mercy didst thou form,
> Teachers of Good through Evil, by brief wrong
> Making Truth lovely . . .

Once again, the way by which good can come out of evil is not made clear. Coleridge, as so often happened in his later life, sees the problem but immediately retreats from it. At this point in the poem he changes the subject and abandons the intractable nature of good and evil. It was to return in a different form in *The Ancient Mariner*.

In *Religious Musings* he now relates the history of the world from primeval times to the coming Millennium. He begins with the shepherd in his tent, goes on to the invention of Property and the oppression of the 'wretched Many'. There is a vision of wild animals who prey upon each other – difficult to explain if God is 'Nature's essence, mind and energy':

> The lion couches: or hyaena dips
> Deep in the lucid stream his bloody jaws;
> Or serpent plants his vast moon-glittering bulk,
> Caught in whose monstrous twine Behemoth yells,
> His bones loud-crashing![2]

Coleridge, in fact, piles on the horrors of every kind of oppression and misery, mounting up to the astonishing climax:

> Yet is the day of Retribution nigh:
> The Lamb of God hath opened the fifth seal:[3]

All earthly wretchedness and evil is thus seen as a prelude to God's vengeance in Revelation. The style also becomes more and more apocalyptic, as in the vision of the Terror of the French Revolution:

> . . . for lo! the Giant Frenzy
> Uprooting empires with his whirlwind arm

[1] *PW*, p. 116.   [2] ibid., p. 119.   [3] ibid., p. 120.

> Mocketh high Heaven; burst hideous from the cell
> Where the old Hag, unconquerable, huge,
> Creation's eyeless drudge, black Ruin, sits
> Nursing the impatient earthquake.

Nevertheless, all this is a prelude to the arrival of the Millennium:

> Old Ocean claps his hands! The mighty Dead
> Rise to new life, whoe'er from earliest time
> With conscious zeal had urged Love's wondrous plan,
> Coadjutors of God.[1]

Chief among God's coadjutors are the Unitarian inspirers of the poem –
Milton, Newton, Hartley and Priestley! The philosopher of Association, after whom Coleridge named his first-born, is hailed as

> . . . he of mortal kind
> Wisest, he first who marked the ideal tribes
> Up the fine fibres through the sentient brain.

while Priestley, driven from his native land,

> . . . mused expectant on these promised years.[2]

Before the poem ends there is a passage which Coleridge (in a note
added later) explains as a reference to Berkeley:

> Believe thou, O my soul,
> Life is a vision shadowy of Truth;
> And vice, and anguish, and the wormy grave,
> Shapes of a dream!

This seems to a mind like Coleridge's the more congenial theory but
he had not yet exorcised the materialist philosophy. Its presence, with
many others, was to haunt *The Ancient Mariner* – shapes of a dream.

The Destiny of Nations, originally written to form part of Southey's
Joan of Arc in 1795, was left unfinished because of Lamb's adverse
criticism. Though finally published in *Sibylline Leaves*, 1817, it was still
confused and fragmentary both in ideas and form. Coleridge had

[1] ibid., p. 122.   [2] ibid., p. 123.

described *Religious Musings* as 'A Desultory Poem'; *The Destiny of Nations* can only be termed chaotic. Yet, formless and turgid though it is, it has at moments a curious imaginative affinity with *The Ancient Mariner*.

It opens in Platonic strain with a vision of God revealed 'through meaner powers and secondary things':

> For all that meets the bodily sense I deem
> Symbolical, one mighty alphabet
> For infant minds; and we in this low world
> Placed with our backs to bright Reality,
> That we may learn with young unwounded ken
> The substance from its shadow.[1]

This, is, of course, a memory of Plato's cave in *The Republic*, where all that we call real is only a shadow of the Absolute Good and Love. Coleridge, however, immediately proceeds to an attack upon the mechanical Newtonian theory of the universe which seemed to be

> Untenanting creation of its God.

This, one feels, expresses his deep distrust of the materialist science and philosophy and his longing for a transcendental explanation. But, once again, he tries to equate the fundamentally opposed views:

> But Properties are God: the naked mass
> (If mass there be, fantastic guess or ghost)
> Acts only by its inactivity.
> Here we pause humbly. Others boldlier think
> That as one body seems the aggregate
> Of atoms numberless, each organized;
> So by a strange and dim similitude
> Infinite myriads of self-conscious minds
> Are one all-conscious Spirit, which informs
> With absolute ubiquity of thought
> (His one eternal self-affirming act!)
> All his involvéd Monads, that yet seem
> With various province and apt agency
> Each to pursue its own self-centering end.[2]

[1] *PW*, p. 132.   [2] ibid., p. 133.

He thus stresses again the divine activity of matter. The Monads are forms of divine energy, personified as spirits of the elements for poetic purposes. This machinery Coleridge borrowed from Erasmus Darwin's *Botanic Garden*, but the spirits are essentially the personification of scientific natural forces. Though I do not agree with the conclusions he draws, H. W. Piper points some very interesting parallels between the winds, the Polar spirit etc. of *The Ancient Mariner* and Darwin's spirits.[1] Coleridge describes the shooting stars and Northern lights of the Polar regions and, in several passages, curiously anticipates his greater poem. Fancy, we are told,

> That first unsensualises the dark mind,
> . . . . peopling air,
> By obscure fears of Beings invisible,
> Emancipates it from the grosser thrall
> Of the present impulse, teaching Self-control,
> . . . .
> . . . . . . Wherefore not vain,
> I deem those legends terrible, with which
> The polar ancient thrills his uncouth throng:
> Whether of pitying Spirits that make their moan
> O'er slaughtered infants, or that Giant Bird
> Vuokho, of whose rushing wings the noise
> Is Tempest, when the unutterable Shape
> Speeds from the mother of Death, and utters once
> That shriek which never murderer heard and lived.[2]

The Ancient Mariner was, unfortunately, not free from 'the thrall of the present impulse', and the association in the Polar legends of the Giant Bird with Death shows that Wordsworth's suggestion of shooting the albatross fell upon ground that was already prepared.

Another curious legend relates how the Spirit of Good assists a magician to release from the depths of the ocean the creatures whom an evil spirit has held captive.[3] This may have played its part in the creation of the water-snakes, transformed from slimy evil creatures to the 'happy living things' sporting on the surface of the sea.

[1] H. W. Piper, *The Active Universe*, pp. 92–102.
[2] *PW*, p. 134.   [3] ibid., p. 135 and note.

Just as we are becoming interested in the polar legends, however, Coleridge abruptly abandons them and reverts to Joan of Arc, inserting the passage he had composed for Southey's poem in 1795. This is bad and pretentious verse with no relevance to *The Ancient Mariner* and, therefore, not worth study. Coleridge concludes the poem with fragments which bear little relation to one another, to Joan or to any other subject. But, at one point, the tutelary power regales Joan with a description of Love whose

> . . . gorgeous wings
> Over the abyss fluttered with such glad noise,
> As what time after long and pestful calms,
> With slimy shapes and miscreated life
> Poisoning the vast Pacific, the fresh breeze
> Wakens the merchant-sail uprising.[1]

The 'pestful calms' and 'the slimy shapes' are, again, a curious foretaste of *The Ancient Mariner*, but, lest we should attach too much importance to them, Coleridge provides us with a salutary and amusing comment:

> These are very fine Lines, tho' I say it, that should not: but, hang me, if I know or ever did know the meaning of them, tho' my own composition.[2]

He concludes the poem with the invocation to God as 'Nature's vast ever-acting Energy' already discussed. Both *The Destiny of Nations* and *Religious Musings* thus try to reconcile the control of the universe by the natural forces of the mechanistic philosophy with the existence of God. Coleridge, however, evades the problems to which this position leads; the Origin of Evil, on which he contemplated writing an epic, is left unsolved. The conflict is summed up in a phrase from his letter to Josiah Wade, discussing Erasmus Darwin, of January 1796:

> Whether we be the outcasts of a blind idiot called Nature, or the children of an all-wise and infinitely good God . . .[3]

The Ancient Mariner shows us the same agonised dilemma, though, this time, in imaginative terms. The winds drive the Mariner's ship helplessly to the South Pole, then north to the Line, where it lies becalmed

[1] *PW*, p. 140.   [2] ibid., p. 140.   [3] Griggs, i, 177.

under the full horror of the tropical sun and the merciless thirst. The moon moves, beautiful but indifferent, over the sailors' tormented sea where the 'slimy things' crawl. The forces of nature seem to behave with the same indifference both before and after the crime. Nor does the Mariner's impulse of love for the water-snakes really release him from his agony; he is still condemned to 'pass like night from land to land'. He seems to be much more 'the outcast of a blind idiot called Nature' than the child 'of an all-wise and good God'. For, if God's essence is inseparable from that of the natural universe, its alien force becomes His too. The sea itself is an image of the terrible desolation of a world without Him:

> O Wedding-Guest! this soul hath been
> Alone on a wide, wide sea:
> So lonely 'twas that God himself
> Scarce seeméd there to be.

We must suffer *Religious Musings* and *The Destiny of Nations* in order to understand *The Ancient Mariner*.

★   ★   ★

Many of Coleridge's other early poems are derivative in style as well as in ideas. Like most young poets, he was searching for his own voice and his revolt against poetic diction was necessary because he had been so much in its power. He tells us much later in the *Biographia Literaria* that he realised '. . . the superiority of an austerer and more natural style'[1] even at the time but was unable to achieve it. Bowyer, his old schoolmaster at Christ's Hospital, to whom Coleridge pays a moving tribute in the *Biographia*, strove to inculcate this lesson. His former pupil relates how

> In our own English compositions (at least for the last three years of our school education) he showed no mercy to phrase, metaphor or image unsupported by a sound sense, or where the same sense might have been conveyed with equal force and dignity in plainer words. Lute, harp and lyre, muse, muses and inspirations, Pegasus,

---

[1] *BL*, p. 3.

Parnassus and Hippocrene were all an abomination to him. In fancy I can almost hear him now, exclaiming, 'Harp? Harp? Lyre? Pen and ink, boy, you mean! Muse, boy, muse? Your nurse's daughter, you mean! Pierian spring? Oh, aye! the cloister-pump, I suppose!'[1]

One would like to have heard Bowyer's comments on, for example, *Lines in the Manner of Spenser*, 1795:

> O Peace, that on a lilied bank dost love
> To rest thine head beneath an Olive-tree,
> I would that from the pinions of thy Dove
> One quill withouten pain yplucked might be!
>
> . . . .
> . . . .
>
> Last night as I my weary head did pillow
> With thoughts of my dissever'd Fair engross'd,
> Chill Fancy droop'd wreathing herself with willow,
> As though my breast entomb'd a pining ghost.[2]

This has all the vices of personification and pretentiousness, with Spenser's archaisms thrown in as well.

Julia, written at Christ's Hospital in 1789, though an obvious imitation of Pope, at least has the merit of lightness:

> 'Twere vain to tell how Julia pin'd away:
> Unhappy Fair! that in one luckless day –
> From future Almanacks the day be crost! –
> At once her Lover and her Lap-dog lost.[3]

The *Ode to the Departing Year*, 1796, is one of Coleridge's most grandiose attempts at bardic prophecy; the style might be described as Milton through Gray:

> Hither, in perplexéd dance,
> Ye Woes! ye young-eyed Joys! advance!
> By Time's wild harp, and by the hand
> Whose indefatigable sweep
> Raises its fateful strings from sleep,
> I bid you haste, a mix'd tumultuous band!

[1] *BL*, p. 4. [2] *PW*, pp. 94–5. [3] ibid., p. 7.

> From every private bower,
> And each domestic hearth,
> Haste for one solemn hour;
> And with a loud and yet a louder voice,
> O'er Nature struggling in portentous birth,
> Weep and rejoice![1]

This, as M. H. Abrams points out in his interesting recent article, *Structure and Style In the Greater Romantic Lyric*,[2] was Coleridge's attempt to assume a public voice. Professor Abrams continues:

> That is to say, he had adopted a visionary and oracular persona – in accordance, as he said in the Dedication to his 'Ode on the Departing Year', with the practice of the ancients, when 'the Bard and the Prophet were one and the same character' – and had compounded Biblical prophecy, the hieratic stance of Milton, and the formal rhetoric, allegorical tactics, and calculated disorder of what he called 'the sublimer Ode' of Gray and Collins, in the effort to endow his subjects with the requisite elevation, passion, drama and impact.[3]

* * *

Coleridge's private and personal voice is, however, also beginning to make itself heard in these early poems. In the Preface to the second edition of his *Poems on Various Subjects*, 1797, he says:

> If I could judge of others by myself, I should not hesitate to affirm, that the most interesting passages in our most interesting Poems are those in which the author developes his own feelings.[4]

Both in the Preface and in the *Biographia Literaria* he ascribed this development of lyric expression and personal feeling to the influence of Bowles. In the *Biographia* he mentions Cowper as well but says he was not familiar with him till later. These two poets were '. . . the first

[1] ibid., p. 161.
[2] M. H. Abrams, 'Structure and Style in the Greater Romantic Lyric', in *From Sensibility to Romanticism*, New York, OUP, 1965, pp. 527–57.
[3] ibid., p. 542.
[4] *PW*, ed. J. Dykes Campbell, p. 540.

B

who combined natural thoughts with natural diction; the first who reconciled the heart with the head.'[1] It need hardly be stressed how important this was to a man of Coleridge's temperament.

M. H. Abrams, in the interesting essay to which I have already referred, traces the development of the genre which he calls 'the greater Romantic lyric'. He sees it as the interpenetration between the reflective mind and feeling of the poet and the observed scene, so that each modifies the other. *Frost at Midnight, Tintern Abbey* and the *Ode to the West Wind* are among its highest achievements and Professor Abrams stresses its uniqueness in Romantic poetry, though he sees its literary ancestor as Denham's *Cooper's Hill*. He believes that the influence of Bowles helped to make Coleridge the real originator of this great Romantic achievement. Coleridge himself, in the *Introduction to the Sonnets*, 1797, stresses the connection between the feeling reflective mind and Nature:

> In a Sonnet then we require a development of some lonely feeling, by whatever cause it may have been excited; but those Sonnets appear to me the most exquisite, in which moral Sentiments, Affections, or Feelings, are deduced from, and associated with, the Scenery of Nature. . . . They create a sweet and indissoluble union between the intellectual and the material world. . . . Hence the Sonnets of BOWLES derive their marked superiority over all other Sonnets; hence they domesticate with the heart, and become, as it were, a part of our identity.[2]

As Professor Abrams says:

> . . . Bowles's sonnets opened out to Coleridge the possibilities in the quite ordinary circumstances of a private person in a specific time and place whose meditation, credibly stimulated by the setting, is grounded in his particular character, follows the various and seemingly random flow of the living consciousness, and is conducted in the intimate yet adaptive voice of the interior monologue.[3]

But Bowles not only helped Coleridge to find a natural and lyrical

[1] *BL*, p. 13.
[2] *PW*, ed. J. Dykes Campbell, p. 543.
[3] M. H. Abrams, 'Structure and Style in the Greater Romantic Lyric', p. 543.

voice. The association between the poet's feeling and the natural scene around him also enabled him, as Professor Abrams points out,[1] to bridge the gulf between subject and object, the internal and the external world. The struggle to reanimate the dead world, to join together what the mechanistic philosophy had put asunder, was, indeed, to be the life-long search of both Coleridge's poetry and philosophy. In his greatest poetry his imagination was to reconcile the inner and the outer world but this was born of his dread of isolation, his deep emotional need for identity. As Mr John Jones points out in *The Egotistical Sublime*, Coleridge's

. . . dread of isolation is therefore both imaginative and intellectual. To be wholly conscious of one's distinctness, he said, is 'to be betrayed into the wretchedness of *division*'.[2]

A little later in his argument Mr Jones adds:

At the same time he saw that neither Wordsworth's acceptance, nor his own rejection, of the condition of subject standing over against a world of objects was a purely intellectual matter . . .[3]

In *Religious Musings* and *The Destiny of Nations* Coleridge had tried intellectually to animate the world of objects; in his other early poems he begins to do this imaginatively.

Coleridge is now drawing upon his personal experience and often describes the scenes of his childhood. Poems like *Song of the Pixies* or *Sonnet to the River Otter* are already full of his favourite images, though here they are not usually metaphors but pictures in the eye of memory. Though he was very young when he wrote them, most of these poems emphasise the importance of memory. Coleridge's unconscious mind was stored with bright images of the natural world which, rising to the surface in his great poetry, became charged with a new and symbolic power. As for Wordsworth, the memories often came 'from hiding-places ten years deep' and the energy of the old associations lends a deeper life to the fresh imaginative creation.

Two of Coleridge's sonnets of Christ's Hospital days, though weak

---

[1] ibid., pp. 544–52.
[2] John Jones, *The Egotistical Sublime*, Chatto and Windus, 1954, p. 26.
[3] ibid., p. 46.

in themselves, are interesting to compare with the one *To the River Otter* where Bowles' influence, slender though his own talent was, has undoubtedly transformed the poetry. The sonnet *To the Autumnal Moon*, 1788, is still full of poetic diction though, like its subject, some clear observation glimmers through:

> Mild Splendour of the various-vested Night!
> Mother of wildly-working visions! hail!
> I watch thy gliding, while with watery light
> Thy weak eye glimmers through a fleecy veil;[1]

The octave describes the movement of the moon, now shrouded and now clear of cloud. The sestet is entirely devoted to a meditation on the changefulness of Hope and Despair; the moon's presence is symbolically there but the clear-cut division of the sonnet into octave and sestet is also a division between subject and object. The reflection is connected with the natural image but there is no real imaginative interfusion. Another sonnet of the following year, called *Life*, describes the river Otter and his native Devon in very hackneyed and lifeless language:

> As late I journey'd o'er the extensive plain
> Where native Otter sports his scanty stream,
> Musing in torpid woe a Sister's pain,
> The glorious prospect woke me from the dream.
> At every step it widen'd to my sight –
> Wood, Meadow, verdant Hill and dreary Steep,[2]

Then, once again, the sestet is devoted to an equally trite reflection on the course of life; the scene and the meditation are firmly separated by the sonnet structure:

> May this (I cried) my course through Life portray!
> New scenes of Wisdom may each step display,

The sonnet, *To the River Otter*, 1793, was probably inspired by Bowles' *To the River Itchen*, and, though by no means a masterpiece, the observation of the scene and the reflection upon it are, here, far more

[1] *PW*, p. 5.   [2] ibid., p. 11.

28

closely interwoven. This time the octave and sestet are not divided but linked closely through rhyme-scheme, syntax and feeling. The memories of careless childhood are superimposed upon the actual scene, thus creating 'a double awareness',[1] a variation on which as Professor Abrams says, the Romantic poets often played:

> Dear native Brook! wild Streamlet of the West!
> How many various-fated years have past,
> What happy and what mournful hours, since last
> I skimm'd the smooth thin stone along thy breast,
> Numbering its light leaps! yet so deep imprest
> Sink the sweet scenes of childhood, that mine eyes
> I never shut amid the sunny ray,
> But straight with all their tints thy waters rise,
> Thy crossing-plank, thy marge with willows grey,
> And bedded sand that vein'd with various dyes
> Gleam'd through thy bright transparence! On my way,
> Visions of Childhood, oft have ye beguil'd
> Lone manhood's cares, yet waking fondest sighs:
> Ah! that once more I were a careless Child![2]

The observation of the scene has a new freshness and clarity:

> And bedded sand that vein'd with various dyes
> Gleam'd through thy bright transparence!

This has something of the concrete brilliance of *The Ancient Mariner* after the vague abstractions of so many of the early poems. The rhythm too has a new liveliness of movement, flexibly suggesting the skimming pebble:

> I skimm'd the smooth thin stone along thy breast,
> Numbering its light leaps! . . .

The scenes 'sink' into the mind and later 'thy waters rise'; it is a statement of the mingling of the conscious and the unconscious in poetic creation which was to recur in the greater river image of *Kubla Khan*.

[1] M. H. Abrams, 'Structure and Style in the Greater Romantic Lyric', p. 533.
[2] *PW*, p. 48.

It is perhaps significant that his sonnet to Bowles in 1794 concludes with an image of Creation. Though the origin is obviously Genesis, the word 'plastic' perhaps anticipates the *Biographia*'s description of the creative Imagination as the 'esemplastic power'. Bowles, after all, first helped Coleridge to write imaginatively:

> While shadowy PLEASURE, with mysterious wings,
> Brooded the wavy and tumultuous mind,
> Like that great Spirit, who with plastic sweep
> Mov'd on the darkness of the formless Deep![1]

Anna and Harland, a curious sonnet from Christ's Hospital days, tells a fictitious love story but already uses the imagery of Coleridge's later love for Sara Hutchinson in the Asra poems. Anna dies of grief after her brother has killed her lover and:

> To Death's dark house did grief-worn Anna haste,
> Yet here her pensive ghost delights to stay;
> Oft pouring on the winds the broken lay –
> And hark, I hear her – 'twas the passing blast.

In the *Ode to Dejection* the moaning of the wind was to be a sad accompaniment to his own sorrowful love. The lovely lines on Memory which becomes the image of the rainbow reflected in the stream are, again, a strange anticipation of the reflection imagery of the Asra poems:

> Then Memory backward rolls Time's shadowy tide;
> The tales of other days before me glide:
> With eager thought I seize them as they pass;
> For fair, tho' faint, the forms of Memory gleam,
> Like Heaven's bright beauteous bow reflected in the stream.[2]

In *Happiness*, 1791, he also uses the image of the mirror which in his last poems was so often to symbolise the search for the self:

> If chance some lovely maid thou find
> To read thy visage in thy mind.[3]

Unfortunately he found her too late.

[1] *PW*, p. 84.   [2] ibid., p. 16.   [3] ibid., p. 32.

There is, indeed, a curious poignancy in reading these early poems with a knowledge of the later ones, the sorrowful irony of life which the writer was, naturally, unaware of at the time. *An Effusion at Evening*, 1792, provides other instances. The voice is still the voice of the eighteenth century but the preoccupation with Imagination looks forward to much of Coleridge's later theory:

> Imagination, Mistress of my Love!
> Where shall mine Eye thy elfin haunt explore?

and, a little later, she is associated with moonlight:

> And on the Lake the silver Lustre sleeps,
> Amid the paly Radiance soft and sad
> She meets my lonely path in moonbeams clad.[1]

In the famous opening of Chapter 14 of the *Biographia Literaria*, so many years later, Coleridge describes his and Wordsworth's attempt to unite the truth of nature with the modifying colours of the imagination, and uses the image of moonlight:

> The sudden charm which accidents of light and shade, which moonlight or sunset diffused over a known and familiar landscape, appeared to represent the practicability of combining both.[2]

In view of the celebration of the later distinction between the two, it is also interesting that Coleridge, in *An Effusion at Evening*, makes Imagination and Fancy synonymous. It is, in fact, 'Propitious Fancy' who meets his lonely path – but he was, of course, still a disciple of Hartley. The poem also describes

> . . . shadowy Memory's wings across the Soul of Love;

and Love 'a crown of thornless roses wears'. Eight years later, when he wrote *The Keepsake* for Sara Hutchinson, only the thorns remain:

> And the rose
> (In vain the darling of successful love)
> Stands, like some boasted beauty of past years,
> The thorns remaining, and the flowers all gone.[3]

[1] ibid., p. 49.   [2] *BL*, p. 168.   [3] *PW*, p. 345.

The Song of the Pixies sprang from a visit Coleridge paid to his native Devonshire in 1793. The note he prefaced to the poem explains its setting:

> The Pixies, in the superstition of Devonshire, are a race of beings invisibly small, and harmless or friendly to man. At a small distance from a village in that county, half-way up a wood-covered hill, is an excavation called the Pixies' Parlour. The roots of old trees form its ceiling; and on its sides are innumerable cyphers, among which the author discovered his own cypher and those of his brothers, cut by the hand of their childhood. At the foot of the hill flows the river Otter.[1]

The scene was, thus, already hallowed by memory and the poem is a storehouse of pictures, many of which were to become the potent images of *Kubla Khan*. The pixies haunt by moonlight and sip the dews of the furze-flower which was associated later with both *Fears in Solitude* and *Kubla Khan*. They retreat to the dark cave away from the sun's light:

> Aye from the sultry heat
> We to the cave retreat
> O'ercanopied by huge roots intertwin'd
> With wildest texture, blacken'd o'er with age:

This was, of course, the real cave described in the note but it is interesting to find it linked in the next verse with Coleridge's awareness of himself as a poet and with the murmur of bees:

> Thither, while the murmuring throng
> Of wild-bees hum their drowsy song,
> By Indolence and Fancy brought,
> A youthful Bard, 'unknown to Fame',
> Wooes the Queen of Solemn Thought,

In *Kubla Khan* also the strange caverns are associated with moonlit magic and with the power of the poet who has fed on honey-dew. The river too, now violent and now gentle, is in both poems:

[1] *PW*, p. 40.

Then with quaint music hymn the parting gleam
By lonely Otter's sleep-persuading stream;
Or where his wave with loud unquiet song
Dash'd o'er the rocky channel froths along;
Or where, his silver waters smooth'd to rest,
The tall tree's shadow sleeps upon his breast.[1]

The image of the tree reflected in the stream was, later, to be a dominant one in the Asra poems; the youthful Coleridge was also indulging
in a little harmless flirtation with one of the young ladies whom he had
taken on a picnic to the Pixies' Parlour! So, though *The Song of the
Pixies* belongs to the real world of Devonshire, its clear boyhood
pictures, with their memories of happiness and hope, may well have
sunk beneath the surface of the poet's mind – to emerge with a strange
new power in *Kubla Khan*.

Lines to a Beautiful Spring in a Village, 1794, also associate the imagery
of fountain and cavern:

Nor thine unseen in cavern depths to well,
The Hermit-fountain of some dripping cell!

Like *The Song of the Pixies*, the poem is a curious mixture of poetic
diction and fresh observation:

Once more! sweet Stream! with slow foot wandering near,
I bless thy milky waters cold and clear.
Escap'd the flashing of the noontide hours,
With one fresh garland of Pierian flowers
(Ere from thy zephyr-haunted brink I turn)
My languid hand shall wreath thy mossy urn.[2]

*   *   *

Perhaps marriage and residence in Somerset induced a greater sense
of reality in Coleridge. Whatever the reason, *The Eolian Harp* and
Reflections on Having Left a Place of Retirement, both written in 1795,
show a far greater poetic maturity. The first draft of *The Eolian Harp*
was short and some of the most beautiful lines were not added till 1828.

[1] ibid., p. 43.   [2] ibid., p. 58.

The 1797 version opens with Sara and himself sitting happily by their cottage door watching the falling of the evening light. Their mood of love is 'soothing sweet' and so blends with the tranquillity of the scene:

How exquisite the Scents
Snatch'd from yon Bean-field! And the world *so* hush'd!
The stilly murmur of the far-off Sea
Tells us of Silence! And that simplest Lute
Plac'd lengthways in the clasping casement, hark!
How by the desultory Breeze caress'd
(Like some coy Maid half-yielding to her Lover)
It pours such sweet Upbraidings, as must needs
Tempt to repeat the wrong.[1]

The feeling of the newly married pair is beautifully continued in the hush of the evening world. By a delicate transition the breeze caressing the strings of the lute also becomes an image of human love. Subject and object, the inner and the outer world, are fused imaginatively with perfect success. This Coleridge was to do again even more skilfully in *Frost at Midnight* and his other Conversation poems. Here we see it fully developing for the first time. The new use of the flexible and gentle blank verse also has an intimacy which follows the movement of feeling and thought with ease. The following lines describing the music of the wind-harp reached a more beautiful final form in the later versions but, even in 1797, they have the authentic Coleridge magic, here heard for the first time:

And now its strings
Boldlier swept, the long sequacious notes
Over delicious Surges sink and rise
In aëry voyage, Music such as erst
Round rosy bowers (so Legendaries tell)
To sleeping Maids came floating witchingly
By wand'ring West winds stoln from Faery land
Where on some magic Hybla MELODIES
Round many a newborn honey-dropping Flower
Footless and wild, like Birds of Paradise,
Nor pause nor perch, warbling on untir'd wing.

[1] *PW*, p. 520.

The 'rosy bowers' were later removed and the lines tautened but the witchery remained.

Coleridge now turns again to Sara, his mood as tranquil still as the scene around him, but his brain, as usual, fairly active, though he himself calls it passive! The wind that stirs the lute becomes this time an image of the movement of fantasies over his mind. Once again the inner and the outer are fused:

> And thus, my Love! as on the midway Slope
> Of yonder Hill I stretch my limbs at noon
> And tranquil muse upon Tranquillity,
> Full many a Thought uncall'd and undetain'd
> And many idle flitting Phantasies
> Traverse my indolent and passive Mind
> As wild, as various, as the random Gales
> That swell or flutter on this subject Lute.[1]

The image of the lute is, again, skilfully continued in the next and more daring thought which occurs to this 'indolent and passive Mind'. It is still Hartleyan and vaguely pantheistic, which explains why the mind is called 'passive', a theory which Coleridge was soon violently to reject and which is, really, the last adjective that fits his own restless intelligence:

> And what if All of animated Life
> Be but as Instruments diversly fram'd
> That tremble into thought, while thro' them breathes
> One infinite and intellectual Breeze
>
> . . . .
>
> Thus *God* would be the universal Soul,
> Mechaniz'd matter as th' organic harps
> And each one's Tunes be that, which each calls I.[2]

This is the Unitarian, Darwinian Coleridge whom we have met before still trying to solve intellectually what, in the first part of the poem, he has been content to convey imaginatively – the fusion of God with 'mechanis'd matter' and each subjective soul. It is suggestive that the poetry immediately descends to the level of *Religious Musings*.

[1] ibid., p. 520.   [2] ibid., p. 521.

Sara, however, had little sympathy with or understanding of 'these Shapings of the unregen'rate Soul' and recalled her husband to a more orthodox position.

> Thou biddest me walk humbly with my God!
> Meek Daughter in the family of Christ.
> Wisely thou sayest, and holy are thy words!

The poem ends with thanks for God's mercy and a return to its starting-point which completes its curve and gives shape to the blending of reflection and description:

> Who with his saving Mercies healèd me,
> A sinful and most miserable man
> Wilder'd and dark, and gave me to possess
> PEACE and this COT, and THEE, my best-belov'd!

But the Coleridge who was so soon to write *The Ancient Mariner* remained conscious of sin, 'wilder'd and dark'.

Reflections on Having Left a Place of Retirement is very similar in feeling and setting to *The Eolian Harp* but much less good. It does, however, contain some delicately accurate observation mingled with reflection:

> Oh! what a goodly scene! *Here* the bleak mount,
> The bare bleak mountain speckled thin with sheep;
> Grey clouds, that shadowing spot the sunny fields;
> And river, now with bushy rocks o'er-brow'd,
> Now winding bright and full with naked banks;

His gaze expands to take in a wider scene:

> The Channel *there*, the Islands and white sails,
> Dim coasts, and cloud-like hills, and shoreless Ocean –
> It seem'd like Omnipresence! God, methought,
> Had built him there a Temple: the whole World
> Seem'd *imag'd* in its vast circumference:[1]

*   *   *

Lines Written at Shurton Bars, another Somerset poem of 1795, is undistinguished except that, as Coleridge watched the Bristol Channel

[1] *PW*, p. 107.

at night, he saw the lighthouse tower and a ship which appeared in a flash of light and then suddenly sank. This was a real scene of distress but, again, curiously anticipates the swift disappearance of the Ancient Mariner's ship:

> Then by the lightning's blaze to mark
> Some toiling tempest-shatter'd bark;
>   Her vain distress-guns hear;
> And when a second sheet of light
> Flash'd o'er the blackness of the night –
>   To see *no* vessel there![1]

The macabre nursery-tale of *The Raven*, 1797, also seems an imaginative foretaste of *The Ancient Mariner*. It tells the strange story of a provident raven who picked up an acorn, left by some swine, and buried it. He came back with a mate many years later to find the acorn grown into a tall oak tree in which they built a nest. But a woodman came with an axe and hewed down the tree:

> At length he brought down the poor Raven's own oak.
> His young ones were killed; for they could not depart,
> And their mother did die of a broken heart.[2]

The wood from the fallen tree was used to make a ship which was then caught in a terrible storm and lost with all hands. The raven reappears above the scene of destruction like an angel of death:

> Round and round flew the raven, and cawed to the blast.
> He heard the last shriek of the perishing souls –
> See! see! o'er the topmast the mad water rolls!
>   Right glad was the Raven, and off he went fleet,
> And Death riding home on a cloud he did meet,
> And he thank'd him again and again for this treat:
>   They had taken his all, and REVENGE IT WAS SWEET!

It is difficult to see what truth, if any, this strange cautionary tale is supposed to enshrine. The suffering of the bird becomes an image of man's guilt, and vengeance is wreaked. But the innocent souls on the

---

[1] ibid., p. 98.   [2] ibid., p. 170.

foundering ship were not responsible for the woodman's original cutting down of the tree, nor did he know it contained a raven's nest. The logic of cause and effect seems entirely lacking; at least the Ancient Mariner committed, in full knowledge, the crime for which he himself suffered. Perhaps we should not examine the structure of a nursery-tale too closely, and, by the time he wrote *The Ancient Mariner*, Coleridge had taken to heart Bowyer's dictum:

> I learnt from him that poetry, even that of the loftiest and, seemingly, that of the wildest odes, had a logic of its own as severe as that of science; and more difficult, because more subtle, more complex, and dependent on more and more fugitive causes.[1]

In *Sibylline Leaves*, 1817, however, Coleridge had second thoughts about the ending of *The Raven* and added two lines after 'REVENGE IT WAS SWEET!':

> We must not think so; but forget and forgive,
> And what Heaven gives life to, we'll still let it live.

Thought an excellent sentiment, this weakens the sombre force of the original whose power lies in its starkness. Nor was Coleridge satisfied with his addition, for he added a curious MS. note:

> *Added thro' cowardly fear of the Goody! What a Hollow, where the Heart of Faith ought to be, does it not betray? this alarm concerning Christian morality, that will not permit even a Raven to be a Raven, nor a Fox a Fox, but demands conventicular justice to be inflicted on their unchristian conduct, or at least an antidote to be annexed.[2]

One wonders whether the moral of *The Ancient Mariner*, similarly tacked on at the end of the poem and with which Coleridge told Mrs Barbauld he was not satisfied, was also 'added through cowardly fear of the Goody!' Lamb referred to *The Raven* as 'Your *Dream*' and *The Ancient Mariner* too has a dream's strange sequence. Yet, as Coleridge added a moral to both, he must take the blame if we search for a deeper meaning. The philosophic and imaginative content of his early poetry makes it difficult to assume that the meaning is simple.

[1] *BL*, p. 3.   [2] *PW*, p. 171.

CHAPTER II

'The Ancient Mariner':
The Natural and the Supernatural

THE vivid brilliance of *The Ancient Mariner* is so different in kind from Coleridge's earlier poems that it is difficult to recognise their common background of thought and feeling. Yet *The Destiny of Nations*, though mostly written in 1796 and partially included in Southey's *Joan of Arc*, was not published till 1817 because of Lamb's adverse criticism, and Coleridge continued to struggle with it under the title of *Visions of the Maid of Orleans*. A letter to Cottle of February 1798 refers to the greater and the lesser poem in the same breath: 'I have finished my ballad – it is 340 lines – I am going on with the Visions . . . '[1] *The Ancient Mariner* when 'finished' in March 1798 had 658 lines, so Coleridge had either miscounted or added a great deal more in the intervening month. Dorothy Wordworth's *Journal* recorded in March:

> Coleridge dined with us. He brought his ballad finished. We walked with him to the Miner's house. A beautiful evening, very starry, the horned moon.[2]

The 'horned moon' shone and for all lovers of poetry still shines above the Mariner's haunted sea, but the 'Visions' are forgotten. If we set a few lines from them beside a verse of *The Ancient Mariner* it is not difficult to see why:

> Shriek'd Ambition's giant throng,
> And with them hissed the locust-fiends that crawled
> And glittered in Corruption's slimy track.[3]

[1] Griggs, i, 387.
[2] D. Wordsworth, *Journals*, ed. H. Darbishire, World's Classics, 1958, p. 15.
[3] *PW*, p. 146.

This shares a common ancestry with the creatures of the terrible calm, but they have certainly undergone a sea-change:

> The very deeps did rot: O Christ!
> That ever this should be!
> Yea, slimy things did crawl with legs
> Upon the slimy Sea.[1]

The abstract has become concrete, the turgid simple, the formless has acquired form. The creative depths have, in every sense, been stirred to a poetry rich and strange beyond our imagining. We must try, as far as we can, to account for the transformation.

Though I believe it is concerned with the same intellectual conflict, *The Ancient Mariner* comes from deeper levels than *The Destiny of Nations* or *Religious Musings*. *The Road to Xanadu* has exhaustively shown that ancient archetypal images from Hellenic and Hebrew sources blended with memories from the old travellers' tales in Coleridge's richly stored mind. Odysseus, like the Mariner, survived the death of his comrades and the wreck of his ship to wander for many years before reaching home. The foundering of the Mariner's ship, Lowes points out, echoes a line from the *Aeneid*:

> And all was still save that the hill
> Was telling of the sound.

and

> . . . pulsati colles clamore resultant.[2]

It is possible, as Lowes says, that Coleridge, who had borrowed Henry Boyd's translation of Dante from the Bristol Library in 1796, also remembered the account in the *Inferno* of the sudden sinking of Ulysses' ship. The noble lines describing the venture into uncharted seas beyond the Pillars of Hercules;

> non vogliate negar l'esperienza,
> diretro al sol, del mondo senza gente,[3]

---

[1] *PW*, p. 531.
[2] Lowes, p. 263.
[3] Dante, *Inferno*, xxvi, l. 116–17.

– the experience of the unpeopled world behind the sun, could have suggested

> We were the first that ever burst
> Into that silent Sea.[1]

But the Wandering Jew with his branded brow and Cain himself, whose story is the subject of one of Coleridge's most haunting unfinished fragments, are also present in the underworld of the poem. The desert setting of *The Wanderings of Cain* with its hot rocks and scorching sands, where the first murderer meets his brother's ghost, has some of *The Ancient Mariner*'s imaginative power. The search for water in the arid waste and Abel's sombre cry: ' "The Lord is God of the living only, the dead have another God",'[2] are paralleled in the poem by the terrible thirst in the desert of the sea amid a universe of death. There is no doubt that *The Ancient Mariner* is concerned with the existence of evil, the spiritual aridity which follows it, and the eternal wandering of the soul which is only partially redeemed. Yet even the fullest awareness of the poem's literary sources and archetypal imagery does not explain the power of its impact upon us. All great poetry must spring from passionate experience and be rooted in its own time as well as in tradition. As Mr T. S. Eliot reminds us:

> The historical sense, which is a sense of the timeless as well as of the temporal and of the timeless and the temporal together, is what makes a writer traditional. And it is at the same time what makes a writer most acutely conscious of his place in time, of his own contemporaneity.[3]

Now Coleridge, of all men, was profoundly aware of the contemporary world but his critics, especially the source hunters, have tended to obscure the fact. The very extent of his learning and his reading have made us regard him as primarily a student whereas his notebooks and letters reveal his passionate preoccupation with the issues of his time.

[1] *PW*, p. 531.
[2] ibid., p. 291.
[3] T. S. Eliot, 'Tradition and the Individual Talent', *Selected Essays*, Faber, 1932, p. 14.

His intellectual conflicts and his never fully satisfied search for truth also underlie his poem. The Mariner's wanderings and desolation of spirit reflect Coleridge's own.

Nor should we forget that much of the subject-matter of *The Ancient Mariner* was quite consciously provided by Wordsworth. Seldom indeed can a great poem have had a more casual and light-hearted origin. It was begun as a joint project by Coleridge and Wordsworth, late on a November afternoon of 1797, to defray the expenses of a walking tour in Somerset upon which the two friends and Dorothy had set out. Many years later Wordsworth gave the following account of it:

In the autumn of 1797, he [Coleridge], my sister and myself, started from Alfoxden pretty late in the afternoon, with a view to visit Linton, and the Valley of Stones near to it; and as our united funds were very small, we agreed to defray the expense of the tour by writing a poem . . . Accordingly we set off, and proceeded along the Quantock Hills towards Watchet; and in the course of this walk was planned the poem of the 'Ancient Mariner', founded on a dream, as Mr Coleridge said, of his friend Mr Cruikshank. Much of the greatest part of the story was Mr Coleridge's invention; but certain parts I suggested; for example, some crime was to be committed which should bring upon the Old Navigator, as Coleridge afterwards delighted to call him, the spectral persecution, as a consequence of that crime and his own wanderings. I had been reading in Shelvocke's Voyages, a day or two before, that, while doubling Cape Horn, they frequently saw albatrosses in that latitude, the largest sort of sea-fowl, some extending their wings twelve or thirteen feet. 'Suppose', said I, 'you represent him as having killed one of these birds on entering the South Sea, and that the tutelary spirits of these regions take upon them to avenge the crime'. The incident was thought fit for the purpose, and adopted accordingly. I also suggested the navigation of the ship by the dead men, but do not recollect that I had anything more to do with the scheme of the poem . . . We began the composition together, on that to me memorable evening. . . . As we endeavoured to proceed conjointly (I speak of the same evening), our respective manners proved so widely different that it would have been quite presumptuous in me to do anything but separate from an undertaking upon which I could only have been a clog.[1]

This is a pleasant reminder of that vital friendship, 'three persons but one soul', which by its deep happiness roused the creative energy of both the young poets. Cruikshank's dream of the 'skeleton ship with figures in it', and the 'spectral persecution', had, as Lowes points out, obviously been in Coleridge's mind from the first, and to this we must return. But the shooting of the albatross and its vengeance by 'the tutelary spirits' of the South Sea were Wordsworth's contribution. If we remember the passage in the *Prelude* describing his night wanderings on the mountains among the woodcock snares, when he yielded to the temptation to steal a captive bird, we can perhaps guess what lay behind his suggestions to Coleridge:

> Sometimes it befel
> In these night-wanderings, that a strong desire
> O'erpowered my better reason, and the bird
> Which was the captive of another's toils
> Became my prey; and when the deed was done
> I heard among the solitary hills
> Low breathings coming after me, and sounds
> Of indistinguishable motion, steps
> Almost as silent as the turf they trod.[2]

The crime of stealing the snared bird was immediately followed by Wordsworth's awareness of the 'low breathings' and silent footsteps which pursued him. The whole context makes clear that these were the presences of Nature rousing the boy's soul to a consciousness of guilt; the passage is introduced by the lines:

> Fair seed-time had my soul, and I grew up
> Foster'd alike by beauty and by fear . . .[3]

The poet's fear of the spirit of Nature, quickened by guilt, thus became the beginning of wisdom. No doubt Wordsworth expected that Coleridge, who shared his pantheistic views to some extent, would also make the death of the albatross and the vengeance of the natural spirit

[1] Quoted by Lowes, p. 203.
[2] Wordsworth, *The Prelude*, ed. E. de Selincourt, OUP, 1933, i, 10.
[3] ibid., p. 9.

of the region instruments of the Mariner's regeneration. The guilty soul, after a period of suffering, would become more deeply reconciled to the Nature it had outraged and a part of the holiness of all life. In effect, however, *The Ancient Mariner* did not work out quite like that. Even on the day the poem was begun Wordsworth recognised that 'our respective manners proved so widely different' that he separated himself from the undertaking. Some of the misinterpretations of later criticism have, I think, arisen from determined attempts to give a Wordsworthian meaning to what was, despite its beginnings, essentially a Coleridge poem.

For, if we turn to his notebooks and letters of the time, it is clear that Coleridge was deeply involved in a continuous conflict between Faith and Reason, God and Nature, the mechanical and transcendental explanations of the universe. This uncertainty was, as I hope to show, reflected and externalised in *The Ancient Mariner*. But first we must look at some of his letters and notebook entries. The letter to Josiah Wade of January 1796, discussing Erasmus Darwin's too readily making up his mind on 'whether we be the outcasts of a blind idiot called Nature, or the children of an all-wise and infinitely good God',[1] has already been quoted in relation to *The Destiny of Nations*. But the phrase epitomises sharply a conflict which recurs in many of the letters of the next two years. In March 1796, the very year in which he published *Religious Musings* with its tribute to Priestley, Coleridge points out to the Rev. John Edwards the difficulties inherent in the Unitarian and pantheistic doctrine. He has referred to the pains of pregnancy and what he (wrongly) took to be his wife's miscarriage:

– Other pains are only friendly admonitions that we are not acting as Nature requires – but here are pains most horrible in consequence of having obeyed Nature. Quere – How is it that Dr Priestley is not an atheist? – He asserts in three different Places, that God not only *does*, but *is*, everything. – But if God *be* every Thing, every Thing is God – : which is all the Atheists assert – . An eating, drinking, lustful *God* – with no *unity* of *Consciousness* – these appear to me the unavoidable Inferences from his philosophy – Has not Dr Priestly [sic] forgotten that *Incomprehensibility* is as necessary an attribute of the First Cause, as Love, or Power, or Intelligence?[2]

[1] Griggs, i, 177. See p. 22.   [2] ibid., pp. 192–3.

Coleridge acutely sees that to make God an immanent part of the material world is to make God Himself material and to deprive the universe of the ultimate mystery of Godhead. A similar dichotomy appears in his postscript of a letter to John Thelwall in June 1796: 'We have an hundred lovely scenes about Bristol, which would make you exclaim – O admirable *Nature*! & me, O Gracious *God*! – '[1] Yet it was to Thelwall, atheist and freethinker as he was, that Coleridge wrote many of his most interesting and revealing letters at this time. Obviously he had a great respect for his friend's intelligence and honesty of mind, though he did not agree with his opinions.

Another letter to him of October 1797, a month before *The Ancient Mariner* was begun, continues the debate which, one comes to feel, was as much with Coleridge himself as with Thelwall:

> – You have my wishes, & what is very liberal in me for such an atheist reprobate, my prayers. – I can *at times* feel strongly the beauties, you describe, in themselves, & for themselves – but more frequently *all things* appear little – all the knowledge that can be acquired, child's play – the universe itself – what but an immense heap of *little* things? – I can contemplate nothing but parts, & parts are all *little* – ! – My mind feels as if it ached to behold & know something great – something *one* & *indivisible* – and it is only in the faith of this that rocks or waterfalls, mountains or caverns give me the sense of sublimity or majesty! – But in this faith *all things* counterfeit infinity![2]

Coleridge hated and feared the disconnected meaningless universe of the mechanical philosophy and longed to be certain of some spiritual power which would give unity and significance to the whole. The same letter, however, continues with a quotation from his own poem, *This Lime-Tree Bower my Prison*, which might be interpreted in a vaguely pantheistic and Wordsworthian way. It certainly betrays Wordsworth's influence:

> and gazing round
> On the wide Landscape gaze till all doth seem
> Less gross than bodily, a living Thing

[1] ibid., p. 222.

[2] ibid., p. 349.

45

> Which acts upon the mind, & with such Hues
> As cloath th' Almighty Spirit, when he makes
> Spirits perceive his presence! –

It is but seldom that I raise and spiritualize my intellect to this height – & at other times I adopt the Brahman Creed, & say – It is better to sit than to stand, it is better to lie than to sit, it is better to sleep than to wake – but Death is the best of all! – I should much wish, like the Indian Vishna, [Vishnu] to float about along an infinite ocean cradled in the flower of the Lotos, & wake once in a million years for a few minutes – just to know that I was going to sleep a million years more.[1]

It is interesting that Coleridge no sooner asserts the pantheistic doctrine of the landscape as a living thing veiling the Almighty Spirit than he disclaims it, longing instead for annihilation in the infinite spaces of the ocean. A month later he was to make the vast solitudes of the 'wide wide sea' the most terrifying image of *The Ancient Mariner*. If all things counterfeit the infinity of God, Coleridge's spirit can rest, but the infinite of measureless space can also suggest the annihilating desolation of a world without Him.

A letter to Poole describing his childhood also betrays the fascination the vast spaces of the sky always held for him:

. . . my father was fond of me, & used to take me on his knee, and hold long conversations with me. I remember, that at eight years old I walked with him one winter evening from a farmer's house, a mile from Ottery – & he told me the names of the stars – and how Jupiter was a thousand times larger than our world – and that the other twinkling stars were Suns that had worlds rolling round them – & when I came home, he shewed me how they rolled round – /. I heard him with a profound delight & admiration; but without the least mixture of wonder or incredulity. For from my early reading of Faery Tales, & Genii etc. etc. – my mind had been habituated *to the Vast* – & I never regarded *my senses* in any way as the criteria of my belief.[2]

An awareness of the infinite had thus always dominated Coleridge's

---

[1] Griggs, i, p. 350.   [2] ibid., p. 354.

imagination but in adult life his childish delight changed to fear and uncertainty, as we shall see in some of his notebook entries.

An important letter to his brother George of March 1798, the month in which he finished *The Ancient Mariner*, shows a continuing incongruity between his awareness of evil and the pantheistic belief that love of the calm beauty of Nature will lead to love of all created things:

> – Of GUILT I say nothing; but I believe most steadfastly in original Sin; that from our mothers' wombs our understandings are darkened; and even where our understandings are in the Light, that our organization is depraved, & our volitions imperfect; and we sometimes see the good without *wishing* to attain it, and oftimes *wish* it without the energy that wills & performs – And for this inherent depravity, I believe, that the *Spirit* of the Gospel is the sole cure . . . [1]

This comment upon the sinful imperfection of the will and its need for Christianity obviously throws interesting light on the evil impulse which slew the albatross and on the lines Coleridge had only just written:

> Instead of the Cross the Albatross
> About my neck was hung.[2]

Nevertheless, later in the same letter, without apparent awareness of the contradiction with 'the *Spirit* of the Gospel', he describes the power of poetry

> . . . to elevate the imagination & set the affections in right tune by the beauty of the inanimate impregnated, as with a living soul, by the presence of Life . . . I love fields & woods & mountains with almost a visionary fondness – and because I have found benevolence & quietness growing within me as that fondness [has] increased, therefore I should wish to be the means of implanting it in others – & to destroy the bad passions not by combating them, but by keeping them in inaction.[3]

The quotation from Wordsworth which follows betrays the strength

[1] ibid., p. 396. [2] *PW*, p. 532. [3] Griggs, i, 397.

of his influence at this time, but *The Ancient Mariner* shows only a doubtful connection between the natural world and 'a living soul'. Nor does Nature in the poem seem benevolent or capable of destroying the bad passions. Original sin and the healing power of the Gospel are equally strongly present. How far Coleridge was aware of the conflict we cannot be sure but it gave a passionate intensity to *The Ancient Mariner*.

The famous Gutch Notebook, which Lowes quarried so extensively for its literary associations in the voyagers' tales, provides equally powerful evidence of Coleridge's strong interest in the scientific and mechanical philosophy of his time and in the Platonic and Neoplatonic doctrines which were its antidote. The notebook, according to Miss Coburn, was used from 1795 to 1800, though not all its entries can be accurately dated. It certainly covers the period of *Religious Musings*, *The Destiny of Nations* and *The Ancient Mariner*, and even a few entries will be enough to show Coleridge's intellectual preoccupations at this date. Many of the notes are short and cryptic and Miss Coburn's elucidation of them is, therefore, especially valuable. Here is one of them:

> Stars twinkle upon us – Suns on other worlds. –
> Double sense of Prophecies.[1]

Miss Coburn explains that in 1796 Coleridge was reading Richard Watson, *An Apology for the Bible*, and had probably been struck by his account of the terrifying spaces of the sky:

> Who can comprehend the distance of the stars from the earth and from each other? . . . It is so great, that it mocks our conception; our very imagination is terrified, confounded, and lost, when we are told that a ray of light, which moves at the rate of above ten millions of miles in a minute, will not, though emitted at this instant from the brightest star, reach the earth in less than six years. . . . But how does the whole of this globe sink, as it were, to nothing, when we consider that a million of earths will scarcely equal the bulk of the sun; that all the stars are suns; and that millions of suns constitute, probably but a minute portion of that material world, which God hath distributed through the immensity of space?[2]

[1] N I, 82 G. 76.   [2] ibid., 82 G. 76 (Notes).

When Coleridge describes the moon in *The Ancient Mariner*,

> Her beams bemock'd the sultry main
> Like morning frosts yspread;[1]

it is possible that the word 'bemock'd' suggests the vast time and distance which baffles our imagination as well as the likeness to frost. Another cryptic entry of 1796 is also concerned with the scientific laws of the universe as expounded by Newton and others:

> World – [? makers / maker]. –
> As if according to Sir Isaac Newton's progression of pores – they had coarct the world to a Ball and were playing with it –[2]

Miss Coburn points out that Sir Isaac Newton's doctrine of centripetal force lies behind this, but that Coleridge had also been reading Russel, *Essay on the Nature and Existence of a Material World*, where the following occurs:

> There is no species of matter known that is not subject to compression by the application of sufficient force; . . . whatever body is not compact enough to have all pores filled up, is necessarily liable to be crushed into less bulk by superior power . . . Thus by the operation of an increasing power, the world may be reduced in bulk *ad infinitum* without making the smallest approach to nihility. . . What will the Materialist say, when he sees the universe in Imagination dwindling down to the size of a cricket ball?[3]

The world, as the scientists explained it, was certainly alien and terrifying and, in our own day, has become more fearful still. This universe, subjected to ruthless and, apparently, impersonal force, was difficult to reconcile with a personal God. In *The Destiny of Nations* Coleridge had tried to link the two:

> Glory to Thee, Father of Earth and Heaven!
> All-conscious Presence of the Universe!
> Nature's vast ever-acting Energy![4]

[1] *PW*, p. 535.
[2] N I, 93 G. 87.
[3] ibid., 93 G. 87 (Notes).
[4] *PW*, pp. 146–7.

But the picture the scientists gave of this energy scarcely suggested any consciousness at all, still less a fatherly one. Their activity seemed more likely to result in

> Untenanting creation of its God.[1]

It is no wonder that two more of Coleridge's 1796 entries show a longing to believe that God can still control these vast and remote spaces:

> God no distance knows,
> All of the whole possessing. – [2]

and

> It surely is not impossible that to some infinitely superior being the whole Universe may be one plain – the distance between planet and planet only the pores that exist in any grain of sand – and the distances between system & system no greater than the distance between one grain and the grain adjacent. – [3]

Both entries reveal a wistful eagerness to believe that these terrifying distances can be comprehended by a God who is equally infinite. But belief was not easy for a mind as subtle and profound as Coleridge's; the terror of a world controlled by alien impersonal forces in a frightening infinity lies behind *The Ancient Mariner*.

One more entry from the Gutch notebook may in its brilliance of colour be evidence of an opium dream.[4] But its last lines show Coleridge's fear of the solitary spaces of the ocean, the Mariner's 'wide wide sea':

> – a dusky light – a purple *flash*
> crystalline splendor – light blue –
>   *Green* lightnings. –
> in that eternal and delirious misery –
> wrathfires –
>   inward desolations –
> an horror of great darkness
>   great things than on the ocean
>   counterfeit infinity.[5]

---

[1] *PW*, p. 132. [2] N 1, 98 G. 92. [3] ibid., 120 G. 114.
[4] M. Abrams, *The Milk of Paradise*. [5] N 1, 273 G. 270.

It is possible that both the brilliance of colour and the desolating terror of the vast sea were due to the influence of opium. Professor Bald points out in his interesting article on Coleridge[1] that he had taken the drug twice in 1796, the date of this entry, probably under medical supervision. The letters refer to it again in March 1798, the month in which *The Ancient Mariner* was finished, and at the time of the composition of *Kubla Khan*. In each case Coleridge speaks of his taking of laudanum quite openly and it was a common prescription for pain at the time; in 1798 he took it to relieve an abscess. Its use did not become habitual till 1801–2 and therefore, in its early stages, the drug may merely have stimulated his senses, sharpening especially his awareness of colour and sound. As Professor Bald says:

> In normal cases of opium addiction the doses produce sensations of relief and pleasure for a period of from six to twelve months, and then the horrors begin . . . [2]

The constant nightmares which made him afraid to go to sleep do not seem to have begun till 1803, the period of *The Pains of Sleep*.

In a notebook entry of October 1803, recasting an earlier one of 1799, Coleridge shows himself aware of the power of association and ascribes it partly to opium:

> – For what is Forgetfulness? Renew the state of affection or bodily Feeling, same or similar – sometimes dimly similar / and instantly the trains of forgotten Thought rise from their living catacombs! – Old men, & Infancy / and Opium, probably by its narcotic effect on the whole seminal organisation, in a large Dose, or after long use, produces the same effect on the *visual*, & *passive* memory / [3]

I have discussed this very important note also in relation to *Kubla Khan* which was composed under the influence of opium and whose imagery of underground caverns seems related to the 'living catacombs' of the mind. Coleridge, with a psychological insight remarkable for his time

---

[1] R. C. Bald, 'Coleridge and "The Ancient Mariner" ', *Nineteenth Century Studies*, Ithaca, 1940.

[2] ibid., p. 29.

[3] N I, 1575 21.296(a). See p. 119.

Coleridge?

but not unusual for him, suggests that opium helps to release the forgotten memories which then rise to the surface of the mind in visual images. This would help to explain not only the vividness of colour and sensitivity to sound in *The Ancient Mariner*, both characteristics of opium dreams, but also its dream-like flow. Its fluid brilliance has the strange logic of a waking dream or reverie, only partly controlled by the conscious mind. This may have been why Wordsworth complained that the events of the poem ' . . . having no necessary connection do not produce each other . . . '[1] The connections are partly unconscious and this may have been due to the influence of opium.

A late notebook entry, quoted by Professor Bald, shows something of the meaning Coleridge attached to the word 'reverie', the sub-title of *The Ancient Mariner* in 1800:

> In short, the Night-mair is not properly *a Dream*; but a species of Reverie, akin to Somnambulism, during which the Understanding & moral Sense are awake, tho' more or less confused, and over the Terrors of which the Reason can exert no influence, because it is not true Terror; i.e. apprehension of Danger, but a sensation as much as the Tooth-ache or Cramp . . . [2]

The understanding and moral sense thus still exerted some control in Coleridge's reveries but it was not complete. Since he had described poetry itself as 'a rationalized dream',[3] Coleridge, with characteristic penetration, had, in fact, analysed the mixture of conscious and unconscious in poetic creation where the power of *The Ancient Mariner* lies.

But the earlier Gutch notebook also contains several references to dreams. An entry of 1796 suggests that the mind's conflict can be externalised in them:

> – Dreams sometimes useful by ~~making~~ [sic] giving to the well-grounded *fears* & *hopes* of the understanding the *feelings* of vivid sense.[4]

We have seen something of Coleridge's fears and hopes at this time but

[1] Quoted by Lowes, p. 475.
[2] Bald, p. 35.
[3] N 2, 2086 15.52, f. 40ᵛ. See Introduction, p. 5.
[4] N 1, 188 G. 184.

have yet to trace how they were given form and vivid life, how his problems were released, if not resolved, in *The Ancient Mariner*.

The psychology of dreams had a great fascination for Coleridge and some of his philosophical reading during this period used them as evidence of the immortality of the soul. In a note on the entry above Miss Coburn tells us that

> At this time Coleridge's chief authority on dreams was Andrew Baxter, *An Enquiry into the Nature of the Human Soul; Wherein the immateriality of the soul is evinced from the Principles of Reason and Philosophy.* (2 vols. 1745), a work Coleridge read in the summer of 1795. In 1827, analysing his own dreams, he remembered it: 'By the bye, I must get the Book – which I have never seen since in my 24th year I walked with Southey on a desperate hot Summerday from Bath to Bristol with a Goose, 2 vol. of Baxter on the Immortality of the Soul, and the Giblets, in my hand – I should not wonder if I found that Andrew had thought more on the subject of Dreams than any other of our Psychologists, Scotch or English – ' (N 35).[1]

If we follow Coleridge through Andrew Baxter (though we cannot recreate the context of the goose and the hot summer day!) we find several passages describing the borderland between sleep and waking which might well have caught his attention. Here is one:

> The soul . . . is often engaged in a dream before we are well fallen asleep; so that we may trace back the perceptions of the soul *in these confines between sleeping and waking*, but shall not find it designing to amuse itself, but rather *suddenly engaged* in beholding things, it knows not how.[2]

This sounds very like Coleridge's 'reverie' where the visual images 'rose up before him as *things*',[3] the process described in the Preface to *Kubla Khan*. In another passage Baxter contrasts the coherence of day-dreams with the inconsequence of real dreams, and, for Coleridge, a day-dream was a species of reverie:

> When one *muses*, the soul moves its attention gradually from one

[1] ibid., 188 G. 184 (Notes).
[2] Andrew Baxter, *An Enquiry into the Nature of the Human Soul*, 1745, ii, 11.
[3] *PW*, p. 296.

object, or one idea, to another; but still with consciousness that it doth so, and according to the connections which have been formerly made between them. There is no hurrying from one thing to another, without coherence or relation. Whence this particular illustrates the incoherence of our dreams a little.[1]

But Baxter's insistence that dreams are evidence of the power of spiritual beings working upon us would have been especially congenial to Coleridge:

> How delightful it is to think that there is a *world* of spirits; that we are surrounded with intelligent living Beings, rather than in a *lonely, unconscious Universe, a wilderness of matter*! It is a *pledge* given us of *immortality itself*, and that we shall not be extinguished all at once, nor cut off from existence . . . Who that is rational would *chuse* to be without these intimations of after-existence?[2]

From his letters and notebook entries we have seen how Coleridge feared a blindly unconscious, material universe as much as Baxter. This conception of dreams as intimations of the soul's immortality would certainly have appealed to him. Baxter thought that spirits could be malicious as well as good (in order to account for disturbing dreams), but God kept the evil ones in subjection.[3] Perhaps Coleridge remembered them when he wrote

> And some in dreams assured were
> Of the Spirit that plagued us so:[4]

If he found evidence of the soul's after-existence in Andrew Baxter, Cudworth's *The True Intellectual System of the Universe* gave him support for the Platonic doctrine of its pre-existence. Another Gutch notebook entry of 1796–7 is largely a quotation from Cudworth who translates the Greek phrase with which it opens, 'Our soul somewhere before it came to exist in this present human form . . . ' Coleridge's entry then goes on:

> [Greek] . . . Plato in Phaedone: and Synesius, the hyper-platonic

---

[1] Baxter, ii, 90.   [2] ibid., pp. 172–3.
[3] ibid., p. 186.   [4] *PW*, p. 532.

Jargonist, would have waved his claims to a Bishopric than allow *his Soul to be younger* than his Body.[1]

On the previous page Cudworth says:

> . . . the assertors of the soul's immortality commonly began here; first to prove its pre-existence, proceeding thence afterwards to establish its permanency after death. This is the method used in Plato . . . [2]

In the first version of his sonnet on the birth of his son, Hartley, in November 1796, which he included in a letter to Poole, Coleridge refers to Plato's doctrine of the soul's pre-existence and, significantly, links it with dreams:

> Oft of *some unknown Past* such Fancies roll
> Swift o'er my brain, as make the Present seem,
> For a brief moment, like a most strange dream
> When, not unconscious that she dreamt, the Soul
> Questions herself in sleep! and Some have said
> We liv'd ere yet this *fleshly* robe we wore.[3]

This conception of the soul's immortality and the dreamer aware that he is dreaming is another intimation of a transcendental world which approaches us in dreams, though, again, through a semi-conscious process. Coleridge thus linked dreams intellectually with a supernatural existence which lies beyond the rational; at the same time, the partially dream-like form of *The Ancient Mariner* both expressed and released this conflict between the transcendental and the material, the supernatural and the natural world. Because it comes from greater depths and is thus more imaginative than intellectual, as much unconscious as conscious, we can be thankful that the searchings of Coleridge's troubled spirit this time issued in *The Ancient Mariner* and not in another *Destiny of Nations*.

★   ★   ★

Now, at last, we can turn to *The Ancient Mariner* itself, as Coleridge first wrote it in 1798. The setting of the wedding-feast provides a

---

[1] N 1, 200 G. 196.
[2] Cudworth, *The True Intellectual System of the Universe*, 1743, p. 38.
[3] Griggs, i, 246.

framework of reality for the strange story by which we are soon hypnotised as fixedly as the wedding-guest. The vivid concreteness of the language, in many ways so like that of the old voyagers and so different from anything Coleridge had written before, helps to cast the spell. After crossing the Line the Mariner's ship is driven inexorably southward to the polar regions:

> Listen, Stranger! Storm and Wind,
> A Wind and Tempest strong!
> For days and weeks it play'd us freaks –
> Like Chaff we drove along.

The sailors are helpless at the mercy of capricious elements which show no trace of benevolence to man. With the speed of a dream we reach the land of ice:

> Listen, Stranger! Mist and Snow,
> And it grew wond'rous cauld:
> And Ice mast-high came floating by
> As green as Emerauld.[1]

The lines have a remarkable pictorial concentration; 'ice mast-high' immediately shows how small the ship is among the ice-bergs and the brilliant 'green as emerauld', whether created by opium or not, has a sinister vividness. If abnormal sensitivity to sound was another characteristic of opium dreams, we certainly have it in the cracking of the ice:

> The Ice was here, the Ice was there,
> The Ice was all around:
> It crack'd and growl'd, and roar'd and howl'd –
> Like noises of a swound.

It also sounds like a wild beast, fierce and cruel to man. In this universe of death the albatross suddenly flies glimmering through the fog and is hailed with joy by the sailors:

> And an it were a Christian Soul,
> We hail'd it in God's name.

[1] *PW*, p. 529.

They greet it almost as an angel of good omen, 'a Christian Soul', and, at its arrival, the ice splits, the south wind rises and the ship sails north-ward away from the ice and snow. The albatross follows, eating the biscuits the sailors give it and perching on the moonlit mast for vespers. Once again we notice the deliberately Christian association with even-ing prayers. This makes the mariner's act seem more evil as he cruelly shoots the friendly and helpless bird. It is no wonder that devils now torment him:

> 'God save thee, ancyent Marinere!
> 'From the fiends that plague thee thus –
> 'Why look'st thou so?' – with my cross bow
> I shot the Albatross.[1]

The shooting of the albatross has led to many and various symbolic interpretations by Coleridge's critics. The difficulty is that they all conflict with one another and try to give the poem the definiteness of allegory which the poet himself would have deplored. Mr Penn Warren, one of the most influential and penetrating of the symbolist critics, thinks the death of the albatross represents the Fall of Man, a crime against the sacramental vision of the 'One Life' which Coleridge had expressed in *The Eolian Harp*:[2]

> O! the one Life within us and abroad,
> . . . .
> Methinks, it should have been impossible
> Not to love all things in a world so fill'd.[3]

This is the most persuasive of the pantheistic interpretations; it gives the poem a good Wordsworthian meaning, and we know that Cole-ridge did have pantheistic leanings at the time. But problems begin to appear when we turn from the theory to the poem itself. Other sug-gestions have been wilder. Professor G. Wilson Knight thinks the slaying of the albatross ' . . . may correspond to the death of Christ in racial history'.[4] Mr Kenneth Burke suggests it represents Coleridge's

[1] ibid., p. 530.
[2] R. Penn Warren, *The Rime of the Ancient Mariner*, Reynal and Hitchcock, New York, 1946, pp. 81–2.
[3] *PW*, p. 101.
[4] G. W. Knight, *The Starlit Dome*, Methuen, 1959, p. 85.

desire to kill his wife[1] (though in 1798 he was still in love with her). They cannot all be right and all have a common rigidity which impoverishes the poem's richness of meaning in order to fit a theory. In the process the poem itself is frequently distorted, for it is difficult to make it conform to any completely consistent pattern. This is, as I have tried to show, because Coleridge was himself uncertain in his beliefs at this time. The attempt to give *The Ancient Mariner* a consistent moral meaning may also be the wrong way to approach it. Coleridge himself confessed to Mrs Barbauld that he thought the poem's chief fault was ' . . . the obtrusion of the moral sentiment so openly on the reader as a principle or cause of action in a work of such pure imagination'.[2] He was, presumably, referring to the moral at the end which he probably regretted. A letter of 1816 to Daniel Stuart suggests a better way to read the poem:

> The truth is that Images and Thoughts possess a power in and of themselves, independent of that act of the Judgement or Understanding by which we affirm or deny the existence of a reality correspondent to them. Such is the ordinary state of the mind in Dreams.[3]

When he called his poem 'a reverie' he probably meant that the images and rhythm should be allowed to do their work at a partly subconscious, dream-like level; the judgment and understanding alone will never arrive at the full meaning.

Mr Penn Warren links the bird, the wind and the moon in what he calls 'a symbolic cluster',[4] but, if this is so, the wind which sprang up at the coming of the albatross should surely drop suddenly at its death. Or, if the powers of Nature have a close moral link with living creatures, as Wordsworth believed, the natural forces of the poem should be seen to sympathise with the albatross. This was, no doubt, what Wordsworth expected, but this is not what happens. Part II opens with the ship speeding northwards, driven by the south wind which seems indifferent to the death of the albatross:

> And the good south wind still blew behind,
> But no sweet Bird did follow

[1] K. Burke, *The Philosophy of Literary Form*, New York, 1957, p. 61.
[2] Coleridge, *Table Talk*, OUP, 1917, p. 106.
[3] Griggs, iv, 641.
[4] R. P. Warren, p. 91.

> Ne any day for food or play
> Came to the Marinere's hollo!

This is followed, moreover, by the curiously ironic verses in which Coleridge himself seems at pains to repudiate any association between the albatross, the forces of nature and the Mariner's moral action:

> And I had done an hellish thing
> And it would work 'em woe;
> For all averr'd, I had kill'd the Bird
> That made the Breeze to blow.

> Ne dim ne red, like God's own head,
> The glorious Sun uprist:
> Then all averr'd, I had kill'd the Bird
> That brought the fog and mist.
> Twas right, said they, such birds to slay
> That bring the fog and mist.[1]

The mariner's shipmates were, in fact, good Pantheists but, since their comments directly contradict each other, we must suppose that Coleridge did not mean them to be taken seriously! The sailors are, apparently, opportunists whose views of morality alter with the circumstances. To make the point still clearer the wind, in the next verse, continues to blow the ship merrily towards the Line. It is obeying the natural rather than the moral law, for, as Lowes points out, 'the breezes' of the 1798 version are the South East Trades, known to the old voyagers as 'the Brises':[2]

> The breezes blew, the white foam flew,
> The furrow follow'd free:
> We were the first that ever burst
> Into that silent Sea.

The verse has in it all the magic of the old discoverers sailing into uncharted seas and moves with an exhilarating rhythm, confident and free. Nothing could be less burdened with guilt or remorse. Coleridge seems deliberately to have rejected any connection between Nature and

---

[1] *PW*, p. 531. [2] Lowes, pp. 118–19.

man's moral life at this point in the poem, and the deliberate irony of the previous verses suggests that he knew quite well what he was doing. A cryptic entry in the Gutch notebook of 1796 is relevant here:

– transfer the proofs of natural to moral Sciences. –[1]

Miss Coburn quotes the extract he had been reading from Burnet, *Sacred Theory of the Earth* (the same Burnet who provided the epigraph for the 1817 edition of *The Ancient Mariner*):

That which gives me the greatest scandal in this doctrine of the vulgar Millennium, is, their joyning things together that are really inconsistent; a natural World of one colour, and a moral World of another.[2]

Now, in *Religious Musings*, Coleridge had had such a vision of the Millennium:

The Saviour comes! While as the Thousand Years
Lead up their mystic dance, the Desert shouts!
Old Ocean claps his hands![3]

Whether he now thought this 'vulgar' we do not know, but Ocean no longer claps his hands in *The Ancient Mariner*. No more personified, it has become the image of desolation itself, a vast solitude from which God has withdrawn. Coleridge's treatment of nature in this section of the poem shows that he was quite aware of the danger of linking the natural with the moral world. It is a pantheistic error into which many of his critics have fallen.

It is true that the wind does now drop but this is because the ship has again reached the Line:

All in a hot and copper sky
The bloody sun at noon,
Right up above the mast did stand,
No bigger than the moon.

Here again the symbolists have been at work. Throughout his essay Mr Penn Warren is at pains to equate the sun of the poem with evil

[1] N 1, 100 G. 94.   [2] ibid., 100 G. 94 (Notes).   [3] *PW*, p. 122.

and the moon with good and redemptive forces. H. House rightly
criticised this in his discussion of *The Ancient Mariner*, pointing out that
the mariners die by the light of the moon in Part III.[1] Mr Beer and
others have not found it difficult to show that Coleridge frequently
identified the sun with God.[2] The equatorial sun has been terrible to
many travellers but this does not mean that the sun is always tor-
menting, even in the poem. In Part V the angelic sounds from the
lips of the dead dart to the sun.[3] Both the sun and moon change with
the geography of the voyage and also with the Mariner's spiritual state;
they cannot be rigidly limited in meaning. The terrible calm and the
rotting sea do seem to suggest the stagnation and corruption of the
soul, a waste land of the spirit, but not because the natural world has
turned against the Mariner. Rather it has become an image of the loneliness and fear the guilty soul feels:

> Water, water, every where,
> And all the boards did shrink;
> Water, water, every where,
> Ne any drop to drink.

Water, the old Christian symbol of life, has become death for the
Ancient Mariner, and in the next verse he calls on Christ:

> The very deeps did rot: O Christ!
> That ever this should be!
> Yea, slimy things did crawl with legs
> Upon the slimy sea.

The brilliant colours that follow have a nightmare quality which may
be due to opium:

> The water, like a witch's oils,
> Burnt green and blue and white.

The word 'burnt' suggests the fiery torment of the blazing colours.
 Then, at last, Coleridge remembers Wordsworth's suggestion of the
vengeance by the tutelary spirits of the region. The powers of Nature

[1] House, p. 103.
[2] J. Beer, *Coleridge the Visionary*, Chatto and Windus, 1959, p. 168.
[3] *PW*, p. 537.

are to assert themselves against the murderer of the albatross. Yet the verse about the Polar Spirit is very curious:

> And some in dreams assured were
> Of the Spirit that plagued us so:
> Nine fathom deep he had follow'd us
> From the Land of Mist and Snow.[1]

Since he is reduced to the vision of *some* of the sailors 'in dreams', the Polar Spirit seems to have a subjective rather than an objective reality. According to Andrew Baxter he might have been an intimation of the immortality of the soul! But this was certainly not what Wordsworth had intended and, though his criticism of *The Ancient Mariner* is pompous and ungenerous, we begin to understand his dissatisfaction:

> The Poem of my Friend has indeed great defects . . . the events, having no necessary connection, do not produce each other; and lastly, that the imagery is somewhat too laboriously accumulated.[2]

In Wordsworth's mind there must have been a 'necessary connection' between the death of the albatross, the polar spirit's vengeance and the Mariner's sufferings. But, in the poem, the spirit is introduced as a possible hallucination of some of the sailors and then immediately abandoned till Part V, where his status is again reduced, as he becomes subordinate to the angelic troop. One is forced to the conclusion that Coleridge found him an embarrassment, a sort of Pantheistic hangover which he included to please Wordsworth.

Part II ends with the terrible thirst and the amazingly vivid and concrete image:

> We could not speak no more than if
> We had been choked with soot.

Then, once again, the awareness of sin is conveyed not through a natural image but by the great Christian symbol:

> Ah wel-a-day! what evil looks
> Had I from old and young;
> Instead of the Cross the Albatross
> About my neck was hung.

---

[1] *PW*, p. 532.   [2] Lowes, p. 475.

In Part III the skeleton ship of Cruikshank's dream, which had been in Coleridge's mind from the beginning, takes possession of the poem with a nightmare abruptness and strangeness. It is not, apparently, called up by the Polar spirit as a part of his vengeance, and Wordsworth's complaint of lack of connection in the events of the poem has here some validity. Nevertheless, the very swiftness and dreamlike inconsequence with which the phantom ship appears has a very powerful imaginative effect. The 'strange shape' drives suddenly between the mariners and the setting sun:

> And strait the Sun was fleck'd with bars
> (Heaven's mother send us grace)
> As if thro' a dungeon grate he peer'd
> With broad and burning face.[1]

The natural world is imprisoned by the supernatural and, in the next verse, the beautiful natural image of 'gossameres' is used to convey the transparency of the skeleton ship's sails:

> Are those *her* Sails that glance in the Sun
> Like restless gossameres?

Wordsworth's imagination suggested the supernatural through the real world; Coleridge suspends our disbelief in the mystery which lies beyond the normal by appealing to our observation of natural things.

The figures in the skeleton-ship, also from Cruikshank's dream, have in the 1798 version all the trappings of Gothic horror. The description of Death is a little crude and was cut out in 1817:

> *His* bones were black with many a crack,
> All black and bare, I ween;
> Jet-black and bare, save where with rust
> Of mouldy damps and charnel crust
> They're patch'd with purple and green.

His female companion is described with a more subtle terror which may have come from Coleridge's own nightmares:

> *Her* lips are red, *her* looks are free,
> *Her* locks are yellow as gold:

---

[1] *PW*, p. 533.

Her skin is as white as leprosy,
And she is far liker Death than he;
Her flesh makes the still air cold.

The change to Present tense also gives her a vivid immediacy, and the image of leprosy creates a more creeping fear than the charnel-house description of Death. But in 1798 we are not told who the two figures are or what they are doing. The significance of the dice-game is made much clearer in *Sibylline Leaves* where Coleridge made many alterations to this part of the poem. In the earlier version we do not even know that the Mariner's soul is the stake; we only hear the leprous figure cry:

'The Game is done! I've won, I've won!'
Quoth she, and whistled thrice.

We are not told what she has won or who she is; the inconsequence of the dice-game itself is made still more haphazard by the poetic method. In 1817, as we shall see, Coleridge gave a greater depth and imaginative clarity to this part of the poem without lessening its nightmare power.

Nevertheless, the skeleton-ship with its two strange figures playing dice remained the imaginative centre of the poem. On the issue of the game the Mariner's and his shipmates' fates depend. This, as Professor E. Bostetter points out in an interesting article,[1] seems to contradict Mr Penn Warren's theory of the 'One Life', the sacramental vision. Professor Bostetter recognises Mr Warren's essay as 'the most influential modern interpretation' but stresses that its emphasis upon crime and punishment, followed by the impulse of love, repentance and redemption, entirely ignores the capricious and irrational elements in the universe of *The Ancient Mariner*. Since the two figures play for the Mariner's soul, 'The most disturbing characteristic of this universe is the caprice that lies at the heart of it; the precise punishment of the Mariner and his shipmates depends upon chance'.[2] He thinks this ' . . . throws into question the moral and intellectual responsibilities of the rulers of the universe', and destroys any attempt to impose a systematic philosophical or religious interpretation on the poem. The Mariner's shipmates, Professor Bostetter points out, are condemned to death also by

[1] E. Bostetter, 'The Nightmare World of "The Ancient Mariner" ', *Studies in Romanticism*, Summer 1962, I, iv, 241-54.
[2] ibid., p. 244.

64

the throw of the dice; this is a primitive and merciless morality. His conclusion questions the whole moral interpretation of the poem, as many critics have expounded it:

> What he (Coleridge) wanted to believe in and increasingly devoted his intellectual energies to asserting was a universe of order and benevolence in which man possessed freedom of will and action to mould his own destiny; what he feared was a universe in which he was at the mercy of arbitrary and unpredictable forces. The *Rime* envisions such a universe.[1]

This seems to point to the same conflict we have already noticed in Coleridge's letters and notebooks. He did want to believe in the relation between cause and effect, sin and expiation, preferably in Christian terms. Even when he veered towards pantheism, 'the beauty of the inanimate impregnated, as with a living soul by the presence of life' was supposed to 'set the affections in right tune',[2] but, as we have seen, this was only a momentary impulse, probably due to Wordsworth's influence. The connection between the natural and moral world is never maintained for long in *The Ancient Mariner*. It is not only the throw of the dice which is 'arbitrary and unpredictable'. The elements themselves, the natural forces of the poem, are equally capricious and remote from man's moral experience. The wind, the moon, the sun and the sea behave, at best, with indifference, obeying their own natural laws but remote and alien to men. The universe of vast and terrifying space, moved according to the scientists by strange and powerful physical forces, was not a comforting one. Coleridge's notebooks show that he feared it because it seemed to reduce man to a mere 'outcast of a blind idiot called Nature'. There are moments in the poem when the wandering Mariner seems such an outcast.

With the departure of the Spectre-ship the horned moon rises and, by its light, the sailors drop dead one by one:

> One after one by the horned Moon
> (Listen, O Stranger! to me)
> Each turn'd his face with a ghastly pang,
> And cursed me with his ee.

---

[1] ibid., p. 251.   [2] Griggs, i, 397. See p. 47.

Four times fifty living men,
With never a sigh or groan,
With heavy thump, a lifeless lump
They dropp'd down one by one.[1]

The horror of his comrades' deaths is brought out by the dead sounds, the heavy monosyllables and internal rhyme, 'with heavy thump, a lifeless lump'. As House points out, this passage makes it impossible to accept Mr Warren's view of the moon as representing good and redemptive forces.[2] It is one more example of the difficulty of relating the natural and the moral world in the poem. The Ancient Mariner's agony of remorse is more vividly brought out in the image of the cross-bow with which he had slain the albatross:

And every soul it pass'd me by,
Like the whiz of my Cross-bow.

At the beginning of Part IV the wedding-guest recalls us from the nightmare to reality:

'I fear thee, ancyent Marinere!
'I fear thy skinny hand;
'And thou are long, and lank, and brown,
'As is the ribb'd Sea-sand.

The Mariner reassures him that he is not a ghost, though death might have been easier than the terrible isolation which he suffered:

Alone, alone, all all alone,
Alone on the wide wide Sea;
And Christ would take no pity on
My soul in agony.

Where Coleridge had once seen God immanent in the natural world,

All-conscious Presence of the Universe!
Nature's vast ever-acting Energy![3]

the sea now becomes an image of a frightening infinity from which

[1] *PW*, p. 534.   [2] House, p. 103.   [3] *PW*, p. 147.

Christ has withdrawn, the loneliness of the forsaken and sinful soul in an empty universe. The Unitarian and pantheistic doctrines provide no answer to the problem of evil with which Coleridge is here deeply concerned. The Mariner suffers the doom of the undying among the dead:

> The many men so beautiful,
> And they all dead did lie!
> And a million million slimy things
> Liv'd on – and so did I.

He tries to pray but cannot; he is conscious only of the vast spaces of sea and sky and the curse in the eyes of the dead men:

> For the sky and the sea, and the sea and the sky
> Lay like a load on my weary eye,
> And the dead were at my feet.

The heavy reiteration of the rhythm and the repeated monosyllables again give the effect of extreme weariness and desolation.

Then, above the stagnant sea and the fixed eyes of the dead, the new moon rises:

> The moving Moon went up the sky,
> And no where did abide:
> Softly she was going up
> And a star or two beside.

The gentle rhythm of the moon's smooth ascent certainly creates in this context an extraordinary feeling of release. Her remote beauty has no part in the terrible sea over which she shines, yet she is a reminder of the unalterable laws of the natural world and, in this universe of death, even that is a consolation. By her light the Mariner becomes aware of the shining beauty and the graceful movement of the water-snakes. Their colours have again a dream-like brilliance:

> Blue, glossy green, and velvet black
> They coil'd and swam; and every track
> Was a flash of golden fire.[1]

[1] ibid., p. 535.

The Mariner's impulse of love towards the living creatures partially redeems his cruelty to the albatross:

> A spring of love gusht from my heart,
> And I bless'd them unaware!

He is able to pray again and the burden of sin is lightened:

> The Albatross fell off, and sank
> Like lead into the sea.

This certainly marks a turning point in the poem and could be taken as the beginning of Christian redemption or as renewed reconciliation with the living world he had outraged. Mr Penn Warren seems to think it a mixture of the two and, in the working of the ship by the dead men, even sees an image 'of regeneration and resurrection'.[1] Earlier, Miss Maud Bodkin saw the poem as an example of the Rebirth archetype.[2] Yet, as *The Ancient Mariner* progresses, the redemption seems only partial and doubtful, nor is the Mariner's return home brought about by natural forces. We must beware of over-simplifying the poem to make a neat moral pattern, since we have seen from Coleridge's notebooks and letters at the time that no solution entirely satisfied him.

Part V indeed opens more gently with the healing sleep and rain which refresh the Mariner's weary soul and body. Wind and storm arise and, under the lightning, the dead men begin to work the ship. Once again the poem assumes the quality of nightmare, as Coleridge himself daringly stresses:

> It had been strange, even in a dream
> To have seen those dead men rise.

The ship begins to move but not by natural forces:

> The helmsman steer'd, the ship mov'd on;
> Yet never a breeze up-blew;

It is sailed by the dead men, yet it would be travesty of Christianity to

[1] Penn Warren, p. 97.
[2] M. Bodkin, *Archetypal Patterns in Poetry*, OUP, 1934, pp. 26–89.

call this resurrection. It is a ghastly mockery of what life had been, another form of Life-in-Death:

> The body of my brother's son
> Stood by me knee to knee;
> The body and I pull'd at one rope,
> But he said nought to me –

No nightmare could be more eerie and terrifying than this, yet, from the midst of the horror, with dream-like strangeness, beauty suddenly flowers.

The text of 1817 and its explanatory gloss again make what happens clearer. The ship is taken over 'by a blessed troop of angelic spirits', as 'sweet sounds' rise from the mouths of the dead sailors. The control of the ship and of the poem has thus become completely supernatural; the transcendental powers have assumed command. Yet the beauty of the angelic music, breathing through the dead bodies, is conveyed in some of the loveliest of Coleridge's natural imagery:

> Sometimes a dropping from the sky
> I heard the Lavrock sing;
> Sometimes all little birds that are
> How they seem'd to fill the sea and air
> With their sweet jargoning.[1]
> . . . .
> It ceased; yet still the sails made on
> A pleasant noise till noon,
> A noise like that of a hidden brook
> In the leafy month of June,
> That to the sleeping woods all night
> Singeth a quiet tune.

This might well have been a familiar brook of Stowey transferred to a strange sea. The natural world which is rejected on one level is affirmed again on another.

The ship sails on, but still by supernatural means:

> Till noon we silently sail'd on
> Yet never a breeze did breathe:

[1] *PW*, p. 538.

This is the second time Coleridge has stressed that there was no wind; if the Mariner is reconciled to Nature, it seems strange that the elements play no part in his return. Then, at this very moment, the Polar spirit reappears in the poem and we are told that he is moving the ship:

> Under the keel nine fathom deep
> From the land of mist and snow
> The spirit slid: and it was He
> That made the Ship to go.

But the gloss of 1817 says that, 'The lonesome Spirit from the south-pole carries on the ship as far as the line, in obedience to the angelic troop, but still requireth vengeance'. In the 1798 version it is by no means clear who *is* propelling the ship. The 'troop of spirits blest', who enter the bodies of the dead in 1817, are not mentioned in the earlier version nor is it clear that the Polar spirit is subordinate to them. By 1817 it is not surprising that Coleridge made the angelic powers superior to the tutelary spirit of the Pole; the transcendental philosophy had now long supplanted pantheism in his mind. The 1798 version is rather confused at this point, and Part V ends with two spirits, presumably angelic, discussing the Mariner's fate. In a sort of dream-trance he overhears them, which, again, Andrew Baxter would have regarded as good evidence of the soul's immortality. These spirits sound like angels in their compassion and their reference to Christ:

> 'Is it he?' quoth one, 'Is this the man?
>   'By him who died on cross,
> 'With his cruel bow he lay'd full low
> 'The harmless Albatross.
>
> . . . .
>
> The other was a softer voice,
>   As soft as honey-dew:
> Quoth he the man hath penance done
>   And penance more will do.

The gloss of 1817 tells us that the Polar spirit, satisfied that the Mariner will still have to do penance, 'returneth southward'. One feels that Coleridge was rather glad to see the last of him.

Part VI continues the angelic dialogue as the two spirits discuss why the ship is moving so fast. One suggests it may be due to the ocean, presumably the power of a current. But the other replies:

> 'Still as a Slave before his Lord,
> 'The Ocean hath no blast;
> 'His great bright eye most silently
> 'Up to the moon is cast –

Therefore neither currents nor the tides which the moon controls seem to be responsible. Once again Coleridge emphasises the supernatural agency:

> 'But why drives on that ship so fast
> 'Withouten wave or wind?

As it is driven onwards by a supernatural power, something of the nightmare horror returns. The Mariner's eyes are again riveted by the dead men's gaze:

> All stood together on the deck,
> For a charnel-dungeon fitter:
> All fix'd on me their stony eyes
> That in the moon did glitter.

This does not suggest that the angelic powers have freed the Mariner from guilt; his redemption still seems far away:

> I could not draw my een from theirs
> Ne turn them up to pray.

Then he feels a wind blowing upon him, but not a physical one, for

> Its path was not upon the sea
> In ripple or in shade.

In the next verse it is compared to a Spring breeze but, if two things are compared by a simile, they cannot be identical. Coleridge is still indicating that no natural forces are bringing the Mariner home;

> It rais'd my hair, it fann'd my cheek,
> Like a meadow-gale of spring –

Then, suddenly, the ship sails back to the Mariner's native land:

> O dream of joy! is this indeed
> The light-house top I see?
> Is this the Hill? is this the Kirk?
> Is this mine own countrée?

This is undoubtedly meant to recall the start of the voyage, with the cheerful company of living men:

> The Ship was cheered, the Harbour cleared –
> Merrily did we drop
> Below the Kirk, below the Hill,
> Below the Light-house top.

It is one of the moments of revelation in the lives of all men. The wheel has come full circle. The familiar landmarks are the same but this only makes more terrible the memory of innocence. But, though it is the familiar bay of home, it is made strange by the crimson shadows rising from the moonlit waters to surround the ship. In the 1798 version much more space and emphasis is given to this rather lurid vision:

> A little distance from the prow
> Those dark-red shadows were;
> But soon I saw that my own flesh
> Was red as in a glare.

The bodies too advance, their right arms burning like torches 'in the red and smoky light'. Presumably the crimson shadows and flame suggest the evil which has returned with the Mariner even to his native shore, which is in one sense the same, yet never to be the same again. So, in *The Family Reunion*, it is when he returns home to Wishwood that Harry sees the Eumenides:

> The contamination has reached the marrow
> And *they* are always near. Here, nearer than ever.
> They are very close here. I had not expected that.[1]

---

[1] T. S. Eliot, *The Family Reunion*, Faber, 1939, p. 32.

In 1817 Coleridge cut this part of the poem and laid more emphasis on the angelic spirits leaving the dead bodies:

> This seraph-band, each wav'd his hand:
> It was a heavenly sight:
> They stood as signals to the land,
> Each one a lovely light:

As the lights vanish and the angels depart, the real world returns; the Mariner again hears human voices and the splashing oars of the pilot's boat. He recognises the Hermit's voice and longs for him to cleanse his sins:

> He'll shrieve my soul, he'll wash away
> The Albatross's blood.

Part VII opens reassuringly with the solidity of earth after wind and sea. The Hermit

> . . . kneels at morn and noon and eve –
> He hath a cushion plump:
> It is the moss that wholly hides
> The rotted old Oak-stump.

There is, perhaps, dramatic irony in his comparison of the ship's tattered sails to the 'skeletons of leaves', since he cannot know that the ship is doomed or what is aboard it. As the Pilot's boat comes close beneath it,

> . . . strait a sound was heard!
>
> Under the water it rumbled on,
> Still louder and more dread:
> It reach'd the Ship, it split the bay;
> The Ship went down like lead.

The dead men disappear with it and only the Mariner is left:

> Like one that had been seven days drown'd
> My body lay afloat:

We are not told directly what mark the horrors he had endured have left upon him, but the effect he has on the Pilot, who falls in a fit, and on the Pilot's boy, 'who now doth crazy go', is far more devastating than any description.

The Mariner turns to the Hermit with a desperate appeal for absolution:

> 'O shrieve me, shrieve me, holy Man!
> The Hermit cross'd his brow –
> 'Say quick,' quoth he, 'I bid thee say
> 'What manner man art thou?'

We are not told whether absolution is given or not; the emphasis is on the terrible confession:

> Forthwith this frame of mine was wrench'd
> With a woeful agony,
> Which forc'd me to begin my tale
> And then it left me free.

But Coleridge does not allow his Mariner to find peace; the anguish and guilt return and he is compelled to tell his terrible story to whoever will listen. The confession goes on and the forgiveness is not made clear. If redemption means the freeing of the soul from sin, the Ancient Mariner is not redeemed. He remains a haunted wanderer, unable to find rest:

> I pass, like night, from land to land;
> I have strange power of speech;
> The moment that his face I see
> I know the man that must hear me;
> To him my tale I teach.

The wedding ceremony is over and, as the more fortunate guests appear, the Mariner hears the bell for evening prayers:

> But in the Garden-bower the Bride
> And Bride-maids singing are;
> And hark the little Vesper-bell
> Which biddeth me to prayer.

This recalls the albatross which had perched upon the mast 'for vespers

74

nine' just before the Mariner's fatal shot. One would like to think that the weary circle of guilt and retribution is now complete and that this vesper-bell can redeem the action of that other evening in the Polar seas. The Mariner has indeed learnt bitterly that

> He prayeth best who loveth best,
> All things both great and small:
> For the dear God, who loveth us,
> He made and loveth all.

Yet God's love should include the sinner; this rather facile view makes no provision for those who reject love. One shares Coleridge's own dissatisfaction with the expressed 'moral' of the poem, for it contains only a small part of its meaning. God's relation to living creatures and to the natural world is what Coleridge wanted to believe, but the very triteness of the poetry of the two 'moral' verses makes it unconvincing. It we set beside it,

> O Wedding-Guest! this soul hath been
> Alone on a wide wide sea:
> So lonely 'twas, that God himself
> Scarce seemed there to be.

the far greater imaginative power suggests his much deeper fear of the desolation of a world without God. The Ancient Mariner's anguished wandering between doubt and faith, the natural and the supernatural, was shared by Coleridge.

★   ★   ★

When Coleridge first published *The Ancient Mariner* under his own name in *Sibylline Leaves*, 1817, he made a considerable number of alterations and additions. Many of these are clearly related to the notebook entries of his Malta voyage in 1804 and thus seem to have a deeply personal content. The notes of the voyage have also a new and almost symbolic quality which throws light on the possible meaning the poem had come to have for him and on the imaginative process itself. This greater subjectivity is also due to a fundamental change in Coleridge's philosophy which we can see taking place from 1801–2.

These were years of deepening personal unhappiness but also of intense mental activity. Coleridge had deserted Poole and Stowey for Wordsworth and the Lake District; Sara Hutchinson, with whom he had fallen deeply in love in the autumn of 1799, was also an attraction to the North. Writing to Poole on March 16th, 1801, he gives an important account of his recent thinking:

> The interval since my last letter has been filled up by me in the most intense Study. If I do not greatly delude myself, I have not only completely extricated the notions of Time, and Space; but have overthrown the doctrine of Association, as taught by Hartley, and with it all the irreligious metaphysics of modern Infidels – especially, the doctrine of Necessity.

He adds that

> . . . the Sleep, which I have is made up of Ideas so connected, & so little different from the operations of the Reason, that it does not afford me the due Refreshment . . . for it seemed to me a Suicide of my very soul to divert my attention from Truths so important, which came to me almost as a Revelation. / [1]

It is interesting to note again that for Coleridge the waking and sleeping mind were not easily distinguishable. Another letter to Poole, a week later, refers with admiration to Newton's mathematical and scientific brilliance but deplores his philosophical conclusions. He thus deposes both Hartley and Newton who, in *Religious Musings*, had been 'Coadjutors of God'.[2] He now says:

> I am exceedingly delighted with the beauty & neatness of his experiments, & with the accuracy of his *immediate* Deductions from them – but the opinions founded on these Deductions, and indeed his whole Theory is, I am persuaded, so exceedingly superficial as without impropriety to be deemed false. Newton was a mere materialist – *Mind* in his system is always passive – a lazy Looker-on on an external World. If the mind be not *passive*, if it be indeed made in God's Image, & that too in the sublimest sense – the Image of the *Creator* – there is ground for suspicion, that any system built on the passiveness of the mind must be false, as a system. / [3]

[1] Griggs, ii, 707.   [2] *PW*, p. 122.   [3] Griggs, ii, 709.

The external world therefore ceases to have an existence independent of the observing and receiving mind. This is still Coleridge's position in 1817 when, in the *Biographia Literaria*, he builds his whole theory of Imagination upon the mind creative in everyday perception:

> The primary imagination I hold to be the living power and prime agent of all human perception, and as a repetition in the finite mind of the eternal act of creation in the infinite I AM.[1]

If our commonest awareness of the external world is thus creative, the secondary or poetic imagination is still more so:

> The secondary I consider as an echo of the former, co-existing with the conscious will, yet still as identical with the primary in the kind of its agency, and differing only in degree, and in the mode of its operation . . . it struggles to idealise and to unify. It is essentially *vital*, even as all objects (as objects) are essentially fixed and dead.[2]

The stress upon the conscious will obviously opposes Hartley and Newton on the mind's passiveness. The active mind becomes similar to God's own creative power and the universe of eighteenth century materialism is dead indeed. When we remember that the *Biographia Literaria* was published in the same year as *Sibylline Leaves*, 1817, and was, indeed, originally intended as a preface to the poetry, the relation between it and Coleridge's philosophy becomes very important.

The epigraph which Coleridge used for the 1817 edition of *The Ancient Mariner* is an extract, with alterations, from Burnet, *Archaeologiae philosophicae*, but we find it already present in the notebooks of 1801–2:

> Facile credo, plures esse naturas invisibiles quam visibiles in rerum universitate – sed horum omnium familiam quis nobis enarrabit? . . . etc.[3]

The belief that there are more invisible than visible beings in the universe is, as Burnet says, something which has always fascinated the human mind. Coleridge's stress upon it in the notebooks of 1801–2 fits in with the movement of his thought from the material to the transcendental nature of reality, from the physical to the spiritual world. The

---

[1] *BL*, p. 167.   [2] ibid., p. 167.   [3] N 1, 1000 H 22.9.

glosses which Coleridge added to *The Ancient Mariner* in 1817, though they may well have been written much earlier, also emphasise the spiritual meaning of the poem. The Polar spirit becomes a Neoplatonic daemon, 'concerning whom the learned Jew, Josephus, and the Platonic Constantinopolitan, Michael Psellus, may be consulted'.[1] The gloss on the water-snakes is 'By the light of the Moon he beholdeth God's creatures of the great calm'.[2] It is 'By grace of the holy Mother', that 'the Ancient Mariner is refreshed with rain'.[3] It is '. . . a blessed troop of angelic spirits, sent down by the invocation of the guardian saint',[4] which enters the bodies of the dead sailors. The meaning of the poem is thus both spiritualised and Christianised in the later version.

But, if external Nature is dead and spiritless, as Coleridge had always feared, the burden of breathing life into it falls wholly upon the creative imagination. As his verse *Letter to Asra* of April 1802, which later became the *Ode to Dejection*, says:

> O Sara! we receive but what we give,
> And in *our* Life alone does Nature live.
> Our's is her Wedding Garment, our's her Shroud –
> And would we aught behold of higher Worth
> Than that inanimate cold World allow'd
> To the poor loveless ever-anxious Crowd,
> Ah! from the Soul itself must issue forth
> A Light, a Glory, and a luminous Cloud
> Enveloping the Earth![5]

The process by which the inanimate cold world of the mechanical universe can be made luminous, the relation between subject and object, the internal and the external, haunted all nineteenth-century philosophy and poetry. The scientific and industrial developments of the twentieth century have made it still more difficult for poets to give imaginative life to a universe which becomes daily more frightening and impersonal. Much modern poetry has retreated from it altogether into a private symbolism which is almost entirely subjective. It is Coleridge's distinction to have first recognised and given poetic voice to the problem and, therefore, he and his poem still 'speak to our condition'.

[1] *PW*, p. 191. [2] ibid., p. 198. [3] ibid., p. 198.
[4] ibid., p. 200. [5] Griggs, ii, 797–8.

In the notebooks of his Malta voyage and in some of the changes he made to *The Ancient Mariner* in *Sibylline Leaves* we can watch the process by which the outer world becomes the inner; the objective reality takes on a subjective and partly symbolic meaning. We can, in fact, see his imagination at work.

He embarked for Malta in April 1804 in the hope of regaining the health and peace of mind which he had lost. The years from 1800–4 had been clouded by constant illness and gradual enslavement to the opium taken to relieve it, by his unhappy love for Sara Hutchinson and by the failure of his marriage. The drying up of his poetic power may have been both the cause and effect of his other distresses. The horror of his nightmares, whether due to opium addiction or to an attempted withdrawal, are described in *The Pains of Sleep* in 1803:

> Desire with loathing strangely mixed
> On wild or hateful objects fixed.
> Fantastic passions! maddening brawl!
> And shame and terror over all![1]

He had also other conscious reasons for shame. Though never physically unfaithful to his wife, his passion for Sara Hutchinson was not easy for either woman. Though he loved his children deeply, he was leaving them and their mother with little visible means of support. His notebooks also betray a growing jealousy of Wordsworth, mainly because Sara had now become an intimate member of the Grasmere circle. Coleridge's sickness was both mental and physical. Like his Mariner, he was 'alone on a wide wide sea'. Unhappiness deepened his natural tendency to introspection, and the notebooks of the Malta voyage reveal the poet himself enduring not only the Mariner's physical experience but also, half-consciously, identified with his guilt and fear and terrible isolation. Coleridge lives out his own poem. This makes the voyage notebook poignant and yet illuminating, for it supplies a little exploited commentary, especially where the entries correspond closely with the additions and alterations Coleridge made to *The Ancient Mariner* in *Sibylline Leaves*.

One of the most interesting of these is the description of the storm

[1] *PW*, p. 390.

which drove the ship southwards in Part I. In the earlier editions this
read:

> But now the Northwind came more fierce,
> There came a Tempest strong!
> And Southward still for days and weeks
> Like chaff we drove along.

Though straightforward and vigorous verse, this entirely lacks the
haunting imaginative power of the *Sibylline Leaves* version:

> And now the STORM-BLAST came, and he
> Was tyrannous and strong:
> He struck with his o'ertaking wings,
> And chased us south along.
>
> With sloping masts and dipping prow,
> As who pursued with yell and blow
> Still treads the shadow of his foe,
> And forward bends his head,
> The ship drove fast, loud roared the blast,
> And southward aye we fled.[1]

This personified storm before whose avenging fury the mariners fled
as though guilty and terror-stricken owes its power, I think, to Coleridge's own experience on his Malta voyage and to Dante's *Inferno*
which he had taken with him. Coleridge gives several vivid descrip-
tions in his notebook of the many storms which buffeted the *Speedwell*:

> All Saturday Night brisk Gales interrupted by Squalls with heavy
> rains, during which variable or varying winds *shuttlecock'd* our poor
> brig . . . But all day it rocked so deep, & the Sea so often gave the
> Ship a smart & lusty Box o' the Ear, that there was neither sitting
> or standing, without danger of Contusions – [2]

About ten days later he records:

> . . . the Vessel began its old trick of Rocking – I was ill after dinner
> which I did not retain / the Mephitis of the Bilge burst forth, like a

[1] *PW*, p. 188.   [2] N 2, 2014 9.120.

Fury / horrid Stench that turned the gold red, & silver black, be-mudded whatever part of the paint had been before soiled, & covered the rest of it with [quick-] silvery grease drops.[1]

I believe the dirty and stinking bilge-water and the storm which boxed the ship on the ear were associated in Coleridge's mind with the 26th canto of the *Inferno*. Here, in the eighth circle of Malebolge, the barrators are submerged in boiling pitch; if they dare to show their heads above it, they are prodded back by the pitchforks of the devils. For all its horror the canto has a grim and vigorous comedy. Its opening is firmly associated with ships, for it describes the Arsenal at Venice where pitch is boiled to repair damaged vessels. This is compared to the pitch of the barrators' torment and, as Dante watches horrified, Virgil suddenly warns him to look behind. He turns to see one of the devils running after him along the causeway with wings outspread,

con l'ali aperte, e sopra il piè leggiero![2]

Now Coleridge's storm has 'o'ertaking wings' and pursues the ship with 'yell and blow'. I believe one of those complex associations has occurred between Coleridge's ship and Dante's, between the stinking Bilge-water and the pitch, the outspread wings of the pursuing devil and the driving storm. The impression of guilt and flight from crime is very strong, though, logically, the verse precedes the shooting of the albatross. One feels that, when Coleridge wrote it, he was himself pursued by the demons of guilt and fear.

Several of the Malta voyage entries were quoted by Professor Bald in the article on Coleridge to which I have referred earlier.[3] Here is one of the most startling which Professor Bald quotes only in part:

Hawk with ruffled Feathers resting on the Bow-sprit – Now shot at & yet did not move – how fatigued – a third time it made a gyre, a short circuit, & returned again / 5 times it was thus shot at / left the Vessel / flew to another / & I heard firing, now here, now there / & nobody shot it / but probably it perished from fatigue, & the

[1] ibid., 2051 15.24.

[2] Dante, *Inferno*, xxvi, l. 33.

[3] R. C. Bald, 'Coleridge and "The Ancient Mariner"', *Nineteenth Century Studies*, Ithaca, 1940.

attempt to rest upon the wave! – Poor Hawk! O Strange Lust of Murder in Man! – It is not cruelty / it is mere ~~un~~ [sic] non-feeling from non-thinking.[1]

Coleridge's stress on the unmotivated thoughtlessness of the shooting and his deep pity for the hawk remind us of the strange impulse which slew the albatross, and set in motion the terrible chain of cause and effect in the poem. The Origin of Evil, on which Coleridge had once contemplated writing an epic, remains mysterious but there is no mistaking its consequences. The agony of the albatross is brief; its murderer is condemned to Life-in-Death. The poet himself, in a notebook entry made at Malta in 1805, shortly after hearing of John Wordsworth's drowning, uses the dying bird as an image of despair:

> . . . indeed I am very, very hopeless & heartless! . . . decrease of Hope and Joy, the Soul in its round & round flight forming narrower circles, till at every Gyre its wings beat against the *personal Self.*[2]

The word 'gyre' recalls the hawk and it, in turn, recalls the albatross which also flew 'round and round'. Perhaps the Mariner by killing the friendly bird destroyed his own soul and the outer death became the inner. An incident from his Malta voyage thus mingles with the memory of the albatross to form a new symbolic whole which is intensely subjective. Though Coleridge's own sins were less dramatic than his Mariner's, he knew the narrowing circles of the sinful soul and the desperate beating of those wings. Nor should we forget the wings that pursued Dante in the ever-narrowing circles of Hell.

Another Malta voyage entry, describing the sudden dropping of the wind, reinforces this correspondence between the inner and the outer world. It becomes difficult to determine whether the breeze was the one which feebly stirred the *Speedwell*'s sails or the creative wind for which the poet also longed:

> Whither have my Animal Spirits departed? My Hopes – O me! that they which once I had to check [. . .] should now be an effort / Royals & Studding Sails & the whole Canvas stretched to catch the feeble breeze! – I have many thoughts, many images; large Stores of

[1] N 2, 2090 15.56.   [2] ibid., 2531 17.89, f. 53ᵛ.

the unwrought materials . . . but the combining Power, the power to do, the manly effective *Will*, that is dead or slumbers most diseasedly – [1]

A year earlier, in November 1803, a notebook recorded his literary plans; 'As to Poems, I have said nothing – the wind bloweth as it listeth'.[2] Both entries suggest that there were moments in *The Ancient Mariner* when the rising wind was identified with spiritual and imaginative power, and its dropping with a stagnation which Coleridge shared with his Mariner. Even though he is discussing his loss of creative power, the passage is itself striking evidence of that imaginative process by which the external becomes internal.

Coleridge must have been aware of this himself, for in the 1804 entry he makes the acutely penetrating comment on the composition of poetry which I have already quoted:

Poetry a rationalized dream dealing [about?] to manifold Forms our own Feelings, that never perhaps were attached by us consciously to our personal Selves –[3]

In this context we have just seen the dream-like manner in which the real Mediterranean breeze becomes also the wind of imaginative power. But Coleridge's unusual awareness of the creative process is, of course, highly rational and analytic. This is the secret of his poetic strength and explains why the rising and falling wind of the poem stirs us so deeply. The imagery comes from the depths of his being but is also clearly controlled by the conscious mind.

Still in the same entry, Coleridge uses the image of the sea, also with great suggestive power:

– O there are Truths below the Surface in the subject of Sympathy, & how we *become* that which we understandly [sic] behold & hear, having, how much God perhaps only knows, created part even of the Form –

An earlier note of 1803 had shown the same awareness of the sub-conscious mind:

. . . the greater & perhaps nobler certainly all the subtler parts of

[1] ibid., 2086 15.52, f. 40.   [2] N 1, 1646 21.392 f. 84.   [3] See Introduction, p. 5.

83

one's nature, must be solitary – Man exists herein to himself & to God alone / – Yea, in how much only to God – how much lies *below* his own Consciousness.[1]

This is a very remarkable observation for 1803, so many years before Freud. But it is not an isolated one. In December of the same year he uses the imagery of sea and ship to describe the subconscious world of sleep and dreams:

> – O then as I first sink on the pillow, as if Sleep had indeed a material *realm* . . . O then what visions have I had, what dreams – the Bark, the Sea, all the shapes & sounds & adventures made up of the Stuff of Sleep & Dreams, & yet my Reason at the Rudder . . . I sink down the waters, thro' Seas & Seas – yet warm, yet a Spirit / [2]

This certainly suggests that the world below the surface of the sea is the subconscious mind from which dreams come; yet, once again, reason is 'at the rudder' and conscious control is also present. One wonders whether the Spirit who followed the ship 'nine fathoms deep' in the sailors' dreams came from those subconscious realms which were haunted inexorably by guilt. By 1817 I think it possible that he represented this to Coleridge, though probably not in 1798 when he was associated, not very satisfactorily, with pantheism. Even in 1804, the poet, like his Mariner, knew this world beneath the surface of the mind where dwelt the pursuing Spirit who was so difficult to exorcise. When the ship, with its dreadful burden of dead men, finally sank, this may mean that it returned beneath the surface of the Mariner's consciousness. He was able to forget for a time, though not for ever, the terrible consequences of his deed.

The crisis of the Ancient Mariner's fate comes in Part III, and it is also here that we find the greatest number of alterations and additions in *Sibylline Leaves*. It opens with the terrible calm and thirst:

> There passed a weary time. Each throat
> Was parched, and glazed each eye.
> A weary time! a weary time!
> How glazed each weary eye,

[1] N I, 1554 21.274.
[2] ibid., 1718 16.105.

Coleridge remembered this hopeless stagnation when he endured a similar experience on his Malta voyage:

> . . . a dead calm . . . Rudder tied (Ropes rotted, yet still the Tiller moved not /) – the ashes thrown over the Vessel's side remaining for Hours.

Later in the same entry, as he enviously watches the swift movement of the porpoises, the poet recalls the poem:

> . . . with a noise of rushing, like that of a Vessel dashing on by steam or other power within itself, thro' the Calm & making the Billows ⟨& the Breeze, which⟩ it did not find / Ancient Mariner / – [1]

This is one of Coleridge's very few direct references to his poem.

The appearance of the spectre-ship and her terrible crew heralds the main alterations of *Sibylline Leaves*. As we have already seen, Coleridge clarified this part by naming the two figures, but the grisly description of Death in 1798, with his black bones and patches of green damp, is removed entirely in 1817 and the more effectively suggestive 'Is Death that woman's mate?' appears instead. Death's companion, for the first three lines, is the same as in the earlier editions, though the point of the italicised 'her',

> *Her* lips were red, *her* looks were free,

is somewhat lost by the removal of her lurid companion. But the last two lines of the 1798 version,

> And she is far liker Death than he;
> Her flesh makes the still air cold.

become in 1817,

> The Night-Mair LIFE-IN-DEATH was she
> Who thicks men's blood with cold.[2]

The terrible and powerful conception of Life-in-Death who wins the Mariner's soul belongs thus to the later versions and, when we read the

---

[1] N 2, 2052 15.25.   [2] *PW*, p. 194.

notebooks of Malta and afterwards, it is not difficult to see why. The record of the years which precede and, indeed, follow *Sibylline Leaves* show us Coleridge's deepening loneliness, the bitterness that crept into his relations with Sara Hutchinson, his estrangement from Wordsworth and, with it, Sara's division from him, the discord of his marriage and the resulting loss of his children. Increasing ill-health and slavery to opium and what seemed the death of his creative power, all created a vicious circle of self-pity and self-disgust, a weariness of life. His bitter knowledge of Life-in-Death could be proved from many entries. Two must suffice. The first was written on his birthday, always a time of melancholy resolutions, in October 1803:

> – O me! my very heart dies! – This *year* has been one painful Dream / I have done nothing! – O for God's sake let me whip & spur, so that Christmas may not pass without something having been done / . . . the Rain Storm pelts against my Study Window! ⌐ O Σαρα Σαρα why am I ⌐ not happy! why have I not an unencumbered Heart! . . .[1]

The second belongs to February 1807 shortly after the 'dreadful Saturday morning' when some incident occurred which aroused Coleridges' intense jealousy of Wordsworth and Sara. The image of the 'nightmair' suggests Life-in-Death, and it is possible both were written about the same time:

> For whenever I seem to be slighted ~~for~~ [sic] by you, I think not what I am to you, but only what I have *claim* to be – & then I sink – & but that it is a dream, & I still half-consciously expect to awake from the night-mair – I could not but *die* – die, / as an *act*! – O! SARA![2]

The stress upon 'die as an *act*' seems to mean suicide as opposed to 'the night-mair Life-in-Death'. Earlier in the same entry he again uses the image of the soul's wings; without Sara he can no longer soar:

> O God! forgive me! – Can even the Eagle soar without Wings? And the wings given by thee to my soul – what are they, but the Love & Society of that Beloved . . .

[1] N 1, 1577 21.297.   [2] N 2, 2998 11.67.

Whatever its personal meaning for Coleridge, in the larger logic of the poem Life-in-Death wins the Ancient Mariner and the dice-game still remains in 1817 the centre of the poem. The significance of this has already been discussed.

Life-in-Death is followed closely in *Sibylline Leaves* by a verse added in 1817 between the departure of the spectre-ship and the rising of the moon:

> We listened and looked sideways up!
> Fear at my heart, as at a cup,
> My life-blood seemed to sip!
> The stars were dim, and thick the night,
> The steersman's face by his lamp gleamed white;
> From the sails the dew did drip – [1]

This is one of the most eerie, yet most vividly concrete, verses in the poem and, when we read with it an entry made on the voyage to Malta, we realise that the guilt and fear were Coleridge's own:

> SICKLY Thoughts about M. mort. & W. ÷ Sā – *Hydrocarb.* / died looking at the stars above the top mast; & when found dead, these Stars were sinking in the Horizon / – a large Star? a road of dim Light? – Light of the Compass & rudderman's Lamp reflected with forms on the Main Sail.[2]

Professor Bald quotes only the reference to the rudderman's lamp,[3] and so, though he links it with the lines added in *Sibylline Leaves*, he omits the most important part of this sombre and cryptic entry. Miss Coburn, in her note on the passage, explains that the 'sickly thoughts' were Coleridge's fear that, if Mary Wordsworth died, William would marry Sara Hutchinson. 'Hydrocarb.', the combination of the unstable element of water and worthless carbon, stands for Coleridge himself. The poet, like his Mariner, was haunted by terror and guilt, with which the eerie gleam of the steersman's lamp and the dim light of the stars become inextricably associated. His unhealthy and jealous fear that, if Mary died, Wordsworth would take Sara from him, is paralleled in

[1] *PW*, p. 195.
[2] N 2, 2001 9.107.
[3] Bald, p. 11.

the poem by the death of the sailors, as the moon rises. In 1817 it became 'star-dogged' instead of 'horned':

> One after one, by the star-dogged Moon,
> Too quick for groan or sigh,
> Each turned his face with a ghastly pang,
> And cursed me with his eye.
>
> Four times fifty living men,
> (And I heard nor sigh nor groan)
> With heavy thump, a lifeless lump,
> They dropped down one by one.[1]

The sombre associations of this passage, both in the poem and in Coleridge's own guilty thoughts, make it impossible, as we have said, to consider the moon a symbol of good. Coleridge himself seems to have inclined to a simpler and less rational explanation.

When his ship left Gibraltar for Malta he was discussing sailors' superstitions with the crew, and *The Ancient Mariner*, not unnaturally, was present in his mind:

> – Comments on Ancient Mariner / – our Capt[n] 'Damn me! I have no superstition, I had as soon sail on Friday as on Saturday; but this I must say, that Sunday is really a lucky day to sail on / indeed to begin any sort of business upon / '[2]

After this it is not surprising to find the entry which immediately follows:

> Poem / dim not feeble is the waning ⟨moon⟩ / the last curse of the waning moon / . The bright moon that follow'd suspended it, that when the moon waned again the Curse began to work, & was finished on the last day of the moon.[3]

This suggests that the waning moon's influence was malevolent but the new moon lightened the curse. Coleridge himself thus helps to disprove Mr Warren's theory that the moon of the poem is allied with the forces of redemption, or indeed that its meaning is fixed at all.

The voyage to Malta continued and Coleridge recorded another

[1] *PW*, p. 196.   [2] N 2, 2048 15.21.   [3] ibid., 2049 15.22.

example of superstition among sailors, this time linked with the 'star-dogged moon' of 1817:

> Tuesday Morning, May Day, 1804!! In the Mediterranean plying wearily to the Windward off Carthagena – a wet foggy oppressive Weather, with the wind impotent or against us! – And the Captn begins to look round for the Jonas in the Fleet . . . Here Vexation, which in a Sailor's mind is always linked on to Reproach and Anger, makes the Superstitious seek out an Object of his Superstition, that can feel his anger – Else the Star, that dogged the Crescent or my 'Cursed by the last Look of the waning moon', were the better[1] –

The last phrase was, apparently, the origin of the 'star-dogged' moon of *Sibylline Leaves*, while J. L. Lowes has shown that Coleridge's interest in the superstition of the star within the horns of the moon goes back to the old voyagers' accounts, and also to the more scientific authority of the Royal Society which recorded this phenomenon in 1794.[2] The travellers' tales which Coleridge had read apparently connected the star with ill-omen. Lowes, quoting Bruce's *Travels to Discover the Source of the Nile*, says, '. . . Coleridge had read how in Abyssinia, "a star passing near the horns of the moon denotes the coming of an enemy." '[3] But Lowes is more anxious to explain the apparent mistake which critics had noted of a rising horned moon at sunset. He continues:

> . . . *is* it at sunset? And is the *crescent* moon (etymologically speaking) the only *hornèd* moon? I fear the charge of ignorance or inadvertence lies against the critics rather than the poet. The *waning* moon each month is hornèd too . . .[4]

and he goes on to explain exactly when the waning moon rises in the early morning. Coleridge's own note, already quoted, about the curse of the waning moon seems to prove Lowes right. Imaginatively, it is fitting that the mariners die beneath the dying moon, and move again, however terribly and strangely, under the light of the new 'moving moon'. Mr J. Beer also discusses this moon problem, quotes Coleridge's notebook entry about the '. . . "star, that dogged the Crescent or my

---

[1] ibid., 2060 15.32, f. 25ᵛ.
[2] Lowes, p. 165.
[3] ibid., p. 168.   [4] ibid., p. 167.

'Cursed by the last look of the waning moon' were the better" ',[1] but without having looked up the previous entry, where Coleridge, after his habit, is quoting himself. Mr Beer concludes:

> This remark complicates, but also helps to solve, the problem before us. The moon remains constant as a beneficent power, and has no part in the dying and cursing. It is the star between its horns that represents the daemonic vengeance upon the Mariner.[2]

But Coleridge's earlier entry about the waning moon[3] proves that the moon *did* have a part in the dying and cursing – in fact, the mariners died with the moon. The problem is not solved by shifting responsibility on to the star and, indeed, the moral of all this slightly lunatic controversy is that, if we read the poem carefully with the notebooks, there *is* no problem. It has been created by critics who try to impose too definite a meaning on the poem, for Mr Beer wants his moon to be continuously beneficent just as much as Mr Warren.

The new moon of Part IV weakens the curse, as, by its light, the Mariner blesses the water-snakes. But, in Part V, we must assume, remembering Coleridge's note, that the moon is now waning again and the power of evil reasserting itself:

> Beneath the lightning and the Moon
> The dead men gave a groan![4]

The horror of the dead men working the ship,

> They raised their limbs like lifeless tools –
> We were a ghastly crew.

could not have seemed to Coleridge an image of resurrection, for, in the drug-ridden despair of Malta, he remembered his own lines:

> – Die, my Soul, die! – Suicide – rather than this, the worst state of Degradation! . . . I work hard, I do the duties of common Life from morn to night / but verily – I raise my limbs "like lifeless *Tools*" –[5]

---

[1] J. Beer, *Coleridge the Visionary*, Chatto and Windus, 1959, p. 160.
[2] ibid, p. 160.
[3] N 2, 2049 15.22. See p. 88.   [4] *PW*, p. 199.   [5] N 2, 2557 17.115.

When Coleridge at last reached harbour in Malta, he recorded his delight again in the words of *The Ancient Mariner*:

> – Found myself light as a blessed Ghost – brought my Things from
> the Boat / [1]

It is clear from all these entries how fully he had relived his own poem and, perhaps, found in it a new and deeper meaning. His identification with his Mariner is also suggested in the manuscript version of the poem Coleridge wrote to Wordsworth after listening to *The Prelude*. Composed shortly after his return from Malta, it is a moving tribute to his friend's genius and to his own happiness in being once more with all whom he best loved. As he thinks of his lonely exile and the death of his own poetic hopes, the images of *The Ancient Mariner* irresistibly recur:

> Comfort from thee, and utterance of thy love,
> Came with such heights and depths of harmony,
> Such sense of wings uplighting, that the storm
> Scatter'd and whirl'd me, till my thoughts became
> A bodily tumult; and thy faithful hopes,
> . . . .
> Were troublous to me, almost as a voice,
> Familiar once and more than musical;
> To one cast forth, whose hope had seem'd to die
> A wanderer with a worn-out heart.
>
> . . . .
> O Friend, too well thou know'st, of what sad years
> The long suppression had benumb'd my soul,
> That even as life returns upon the drown'd,
> The unusual joy awoke a throng of pains –

The poem later uses the imagery of sea, moon and stars:

> My soul lay passive, by thy various strain
> Driven as in surges now beneath the stars,
> . . . .
> Into the darkness; now a tranquil sea,
> Outspread and bright, yet swelling to the moon. [2]

[1] ibid., 2100 10.3.   [2] *PW*, pp. 406–8.

The wings of the soul were only momentarily uplifted; Coleridge, like his Mariner, returned from the drowned only to become again 'alone on a wide wide sea', but there were times when the waves remained tranquil and he found temporary harbour.

The beautiful gloss on the moving moon which he added to *The Ancient Mariner* in 1817 reveals his own feeling too:

> In his loneliness and fixedness he yearneth towards the journeying Moon, and the stars that still sojourn, yet still move onward; and everywhere the blue sky belongs to them, and is their appointed rest, and their native country and their own natural homes, which they enter unannounced, as lords that are certainly expected and yet there is a silent joy at their arrival.[1]

He had often watched the sky from the *Speedwell*'s deck and knew the movement of moon and stars. Yet I think the gloss expresses not only his personal loneliness but a deeper philosophical awareness of man's place in the cosmos. The moon and stars pursue their appointed paths in the heavens according to the unalterable laws of the natural world. Man only is left outside, an eternal wanderer in a universe where he has no assured place. Like the Mariner, he is the 'outcast of a blind idiot called Nature',[2] though the beauty of the gloss shows that Coleridge has performed the poet's task of endowing the 'inanimate cold world' with imaginative life. The terrifying isolation of the Ancient Mariner is, to some extent, the predicament of modern man. This is why the poem haunts us, as it did its author.

Yet, another entry made in Malta, which also describes the moon, sees it this time as an image of that inner world which Coleridge also knew so well:

> April 14th, 1805 – In looking at objects of Nature while I am thinking, as at yonder moon dim-glimmering thro' the dewy window pane, I seem rather to be seeking, as it were *asking*, a symbolical language for something within me that already and forever exists, than observing anything new.[3]

There are moments in *The Ancient Mariner* when the two worlds meet, and, through the power of imagination, the outer world becomes the

---

[1] *PW*, p. 197.   [2] Griggs, i, 177.   [3] N 2, 2546 17.104.

inner. The rising wind, the moving moon, the free flight of wings do seem to suggest the release of the soul from its guilt and imprisonment beneath the dead bird's weight, the dying moon, the dead calm. This is the imaginative process which the notebooks help us to see. But even Coleridge could not fit together the whole pattern of that symbolical language, though this underlay his desire that Wordsworth should write the great philosophical poem which would give meaning to 'all this unintelligible world'. His own Logosophia was to accomplish the same immense task. It is no real criticism of either poet that the work was never achieved. By the nineteenth century it was no longer possible to give unity and vital meaning to the baffling complexity of the universe. In our own century the division between man and his world has become wider still.

It is no wonder that Coleridge was haunted by Dante, for in the achievement of this greatest of metaphysical poets he recognised the unity missing in his own century. When discussing the third canto of the *Inferno*, he sees, above all, the *wholeness* of Dante:

> In this canto all the images are distinct, and even vividly distinct; but there is a total impression of infinity; the wholeness is not in vision or conception, but in an inner feeling of totality and absolute being.[1]

He who had always dreaded seeing the universe as 'an immense heap of little things' pierces swiftly to the heart of Dante's greatness. A note of 1807-8 speaks of the difficulty of fully understanding his arduous poetry:

> Canzon, i'credo, che saranno radi
> Color, che tua ragione intendan bene,
> Tanto lor parli faticosa e forte /
>   Convito di Dante
> Voi che'ntendendo, il terzo ciel movete etc.[2]

This is a quotation from the *Convivio* (or *Convito*), but the last line shows that Coleridge himself understood. It is used again in the eighth canto of the *Paradiso*, 'You who by intellect move the third heaven'.

[1] Coleridge, *Miscellaneous Criticism*, ed. T. M. Raysor, 1936, p. 152.
[2] N 2, 3219 22.126.

The circle of Venus, the third from the earth in medieval cosmology, is moved by the heavenly intelligences, and, as it goes singing on its way, makes with its fellows the music of the spheres. Nothing could be more different from the sky the Mariner watched in 'loneliness and fixedness'. For Dante the physical universe is controlled by the heavenly spirits in a harmony which comes ultimately from God. Modern man stands outside yearning 'towards the journeying Moon' and the celestial order from which he is forever exiled. But, in the shining vision which closes the *Paradiso*, Dante's own will and desire is moved like a wheel by the Love which moves the sun and the other stars:

> ma già volgeva il mio disiro e il *velle*,
> sì come rota ch'egualmente è mossa,
> L'amor che move il sole e l'altre stelle.

CHAPTER III

Belovéd Stowey

The Ancient Mariner was not all Coleridge wrote at Nether Stowey from 1797 to 1798. Four other shorter poems belonged to this brief period of happiness, security and love. They were deep rooted in the countryside of Somerset and in the young Coleridge's affection for his family and dearest friends. *This Lime-Tree Bower My Prison* was addressed to Charles Lamb who paid Coleridge a brief visit in June 1797. *Frost at Midnight* was written in the peace of his cottage home at Stowey in February 1798, and its main impulse is his deep affection for his baby son, Hartley. *Fears in Solitude*, composed during the alarm of a French invasion in April 1798, begins and ends with his love for Stowey, for his wife and child, and Tom Poole. *The Nightingale* too belonged to a Spring evening in April 1798 when he had been walking with William and Dorothy Wordsworth, though it also contained 'a father's tale' of Hartley. All four, at their best, describe the natural scene with a spontaneity, freshness and delicacy of observation which Coleridge had never achieved in poetry before and was never quite to possess again. In contrast with the turgid didacticism of *Religious Musings* or *The Destiny of Nations*, the Conversation poems, as they are often called, have a natural ease of tone and flexibility of movement. They reveal the young Coleridge his friends loved, affectionate, sensitive and gay, the most fascinating conversationalist of his time.

Yet, if we read them carefully, I believe the darker world of *The Ancient Mariner* shadows the Conversation poems also. Though there are many moments of beautiful and exact observation where Coleridge feels at one with his surroundings, when he comes to philosophise upon this identity between Nature and Man, the tone of the poetry immediately changes. The style seems to become pompous, self-conscious and artificial; Coleridge loses his own voice and sounds like an unconvincing echo of Wordsworth. Though human love and natural beauty often made him feel at one with the world about him, I do not think his intellect, that 'self-watching subtilising mind',[1] ever really accepted this identity. His deeper conviction, both rational and instinctive, was, I think, expressed through the Ancient Mariner's terrible estrangement from the natural world and '. . . all the numberless goings-on of life.'[2] *Frost at Midnight*, from which the last two quotations come, shows, perhaps, most clearly Coleridge's fear of loneliness, as if he were already dimly aware how few the years of security and affection were to be.

The unfortunate accident which occasioned the writing of *This Lime-Tree Bower my Prison* is described by Coleridge in a letter to Southey:

The second day after Wordsworth came to me, dear Sara accidentally emptied a skillet of boiling milk on my foot, which confined me during the whole time of C. Lamb's stay.[3]

As Lowes remarks, 'One lingers fascinated over the unutterable volumes in "dear Sara".'[4] Imprisoned in his garden-bower, Coleridge was forced to follow the footsteps of his friends in imagination only. He sees them striding among the familiar scenes of hill and dell and waterfall:

> . . . . and there my friends
> Behold the dark green file of long lank weeds
> That all at once (a most fantastic sight!)
> Still nod and drip beneath the dripping edge
> Of the blue clay-stone.[5]

Was this what he remembered in Malta eight years later?

O the beautiful Fountain or natural Well at Upper Stowey [. . .] The images of the weeds which hung down from its sides, appeared as plants growing up, straight and upright, among the water weeds that really grew from the Bottom / & so vivid was the Image, that for some moments & not till after I had disturbed the water, did I perceive that their roots were not neighbours, & they side-by-side

---

[1] *PW*, p. 241.   [2] ibid., p. 240.   [3] Griggs, i, 334.
[4] Lowes, p. 23.   [5] *PW*, p. 179.

companions. So – even then I said – so are the happy man's *Thoughts* and *Things* . . .[1]

In 1797 unhappiness had not yet divorced the inner and the outer world. The familiar images of Coleridge's poetry are already present, but the water and weeds of *This Lime-Tree Bower* exist in the solid objective world and are not yet burdened with the weight of introspection and sadness.

Coleridge next imagines his friends viewing the sea, but not the 'wide wide sea' of *The Ancient Mariner*. This is familiar, gentle and enclosed:

> The slip of smooth clear blue betwixt two Isles
> Of purple shadow!

His affection for Lamb, his friend since Christ's Hospital days, is moving and sincere:

> . . . thou, methinks, most glad,
> My gentle-hearted Charles! for thou hast pined
> And hunger'd after Nature, many a year,
> In the great City pent, winning thy way
> With sad yet patient soul, through evil and pain
> And strange calamity!

Whether Lamb, that devoted Londoner, objected to this picture of him or to the publicising of his troubles, his response was a little tart:

> For God's sake . . . don't make me ridiculous any more by terming me gentle-hearted in print, or do it in better verses.[2]

Coleridge now apostrophises the setting sun in a somewhat pretentious and conceited style:

> Ah! slowly sink
> Behind the western ridge, thou glorious Sun!
> Shine in the slant beams of the sinking orb,
> Ye purple heath-flowers! richlier burn ye clouds![3]

[1] N 2, 2557 17.115. See pp. 176 and 202.
[2] C. Lamb, *Letters*, ed. E. V. Lucas, i, 198.
[3] *PW*, p. 180.

In a closely parallel notebook passage, he adds a line which is still more reminiscent of the poetic diction of the eighteenth century:

> Expecting Ocean smiled with dimpled face.[1]

In contrast, the lime-tree bower itself is described with beautiful and delicate exactitude and naturalness:

> Pale beneath the blaze
> Hung the transparent foliage; and I watch'd
> Some broad and sunny leaf, and lov'd to see
> The shadow of the leaf and stem above
> Dappling its sunshine!

His ear is as acute as his eye; he listens to the bee singing in the bean-flower or the last rook 'creeking' overhead. But, when he turns to philosophy and meditation on the scene before him, the style immediately becomes sententious:

> Henceforth I shall know
> That Nature ne'er deserts the wise and pure;
>
> . . . .
> . . . .   and sometimes
> 'Tis well to be bereft of promis'd good,
> That we may lift the soul and contemplate
> With lively joy the joys we cannot share.[2]

Frost at Midnight, written in February 1798, as *The Ancient Mariner* was nearing completion, is the most successful and beautiful of all these early poems. Its delicate balance of reflection and description, the introspective mind and the sensitively observed scene, is also most purely Coleridgean. The quiet and meditative atmosphere is created at once in the opening lines describing the stillness of the frosty midnight, broken only by the hooting of owls and the breathing of the sleeping baby. The feeling of peace in which only the mind moves in reverie is skilfully suggested in the dreamy rhythm, the flexible run-on lines and interwoven repetitions:

> 'Tis calm indeed! so calm, that it disturbs
> And vexes meditation with its strange

[1] N I, 157 G. 152.   [2] *PW*, p. 181.

> And extreme silentness. Sea, hill, and wood,
> This populous village! Sea, and hill, and wood,
> With all the numberless goings-on of life,
> Inaudible as dreams![1]

Only the film which flutters in the grate has movement, and Coleridge explains in a note: 'In all parts of the kingdom these films are called *strangers* and supposed to portend the arrival of some absent friend.' The poem then passes easily to reflection, the fluttering film becoming an image of the fluctuation of the mind itself:

> Methinks, its motion in this hush of nature
> Gives it dim sympathies with me who live,
> Making it a companionable form,
> Whose puny flaps and freaks the idling Spirit
> By its own moods interprets, everywhere
> Echo or mirror seeking of itself,
> And makes a toy of Thought.[2]

Once again, in a dream-like manner, Coleridge has attached his own feeling to an external form so that the one becomes an echo of the other.

By another easy and delicate transition, the poet's memory flutters back into the past, his Christ's Hospital schooldays. Coleridge gives a touching and unselfconscious picture of his childhood loneliness when, having seen the 'stranger' in the grate, he looked up eagerly from his books, hoping to find a visitor from home:

> Awed by the stern preceptor's face, mine eye
> Fixed with mock study on my swimming book:
> Save if the door half opened, and I snatched
> A hasty glance, and still my heart leaped up,
> For still I hoped to see the *stranger's* face,
> Townsman, or aunt, or sister more beloved, . . .[3]

He had dreamt of his 'sweet birth-place and the old church-tower', and one is sadly reminded how seldom the lonely schoolboy went back to Ottery, even for holidays. This might well have been the beginning of

[1] *PW*, p. 240. [2] ibid., pp. 240-1. [3] ibid., p. 241.

that deep insecurity which haunted Coleridge's life. Like his Mariner, he dreaded isolation and longed

> To walk together to the kirk
> With a goodly company! – [1]

So, as he listens with tenderness to his baby son's gentle breathing, his mind moves forward to the future and he wishes for Hartley a happier, freer, more secure childhood than his own:

> For I was reared
> In the great city, pent 'mid cloisters dim,
> And saw nought lovely but the sky and stars.
> But *thou*, my babe! shalt wander like a breeze
> By lakes and sandy shores, beneath the crags
> Of ancient mountain and beneath the clouds . . .

The ending completes the curve of the poem, as he imagines his son enjoying the changing beauty of the country seasons, and so brings us back gently to reality and the present. The last lines again show Coleridge's power of exact observation and expression:

> Therefore all seasons shall be sweet to thee,
> Whether the summer clothe the general earth
> With greenness, or the redbreast sit and sing
> Betwixt the tufts of snow on the bare branch
> Of mossy apple-tree, while the nigh thatch
> Smokes in the sun-thaw; whether the eave-drops fall
> Heard only in the trances of the blast,
> Or if the secret ministry of frost
> Shall hang them up in silent icicles
> Quietly shining to the quiet Moon.

A notebook entry of 1797–8 shows the poet playing with some of these phrases; the vividness was not achieved without effort:

> The reed-roof'd Village, still bepatch'd with snow
> Smok'd in the sun-thaw.[2]

The gently falling close reminds us of the 'moving moon' above the Mariner's 'rotting sea', but, in the stillness of Coleridge's village home, the moon is quiet like the feeling.

Fears in Solitude, written during the alarm of an invasion in April 1798, is rather bad as poetry but interesting in its relation to *The Ancient Mariner* and *Kubla Khan*. The didactic but straightforward statement of the lesser poem throws light on the mind which created the greater. *Fears in Solitude* opens, as Lowes noted,[1] with an echo from Bartram's *Travels through North and South Carolina*. Coleridge, in his Gutch Notebook, jots down a short reminder of one of Bartram's earthly paradises:

– Some wilderness-plot, green and fountainous and unviolated by Man.[2]

This may well have contributed to *Kubla Khan*, probably written at this time. It certainly reappears at the beginning of *Fears in Solitude*:

A green and silent spot, amid the hills,
A small and silent dell![3]

Two entries later in the notebook comes Bartram's description of the Gordonia Lasianthus, an exotic tree of perpetual flower which seems to suggest immortality. With it, however, appears the 'never-bloomless Furze', of *Fears in Solitude*:

The hills are heathy, save that swelling slope,
Which hath a gay and gorgeous covering on,
All golden with the never-bloomless furze,
Which now blooms most profusely: . . .

Miss Coburn, commenting on the notebook passage, says she has not found the furze in Bartram and suspects '. . . it is good Somersetshire furze', but adds that, 'The Gordonia Lasianthus is in Bartram, 159–60; and for the Snake birds Coleridge turned back the pages to 130–1.'[4] Here is part of the notebook passage itself:

Describe –
– the never-bloomless Furze –
and the transi to the Gordonia Lasianthus. Its thick foliage of a dark

[1] Lowes, p. 332. [2] N I, 220 G. 216.
[3] *PW*, p. 256. [4] N I, 222 G. 218 (Notes).

green colour is flowered over with large milk white fragrant blossoms
. . . from the bosom of the leaves, & renewed every morning – and
that in such incredible profusion that the Tree appears silvered over
with them & the ground beneath covered with the fallen flowers. It
at the same time continually pushes forth new twigs, with young
buds on them. . . . So that the Gordonia Lasianthus may be said to
change & renew its garments every morning thro'out the year.[1]

There seems little doubt that, in Coleridge's mind, both the exotic and
the English flower were images of immortality, and the 'never bloom-
less furze' represented his own earthly paradise of Stowey. A few lines
later in the same entry we find the Snake-birds. Why did Coleridge
turn back thirty pages in Bartram in order to associate them with the
ever-flowering tree? England and Stowey were threatened by invasion;
perhaps there was also a deeper paradise of the mind which was already
menaced by the snake. The same image was to recur much later in the
Asra poems where it certainly represents Coleridge's lost happiness.
Here it may have been linked unconsciously with the joy of creation,
which produced *Kubla Khan* and *The Ancient Mariner* and was so soon
to disappear. In the Asra poems also the reflection image is associated
with creative power; the Gordonia Lasianthus and the Snake-birds are
mirrored in water. The entry continues:

– It grows by ponds & the edges of rivers – Perhaps – the Snake-bird
with slender longest neck . . . glossy black, like fish-scales except on
the breast which is cream-coloured. . . . They delight to sit in little
peaceable communities on the dry limbs of trees, hanging over
the still waters, with their wings & tails expanded – I suppose to
cool themselves, when at the same time they behold their images
below . . .

In *The Devil's Thoughts*, distant though it is in mood, Coleridge
describes Satan, that other snake-bird who sat upon a tree and
threatened Paradise:

He peep'd into a rich bookseller's shop,
Quoth he! we are both of one college!

> For I sate myself, like a cormorant, once
> Hard by the tree of knowledge.[1]

We seem to be dealing with one of those complex webs of association spun by Coleridge's 'subtilising mind'; the shadow lies on both the inner and the outer paradise of creation.

The poet rests in the 'fern or withered heath' of *Fears in Solitude*, listening to the

> . . . singing lark,
> That singest like an angel in the clouds![2]

Did he remember *The Ancient Mariner*, completed only a month earlier, where

> Sometimes a–dropping from the sky
> I heard the sky-lark sing;
>
> . . . .
>
> And now it is an angel's song,
> That makes the heavens be mute?[3]

The strange sweet sounds which rose from the bodies of the dead men introduces the note of melancholy in *Fears in Solitude* also. Coleridge continues with a long passage on the evils of war which threaten his home and the sins of England which have made it possible. It is a long and melancholy catalogue in the style of Coleridge, the preacher, rather than Coleridge, the poet. Abroad there is war, the threat of invasion and tyranny, from which England is not free. At home he sees hypocrisy, greed, religious apathy or atheism, but, above all, lack of imagination. We speak of victories and defeats,

> Terms which we trundle smoothly o'er our tongues
> Like mere abstractions, empty sounds to which
> We join no feeling and attach no form!
> As if the soldier died without a wound;
> As if the fibres of this godlike frame
> Were gored without a pang;[4] . . .

[1] *PW*, p. 321. [2] ibid., p. 257.
[3] ibid., p. 200. [4] ibid., p. 260.

Lack of imagination, the sin of the Ancient Mariner, the failure to attach the feeling to the form, is also the sin of England, for which Coleridge fears a retribution similar to the Mariner's:

> Therefore, evil days
> Are coming on us, O my countrymen!
> And what if all-avenging Providence,
> Strong and retributive, should make us know
> The meaning of our words, force us to feel
> The desolation and the agony
> Of our fierce doings?[1]

Behind the pompous admonitory style lies the feeling of the greater poem:

> And never a saint took pity
> On my soul in agony.[2]

But the bond between Nature and Man, which the Mariner broke and found himself desolate in an alien universe, is one to which Coleridge here clings. He ends *Fears in Solitude* with gratitude for all natural ties which link him to country and home:

> But, O dear Britain! O my Mother Isle!
> Needs must thou prove a name most dear and holy
> To me, a son, a brother, and a friend,
> A husband, and a father! who revere
> All bonds of natural love, and find them all
> Within the limits of thy rocky shores.
> O native Britain! O my Mother Isle!
> How shouldst thou prove aught else but dear and holy
> To me, who from thy lakes and mountain-hills,
> Thy clouds, thy quiet dales, thy rocks and seas,
> Have drunk in all my intellectual life,
> All sweet sensations, all ennobling thoughts,
> All adoration of the God in nature, . . .[3]

This sounds like a parody of Wordsworth. The more pompous and sentimental Coleridge becomes, the more unconvincing he is. I feel

[1] *PW*, p. 260   [2] ibid., p. 196.   [3] ibid., p. 262.

here that he is himself unconvinced and therefore protests too much. His intellectual life was in the realm of ideas and was not dependent upon rocks and seas; if it had been, the waves of desolation might never have drowned him.

It is a relief when he returns to 'the golden furze' and sees the village and its well-loved landmarks in the distance:

> And now, belovéd Stowey! I behold
> Thy church-tower, and, methinks, the four huge elms
> Clustering, which mark the mansion of my friend;
> And close behind them, hidden from my view,
> Is my own lowly cottage, where my babe
> And my babe's mother dwell in peace! . . .[1]

The Nightingale was written on a still Spring evening of April 1798 when Coleridge had been walking with William and Dorothy Words-worth. The 'dim stars' and the murmuring stream which appeared in *The Ancient Mariner* are here too, but it is the nightingale, not the skylark, to which the friends are listening. Inevitably, the song recalls Milton:

> And hark! the Nightingale begins its song,
> 'Most musical, most melancholy' bird![2]

Then Coleridge suddenly repudiates this association:

> A melancholy bird? Oh! idle thought!
> In Nature there is nothing melancholy.
> But some night-wandering man whose heart was pierced
> With the remembrance of a grievous wrong,
> Or slow distemper, or neglected love,
>
> . . . .
>
> First named these notes a melancholy strain.

It is ironic that four years later Coleridge was himself to be such a man; he discovered in *Dejection* that without Joy, the 'strong music in the soul', he no longer felt a part of the natural world. Now, he says, the poet should surrender himself to the shapes and sounds around him and drink in the happiness of Nature:

[1] *PW*, p. 263.   [2] ibid., p. 264.

> . . . and so his song
> Should make all Nature lovelier, and itself
> Be loved like Nature![1]

Only those who cut themselves off from 'the deepening twilights of the spring', in the unnatural surroundings of 'ball-rooms and hot theatres', attribute sadness to the nightingale. We are not surprised when he turns to Wordsworth and Dorothy, but it is significant that the style immediately becomes a little self-conscious and itself unnatural:

> My Friend, and thou, our Sister! we have learnt
> A different lore: we may not thus profane
> Nature's sweet voices, always full of love
> And joyance!

However, when Coleridge abandons philosophy and apostrophe, to describe the nightingale's song itself, the poetry immediately becomes spontaneous, lyrical and fresh:

> 'Tis the merry Nightingale
> That crowds, and hurries, and precipitates
> With fast thick warble his delicious notes,
> As he were fearful that an April night
> Would be too short for him to utter forth
> His love-chant, and disburthen his full soul
> Of all its music![2]

His keen and sensitive ear has caught the urgency and volume of the song and translated it perfectly in the cumulative rhythm of the run-on lines. A little later, in the delicately balanced movement of the verse, he conveys the intricate phrasing of the nightingale's music:

> They answer and provoke each other's song,
> With skirmish and capricious passagings,
> And murmurs musical and swift jug jug,
> And one low piping sound more sweet than all –
> Stirring the air with such a harmony,
> That should you close your eyes, you might almost
> Forget it was not day!

[1] *PW*, p. 265. [2] ibid., p. 265.

The poetry is as musical and unselfconscious as the song it describes and among the best that Coleridge ever wrote. It reappears almost verbatim in the Gutch Notebook,[1] and it is pleasant to imagine that he may have jotted down the lines on his return from his walk.

The mysterious Lady who suddenly glides into the poem like a moon-maiden and listens to the nightingales by its light disappears as silently as she had come. Coleridge says good-night to William and Dorothy, but only the short unclouded farewell of friends who will see each other the next day. The poem ends with 'a father's tale' of Hartley which is also present in the notebook:[2]

> ... once, when he awoke
> In most distressful mood (some inward pain
> Had made up that strange thing, an infant's dream –)
> I hurried with him to our orchard-plot,
> And he beheld the moon, and, hushed at once,
> Suspends his sobs, and laughs most silently,
> While his fair eyes, that swam with undropped tears,
> Did glitter in the yellow moon-beam! Well! –
> It is a father's tale:

Did Coleridge remember the eyes of the dead which also shone in the moonlight?:

> All fixed on me their stony eyes,
> That in the Moon did glitter.[3]

The Nightingale, however, ends happily in the peace of his love for Hartley and the Wordsworths and the gentle Stowey spring. If only the wish of the last lines could have been fulfilled and he had never drifted into the wide sea of isolation and estrangement, what more might he not have given to English poetry:

> But if that Heaven
> Should give me life, his childhood shall grow up
> Familiar with these songs, that with the night
> He may associate joy. – Once more, farewell,
> Sweet Nightingale! once more, my friends! farewell.

[1] N I, 231 G. 227.   [2] ibid., 219 G. 215.   [3] *PW*, p. 203.

CHAPTER IV

'Kubla Khan' and the Underworld

Kubla Khan was for long acclaimed as the miraculous product of an opium dream whose shining visions flowed into one another with brilliant inconsequence. Emphasis has been laid more on its mysterious dream origin than on the poem itself, and for this Coleridge was largely responsible. In his famous Preface, written in 1816, nearly twenty years after the poem, he described how he

> . . . continued for about three hours in a profound sleep, at least of the external senses, during which time he has the most vivid confidence, that he could not have composed less than two to three hundred lines; if that indeed can be called composition in which all the images rose up before him as *things*, with a parallel production of the correspondent expressions, without any sensation or consciousness of effort.[1]

This abdication of conscious control, induced by the sleep of opium, also formed the basis of J. L. Lowes' interpretation of the poem in *The Road to Xanadu*. So he comments:

> Volition for the moment was asleep; it was the sleeping images that were awake and in motion. And with only the radiating streams of spontaneous association to determine their combining, they followed one another in that strange self-evolving succession which replaces ordered sequence in the world of dreams.[2]

Later he describes how '. . . the linked and interweaving images irresponsibly and gloriously stream. . . . And their pageant is as aimless as it is magnificent.'[3] The pageant, however, was interrupted by the

[1] *PW*, p. 296.   [2] Lowes, p. 375.   [3] ibid., p. 377.

'. . . person on business from Porlock', and, when the poet returned to writing down the lines which had been so strangely '. . . given to him', he found,

> . . . to his no small surprise and mortification, that though he still retained some vague and dim recollection of the general purport of the vision, yet, with the exception of some eight or ten scattered lines and images, all the rest had passed away like the images on the surface of a stream into which a stone has been cast, but, alas! without the after restoration of the latter![1]

There has in recent years been a violent critical reaction against both Coleridge's account of the poem's dream origin in the unconscious and Lowes' elaboration of it. Miss E. Schneider led the attack in her interesting and pugnacious book, *Coleridge, Opium and 'Kubla Khan'*, 1953, in which she cast serious doubt on the truth of the Preface, written so long after the poem itself by a poet notoriously unreliable about facts who had already been proved to have got the date of composition wrong. She pointed out that the Crewe manuscript of *Kubla Khan* differed from the Preface by claiming that the poem was composed in a 'reverie' or day-dream and therefore largely conscious. According to Miss Schneider, Coleridge, in the Preface, tried to make *Kubla Khan* seem more remarkable than it really was in order to reassure himself psychologically of his own genius, and Lowes made the poem's genesis '. . . more purely Hartleyan than Coleridge himself, except in quite early years, might have approved.'[2] Others have followed Miss Schneider in thinking that the Preface cannot be trusted. E. Bostetter[3] says it represents Coleridge's attempt to evade responsibility for the poem's incompleteness and to gain for it the special attention he craved. A. C. Purves,[4] in a recent article, argues interestingly that the form and rhyme-scheme of the poem are too carefully wrought and elaborate to be a product of the unconscious. G. Watson thinks it entirely coherent and goes so far as to suggest that the poem is '. . . not emotionally

[1] *PW*, p. 296.

[2] E. Schneider, *Coleridge, Opium and 'Kubla Khan'*, Chicago, 1953, p. 115.

[3] E. Bostetter, *The Romantic Ventriloquists*, University of Washington Press, 1963, p. 85.

[4] A. C. Purves, 'Formal Structure in *Kubla Khan*', *Studies in Romanticism*, Spring 1962, I, iii, 187-91.

intense, apart from the last half dozen lines. Its characteristic tone is matter-of-fact, informative, even slightly technical.'[1] Reaction from the streaming of the dream pageant could hardly go any further.

The truth, as so often, may perhaps lie somewhere between these extremes. The poem still exerts its strange power and its images must have come from *somewhere* in the poet's mind, though it can also be seen to have order and meaning and is not merely an inconsequent assemblage of subconscious memories from Coleridge's reading of travel books, as Lowes seemed to suggest. The Crewe manuscript gives, perhaps, the most helpful account. A reverie or waking dream, induced by opium, would open the gates of the unconscious so that the images would rise to the surface more freely, yet the poet would still have enough conscious control to shape and order them into a signi-ficant unity. This was pointed out by M. H. Abrams in his discussion of *Kubla Khan*:

> Coleridge should have written 'opium revery' which is a different thing from an actual dream. This would explain away the difficulty, for composition in an 'opium revery' could still be conscious enough to be remembered, yet have all the flux and other characteristics of opium vision.[2]

Coleridge's own stress in the Preface upon the unconscious origin of the poem is, as Miss Schneider pointed out, surprising, for, by 1816, he had long repudiated Hartley and the doctrine of Association and, in the following year, the *Biographia Literaria* emphasised very strongly the shaping power of the imagination and the conscious will. The Preface must, therefore, presumably contain some measure of truth, since it seems unlikely that Coleridge, at this date, would have gone out of his way to corroborate Hartley. His Malta notebook comment upon poetry as 'a rationalized dream', where Truths are 'below the Surface'[3] and feeling is attached unconsciously to form, probably brings us nearest to the truth of *Kubla Khan* also. It is important, therefore, in studying the poem, to remain sensitive, as Lowes was, to its linked and merging associations, but also to notice the order of the images and

[1] G. Watson, 'The Meaning of *Kubla Khan*', *Review of English Literature*, Jan. 1961, II, i, 22.
[2] M. H. Abrams, *The Milk of Paradise*, Cambridge, Mass., 1934, p. 78.
[3] N 2, 2086 15.52, f. 40ᵛ. See Introduction, p. 5.

the shaping power of the rhythm. If, in addition, we can interpret the feelings that Coleridge, consciously or unconsciously, attached to these forms, we may then be able to come closer to the total meaning of the poem.

The magic of *Kubla Khan* compels us immediately in its opening lines:

> In Xanadu did Kubla Khan
> A stately pleasure-dome decree;
> Where Alph, the sacred river, ran
> Through caverns measureless to man
> Down to a sunless sea.[1]

Coleridge tells us himself that he had been reading Purchas's *Pilgrimage* before he fell asleep or drifted into his reverie. The sentence which suggested the opening lines was:

> In Xamdu did Cublai Can build a stately Palace, encompassing sixteen miles of plaine ground with a wall, wherein are fertile Meddowes, pleasant Springs, delightfull Streames, and all sorts of beasts of chase and game, and in the middest thereof a sumptuous house of pleasure.[2]

So Coleridge found his lordly Eastern potentate surrounded by bright and sensuous luxury in a kind of earthly paradise. The dome may have come, as Lowes suggests, from Bernier's account of his travels in Cashmere, where it is found in the king's pleasure-garden.[3] It is interesting also, in view of the influence it had later in the poem, to discover the same source mentioned in Maurice's *History of Hindostan*:

> For myself, were it consistent with sacred writ to place the seat of Paradise any where but in the immediate neighbourhood of the Euphrates, I should incline with Bernier to conclude it was indeed in India, through not in the parched land of Ceylone, but in the warm, delicious and fertile valley of Cashmere, the present Paradise of Asia . . .[4]

[1] *PW*, p. 297.
[2] Quoted by E. H. Coleridge, ibid., p. 296.
[3] Lowes, p. 353.
[4] T. Maurice, *History of Hindostan*, London, 1795, i, 365.

The dome which Kubla so magnificently decreed may, perhaps, as Professor Wilson Knight[1] and others have suggested, stand for the achievement of civilisation, the artifact created by man from the wilderness. This was the vision Yeats had of it in *Byzantium*:

> A starlit or a moonlit dome disdains
> All that man is,
> All mere complexities,
> The fury and the mire of human veins.[2]

It is the poetry of great rulers, their power to shape their world; the poet, later in the poem, wishes to recreate it in his own medium of words:

> I would build that dome in air.

In a note Coleridge made on the Greek phrase usually translated, 'that only a poet is king', cited in Porphyry's *Life of Plotinus* as the title of a work of Origen, addressed to the Emperor Gallienus, he questions this interpretation:

> *Qy.* Is it not possible that Origen's Title might be rendered. That the only Poet is the Emperor – instead of, That the Poet alone is a King? . . . And is it not probable that the theme of a work done *in praise* of the Emperor Galienus, was to prove, that the true *poesy*, = making, was that of giving objectivity, form and life to the Ideas of legislative Reason, the reducing the rude materials of a multitude to measure & harmony etc. . . .[3]

This comment upon the emperor as creator throws interesting light upon Kubla and his dome; but, almost as soon as this splendid vision of civilisation has been evoked, it vanishes and we are plunged into a different and darker world. Why did Coleridge's imagination suddenly descend from the sunlit dome to the frightening depths of the 'caverns measureless to man'? I believe that Lowes provides us with a clue, though not in the way he intended. He tells us that

The last sentence Coleridge had read before his eyes rested on the

---

[1] G. W. Knight, *The Starlit Dome*, p. 97.
[2] W. B. Yeats, *Collected Poems*, Macmillan, 1934, p. 280.
[3] Quoted by Miss Coburn in N 1, 1057 21.181 (Notes).

words 'In Xamdu did Cublai Can build a stately Palace', was a remarkable expression of the belief among the Tartars of the survival of the dead.[1]

Within less than a page, Lowes adds, Purchas records, ' "Their Priests were diviners . . . They foretell holy dayes, and those which are unlucky for enterprises." '[2] Here, surely, one of those strange mergings took place in the stream of the poet's unconscious mind. The description of the survival of the dead among the *Tartars* became linked with *Tartarus*, the Greek underworld of death, and the legendary rivers that flowed through it. The Tartar priests who could foretell the future also point forward to the

Ancestral voices prophesying war!

Alpheus did not, indeed, flow through the underworld, but it was the sacred river associated with the religious festivals of Olympia, and part of its legendary course was beneath the earth. Lowes reminds us of an interesting quotation from Pausanias' *Description of Greece*, translated by Thomas Taylor in 1794, which it seems unlikely that Coleridge would have neglected, Classical scholar and lover of Taylor, the Platonist, as he was:

'But the Alpheus seems to possess something different from other rivers; for it often hides itself in the earth, and again rises out of it. Thus it . . . merges itself in the Tegeatic land. Ascending from hence in Asaea, and mingling itself with the waters of Eurotas, it falls a second time into the earth, emerges from hence, in that place which the Arcadians call the fountains, and running through the Pisaean and Olympian plains, pours itself into the sea. . . .'[3]

If we leave Lowes and turn to Pausanias himself, we find that the Alpheus was not the only river with these subterranean habits. The river Pausanias describes flowing past the tomb of Orpheus on Mount Helicon is even more important for lovers of poetry:

The river Helicon flows through this part of the country, and at a

[1] Lowes, p. 362.
[2] ibid., p. 363.
[3] Quoted by Lowes, p. 359. In N 1, 1170 6.98, Coleridge refers to the statue of Venus by Praxiteles in Pausanias' description of Megara.

distance of eighty-five stadia, hides itself in the earth. Afterwards, having concealed itself for about twenty-two stadia, it again rises, and, assuming the name of Baphyrae instead of Helicon, becomes a navigable river and pours itself into the sea. The Dietae say, that the river at first ran in an open channel; but that when the women who slew Orpheus attempted to wash themselves from his blood in it, then it sunk into the earth, that its water might not be the means of purifying them from his murder.[1]

This legendary river whose name is synonymous with poetry is, thus, indissolubly linked with Orpheus, the sweet singer of the ancient world, who descended into Tartarus by the magic of his lyre but returned again to life and light. The descent and rising of the river might well symbolise this also. Since the Alpheus and the Alph of *Kubla Khan* also sink to the underworld and rise again, a further legend Pausanias records of Orpheus' power may have relevance to the poem:

A shepherd about mid-day, being weary, laid himself down by the tomb of Orpheus, and in his sleep began to sing the verses of that poet with a loud and sweet voice. . . .[2]

Kubla Khan also came to Coleridge unbidden in sleep, or in that reverie where the well-loved myths of Greece merged in his dreaming mind.

Miss J. Harrison, in *Prolegomena to the Study of Greek Religion*, gives an account of the curious religious rites practised by the Orphics, the sect to which Orpheus who was both priest and poet had given his name. Some of these Coleridge could have read in Pausanias or in Plato who was certainly influenced by Orphism. Among the supposedly Orphic tablets, found inscribed in thin gold in the tombs of Southern Italy and Crete, is one from Petelia which provides instructions for the conduct of the dead in the world below. Miss Harrison gives the following translation:

The Petelia tablet

Thou shalt find on the left in the House of Hades a Well-spring
And by the side thereof standing a white cypress.

[1] Pausanias, *The Description of Greece*, trans, Thomas Taylor, London, 1794, iii, 68.
[2] ibid., p. 69.

To this Well-spring approach not near.
But thou shalt find another by the Lake of Memory,
Cold water flowing forth, and there are Guardians before it,

Say: 'I am a child of Earth and of Starry Heaven'.[1]

The spring on the left, which the soul is warned not to touch, is Lethe,
the legendary river of Forgetfulness, which flowed through Hades. The
well which other tablets locate on the right is Mnemosyne, 'the lake
of Memory'. These streams, of course, flowed through all Greek literature and Coleridge might have met them in many places, though
perhaps most notably, as Miss Harrison points out, in Book 10 of
Plato's *Republic*, where the souls took shelter by the river of Unmind-
fulness. Some lines from Coleridge's *The Snowdrop* are startlingly
close to the description of Lethe in the Orphic tablet:

> . . . the insuperable steep,
> On whose vast summit broad and smooth
> Her nest the Phœnix bird conceals,
> And where by cypresses o'erhung
> The heavenly Lethe steals.[2]

The 'insuperable steep' might well have been Helicon or Parnassus, the
mountains of the Muses, where Orphic rites were performed of which
Coleridge had probably read in Pausanias and elsewhere.

If, as I have suggested, he was interested in Orpheus and the river
Helicon, it is unlikely that he would have missed Pausanias' further
account of the oracle of Trophonius at Lebadea which lies between
Helicon and Parnassus. Pausanias gives an extraordinary but circum-
stantial account of this Orphic ritual in which he himself took part.
The initiate, he says,

> . . . is not immediately after this led by the sacrificers to the oracle,
> but is first brought to the fountains of the river, which are very near
> to each other. Here he is obliged to drink of that which is called the

---

[1] J. Harrison, *Prolegomena to the Study of Greek Religion*, CUP, 1922, p. 572.
Later scholars such as E. R. Dodds, *The Greeks and the Irrational*, 1951, pp. 147–9,
are less fully convinced of the Orphic origin of the tablets.
[2] *PW*, p. 358.

water of Lethe, that he may become oblivious of all the former objects of his pursuit. Afterwards, he must drink of another water, which is called the water of *Mnemosyne*, or *memory*, that he may remember the objects which will present themselves to his view on descending into the grove . . . within the inclosure there is a chasm of the earth, which was not formed by nature but was made by art . . . He, therefore, who descends to the bottom of this chasm lays himself down on the ground, and holding in his hand sops mingled with honey, first of all places his feet in a small cavern, then hastens to join his knees to his feet; and immediately after the rest of his body contracted to his knees, is drawn within the cavern, just as if he was hurried away by the vortex of the largest and most rapid river. But those that have descended to the adytum of this place are not all instructed in the secrets of futurity in the same manner.[1]

The fountains; the descent into the chasm; the offering of honey to the Gods of the underworld; the rushing force of the river and the learning of the secrets of futurity; all have their obvious parallels in *Kubla Khan*. After his terrifying experience, the initiate is seated 'on the throne of Mnemosyne' to describe what he has seen and heard. Then he is brought, Pausanias continues,

. . . to the temple of Good Fortune, and the Good Daemon, while he is yet full of terror, and without any knowledge either of himself, or of those that are near him . . .[2]

He is then questioned by the priests of the things that are to be. It seems very probable that the Alpheus merged in Coleridge's mind with Lethe and Mnemosyne and Helicon; the Tartar priests with their gift of prophecy became linked with Orpheus and his followers who returned to life burdened with the strange and terrible knowledge of the underworld. Surely *Kubla Khan* means that the poet, when divinely inspired, remembers the inscrutable secrets of the world below, singing of a mystery and terror which seems to men like the gift of prophecy. The poem, which begins with the river plunging into the underworld and ends with the divine madness of the poet, is, also, I believe, about the

[1] Pausanias, iii, 93.   [2] ibid., p. 94.

mysterious unconscious sources of creative inspiration and the poet's brief singing of this memory on his return to the sunlit conscious world.

Coleridge, after all, in his moving tribute to Wordsworth's greatness, described *The Prelude* as

> – An Orphic song indeed,
> A song divine of high and passionate thoughts
> To their own music chaunted![1]

and, in the first manuscript version of his poem to Wordsworth, which was later altered, he speaks of his friend's inner power and sees his brows garlanded; this was certainly a reference to Orphic ceremony:

> Theme as hard as high!
> Of Smiles spontaneous, and mysterious Fears;
>
> . . . .
>
> Or by interior Power; of Moments aweful,
> Now in thy hidden Life; and now abroad,
> Mid festive Crowds, *thy* Brows too garlanded,
> A Brother of the Feast; . . .[2]

This is describing the hidden mystery of poetry, and Miss Harrison tells us that, in the Orphic Mysteries, 'the putting on of garlands was the final stage of initiation for Hierophants and other priests.'[3] It is not without reason that Coleridge speaks of 'a song divine', or, at the end of *Kubla Khan*, describes the poet as surrounded by 'holy dread.' It is a curious coincidence also that Pausanias, as Taylor translates him, when about to describe the mysteries of Eleusis which was connected with the underworld and Orphic ritual, '. . . *was restrained from the execution of this design by a vision in a dream*. . . .' He gave only '. . . such particulars as it is lawful to disclose.'[4] Did Coleridge remember the underlined phrase, and, when trying to describe the mystery of poetic creation, call his unfinished poem, 'A Vision in a Dream. A Fragment'?

*   *   *

The poet had, indeed, drunk from Mnemosyne, for the Preface tells us that, 'On awaking he appeared to himself to have a distinct recollection of the whole', but the man from Porlock plunged him back

---

[1] *PW*, p. 406. [2] ibid., p. 579.
[3] J. Harrison, p. 593. [4] Pausanias, i, 38.

again into Lethe and '. . . with the exception of some eight or ten scattered lines and images, all the rest had passed away like the images on the surface of a stream into which a stone has been cast, but, alas! without the after restoration of the latter!' It is significant that Coleridge himself here uses the image of the stream to suggest poetic consciousness and there are also places in the notebooks where it is employed in the same way. In an entry of December 1803, he writes:

> I will at least make the attempt to explain to myself the Origin of moral Evil from the *streamy* Nature of Association, which Thinking = Reason, curbs & rudders / how this comes to be so difficult / Do not the bad Passions in Dreams throw light & shew of proof upon this Hypothesis?[1]

and about a month later, in January 1804, he recurs to this:

> . . . I saw great Reason to attribute the effect wholly to the streamy nature of the associating Faculty and especially as it is evident that *they most* labor under this defect who are most reverie-ish & streamy – Hartley, for instance & myself.[2]

The connection Coleridge makes in these two passages between the image of the stream and the faculty of association, and the further linking of it with dreams and reverie, obviously throw interesting light on *Kubla Khan*; it strengthens the suggestion that the river flowing through Kubla's garden is consciousness, while 'the caverns measureless to man' are the unconscious. In 1798, presumably, Coleridge would not have linked association with the origin of evil. J. V. Baker, in *The Sacred River*, also remarks on this notebook entry of Coleridge, seeing him as a pioneer in psychology: '. . . a hundred years before William James and James Joyce he was aware of the stream of consciousness . . .'[3] In an entry of November 1803 Coleridge uses the image of the stream to suggest Memory:

> – The town with lighted windows & noise of the *Clogged* Passengers in the Streets – sound of the unseen River – Mountains scarcely perceivable except by eyes long used to them, & supported by the

---

[1] N 1, 1770, 16.156. See p. 150.   [2] ibid., 1833 16.216.
[3] J. V. Baker, *The Sacred River*, Louisiana University Press, 1957, p. 153.

images of Memory flowing in on the impulses of immediate Impression – [1]

An earlier note of September 1801, written with Sara Hutchinson in mind, seems even closer to Mnemosyne:

> Item – Murmur of a stream – Item – *well** *with* Shadows. Item – Why aren't you here? – *images & realities in the eye & memory – fantasticaly [sic], soul going into the heart of the survivor, & abiding there with its Image.[2]

In a later entry of April 1805, discussing metre in poetry with his usual acuteness, Coleridge describes the stream of Memory with the brighter light of consciousness upon it:

> . . . two ~~sources~~ [sic] kinds of pleasure are procured, in the two master-movements & impulses of man, the gratification of the Love of Variety with the grat. of the Love of Uniformity – and that by a recurrence, delightful as a painless and yet exciting act of memory, tiny breezelets of surprise, each one destroying the ripplets which the former had made, yet all together keeping the surface of the mind in a bright dimple-smile – [3]

The very interesting notebook entry of October 1803, which recalls an earlier one of November 1799, recording his first meeting with Sara Hutchinson, describes the unconscious or semi-conscious mind in the image of catacombs from which association calls up memories:

> Print of the Darlington Ox, sprigged with Spots. – Viewed in all moods, consciously, uncons. semiconsc. – with vacant, with swimming eyes – made a Thing of Nature by the repeated action of the Feelings. O Heaven when I think how perishable Things, how imperishable Thoughts seem to be! – For what is Forgetfulness?†
> Renew the state of affection or bodily Feeling, same or similar – sometimes dimly similar / and instantly the trains of forgotten Thought rise from their living catacombs! – Old men, & Infancy / and Opium, probably by its narcotic effect on the whole seminal

[1] N 1, 1648 21.394. See p. 177.
[2] ibid., 981 21.133. See p. 176.   [3] N 2, 2516 17.81.

organisation, in a large Dose, or after long use, produces the same effect on the *visual* & *passive* memory /† so far was written in my b. pocket [book] Nov. 25th. 1799 – [1]

This is a very clear statement of the power associations of feeling have to call up memories from the deep caverns of the mind through unconscious or semi-conscious processes. This happens more easily through the action of opium, Coleridge says, and we immediately recall the 'anodyne' of *Kubla Khan*'s Preface, which 'flung up momently the sacred river' from the 'caverns measureless to man'. This underworld of the mind had a great fascination for Coleridge. Indeed, Miss Coburn notes that he used the words 'subconscious' and 'psycho-analytical' in the notebooks of 1805, nearly a hundred years before their earliest recorded use in NED. In December 1801, for example, we find the following:

> To *fall* asleep – is not a real *event* in the body well represented by this phrase – is it in *excess*, when on first *dropping* asleep we *fall* down precipices, or *sink* down, all things *sinking* beneath us, or *drop down*, . . .[2]

Or, again, he describes falling asleep:

> – O then as I first sink on the pillow, as if Sleep had indeed a material *realm* . . . O then what visions have I had, what dreams . . . I sink down the waters, thro' Seas & Seas – yet warm, yet a Spirit – [3]

Was this perhaps 'the sunless sea' of *Kubla Khan*? The difficulty of reaching or understanding this subterranean world of one's own mind is expressed in another note of 1803:

> . . . the greater & perhaps nobler certainly all the subtler parts of one's nature must be solitary – Man exists herein to himself & to God alone / – Yea, in how much only to God – how much lies *below* his own Consciousness.[4]

Much later, in the *Biographia Literaria*, Coleridge praises Wordsworth's

---

[1] N I, 1575 21.296(a). See p. 51.   [2] ibid., 1078 21.203.
[3] ibid., 1718 16.105. See p. 84.   [4] ibid., 1554 21.274. See p. 84.

Ode on the Intimations of Immortality in a fine passage which could also describe himself and his own poetry, not least *Kubla Khan*:

> But the ode was intended for such readers only as had been accustomed to watch the flux and reflux of their inmost nature, to venture at times into the twilight realms of consciousness, and to feel a deep interest in modes of inmost being, to which they know that the attributes of time and space are inapplicable and alien, but which yet cannot be conveyed, save in symbols of time and space.[1]

No one knew these twilight realms better than Coleridge and, though symbols are inadequate to express the deepest truths of this underworld, we have, perhaps, gained a glimpse of what the imagery of *Kubla Khan* meant to its author.

* * *

The description of the earthly paradise of Kubla with the gardens and forests which the river makes fertile, before it plunges back into the earth, may have many associations. Elysium, the gardens of the Hesperides, the Promised Land of Canaan, Milton's Paradise, the mountain gardens of Cashmere, Purchas' description of Aloadine's Mohammedan paradise; all may lie behind the following lines:

> So twice five miles of fertile ground
> With walls and towers were girdled round;
> And there were gardens bright with sinuous rills,
> Where blossomed many an incense-bearing tree;
> And here were forests ancient as the hills,
> Enfolding sunny spots of greenery.

It is, however, a paradise made by man, encircled with walls and towers, where the trees are heavy with fragrant flowers, and even the dark force of the sacred river has been tamed into 'sinuous rills' which ornament and water the gardens. This is a cultivated rather than a natural world, or, as E. Bostetter says:

> Upon the primitive, inchoate world of nature the gardens have been imposed, a portion of the wilderness has been tamed and cultivated,

---

[1] *BL*, p. 268.

and the fabrics of art have been erected. . . . The origin and end of
the river are terrifying and inscrutable but in the midst is meaning.[1]

The description also has a distinctly Eastern atmosphere – the garden
is dominated by the dome, as the very sound of the word suggests.
Though Coleridge tells us the poem was written on Exmoor, neither
its wild beauty nor the freshness of spring in the coombs of Somerset
has crept into the landscape of *Kubla Khan*, as they did into *The
Ancient Mariner* and *Christabel*. The very rhythm of the lines has a
fluctuating dreamy movement which seems to suggest the lazy, sunlit,
scented world where, according to Lowes and Purchas, ' "Mahomet
had promised such a sensuall Paradise to his devout followers." '[2]

Coleridge and Southey had been planning a joint poem on Mahomet
and, in a letter to his brother-in-law of September 1799, Coleridge
writes 'I shall go on with the Mohammed.'[3] A notebook entry of
November 1803, which makes tragi-comic reading, lists, not for the
first time, the many works that the poet was going to write, '. . . with
a fervent prayer that I may build up in my Being enough of Manly
Strength and Perseverance to do one thing at a time . . .'[4] Coleridge's
plans were nothing if not grandiose, one being,

> On Man, and the probable Destiny of the Human Race –
> ⟨*My last & great* work – always had in mind⟩

But more immediate to our purpose is the last sentence of this entry:

– Conquest of India by Bacchus in Hexameters. –

Miss Coburn points out in her note on this passage that 'India was the
subject of considerable reading: Maurice's *Hindostan*, Wilkins's translation of the *Bhagavadgita*, and T. A. Dubois *The People of India*.' A
fragment of Coleridge's *Mahomet* has survived, beginning with the
following lines:

Utter the song, O my soul! the flight and return of
Mohammed,

---

[1] E. Bostetter, *The Romantic Ventriloquists*, University of Washington Press,
1963, p. 87. [2] Lowes, p. 330.
[3] Quoted by E. H. Coleridge, *PW*, p. 329. [4] N I, 1646 21.392 and Notes.

Prophet and priest, who scatter'd abroad both evil
    and blessing,
Huge wasteful empires founded and hallow'd slow
    persecution,
Soul-withering, but crush'd the blasphemous rites of
    the Pagan . . .[1]

If this is a fair specimen, we need not, perhaps, too much regret 'The Conquest of India by Bacchus in Hexameters'! It is, however, important that Coleridge was fascinated by Mohammed, 'prophet and priest' and 'the huge wasteful empires' he founded, by the civilisation of India and by Bacchus with whom he connected it. The dome and its sunlit pleasure-gardens which stand above the dark caverns where the river rises seem, then, to suggest a great civilisation which the creative spirit of man has won from the darkness. The caves of ice, associated later with the dome, were in Cashmere, the musical damsels were in Mahomet's Paradise in Purchas and became linked with Milton's Abyssinian garden, so Coleridge does seem to have been enchanted at this time by the luxurious beauty of the East. He wished to recreate its magic in poetry:

I would build that dome in air,
That sunny dome, those caves of ice!

But, before the poet himself comes into his poem, we must return from the earthly paradise to the deep and savage chasm, from Tartary to Tartarus.

Coleridge now takes us back to the origin of the sacred river, the chasm from which the fountain bursts forth:

But oh! that deep romantic chasm which slanted
Down the green hill athwart a cedarn cover!
A savage place! as holy and enchanted
As e'er beneath a waning moon was haunted
By woman wailing for her demon-lover!

The 'forests ancient as the hills' in the background of the garden seem to lead down to the primitive savage scene of the chasm with its

[1] *PW*, p. 329.

'cedarn cover' which, in turn, suggests a strange, sacred but terrifying landscape. Now Bacchus, as we have seen, was associated in Coleridge's mind with India and so, probably, was the dome, but he is, of course, more usually thought of as the Greek god who intoxicated his worshippers with wine or possessed them with the divine madness of spiritual ecstasy. In Greece he had many names, most commonly Dionysus or Bromius, and he was connected with Hades and with Orpheus who was his priest. Miss Harrison points out that the ancient vase paintings show no evidence of Eurydice and explains Orpheus' descent to the underworld as follows:

> Semele, the green earth, comes up from below, year by year; with her comes her son, Dionysos, and by a certain instinct of chivalry men said he had gone to fetch her. The mantle of Dionysos descends on Orpheus . . . Orpheus, priest of Dionysos, took on his resurrection as well as his death; that is the germ from which sprang the beautiful love-story. A taboo element, common to many primitive stories, is easily added. You may not look back when spirits are about from the underworld. If you do, you may have to join them.[1]

Greek tragedy originated in the rites of Dionysos and the theatre of Athens is still called by his name. Like his priest, Orpheus, he is connected with music and poetry, and Miss Harrison describes an ancient vase-painting which shows him holding a lyre: 'His head is thrown back in ecstasy; he is drunken, but with music not with wine.'[2]

Coleridge, in one of his lectures of 1813–14 on the origin of drama, shows himself aware of what the god stood for in the deepest sense:

> In his earthly character [Bacchus was] the conqueror and civiliser of India, and allegorically the Symbol – in the narrower and popular notion – of festivity, but worshipped in the mysteries as representative of the organic energies of the Universe, that work by passion and joy without apparent distinct consciousness, and rather as the cause or condition of skill and contrivance than the result . . . with the

[1] J. Harrison, p. 603.
[2] ibid., p. 451.

ancients Bacchus or Dionysus was among the most awful and
mysterious deities – in his earthly character etc. to such passions.[1]

Professor Wind, in his interesting study of *Pagan Mysteries in the
Renaissance*, records a very similar interpretation of Dionysus held in
the famous Neoplatonic circle of Florence which surrounded Lorenzo
de Medici. Two of its outstanding figures were Pico della Mirandola
and Ficino, with both of whom Coleridge's notebooks show him to
have been familiar. An entry of 1798–9, discussing Unity and Entity,
comments:

> We can predicate Unity of God, but not Entity. The Aristotelians
> denied this – / The Thing was learnedly disputed in the year 1490
> by Politian & Mirandula on the side of the Aristotelians, & Lorenzo
> de Medicis, on the Platonic Party.[2]

Professor Wind quotes a passage from Ficino's preface to the *Mystical
Theology* of Dionysus, the Areopagite, 'whose name offered the occasion for describing as Bacchic the approach to God through a negation
of the intellect'. The Renaissance interpretation of Bacchus is very
similar to Coleridge's in his lecture on drama; both had a common
origin in Plato:

> . . . 'The spirit of the god Dionysus', Ficino explained, 'was
> believed by the ancient theologians and Platonists to be the ecstasy
> and abandon of disencumbered minds, when partly by innate love,
> partly at the instigation of the god, they transgress the natural limits
> of intelligence and are miraculously transformed into the beloved
> god himself: where, inebriated by a certain new draft of nectar and
> by an immeasurable joy, they rage, as it were, in a bacchic frenzy.'[3]

Another comment Coleridge made on Bacchus anticipates by half
a century the distinction Nietzsche drew in *The Birth of Tragedy*
between Apollo and Dionysus:

> The Greek stage had its origin in the ceremonies of a sacrifice,
> such as the goat to Bacchus. It was erroneous to call him only the

[1] Coleridge, *Shakespearean Criticism*, ed. T. M. Raysor, 1930, i, 184.
[2] N I, 374 3½.9, f. 4.
[3] E. Wind, *Pagan Mysteries in the Renaissance*, Faber, 1958, p. 64.

jolly god of wine; among the ancients he was venerable; he was the symbol of that power which acts without our consciousness from the vital energies of nature, as Apollo was the symbol of our intellectual consciousness.[1]

Coleridge's awareness of Apollo and Dionysus as symbols of the conscious and unconscious powers in man seems also to have had a Renaissance tradition. Professor Wind, commenting on Pico della Mirandola, says:

All the particular gods, in the Orphic theology as outlined by Pico, seem animated by a law of self-contrariety, which is also a law of self-transcendence . . . The wild Dionysus, on Mount Parnassus, finds himself checked by a stern Apollo, who in his turn, when he appears opposite to Minerva, softens her severity.[2]

In illustration of this, Professor Wind adds an illuminating note on a Renaissance painting:

For Dionysus-Apollo see the portrait of Alberto Pio, which should be ascribed, I believe, to Giacomo Francia. It shows the Muses divided between Apollo and Dionysus, whose temples inscribed with their names, occupy the two peaks of Parnassus.[3]

Professor Wind further adds that this theme of union and division between the gods, each god containing his opposite in himself, has its origin in Proclus, translated by Thomas Taylor, and in the *Orphic Hymns*.[4] Coleridge's favourite theory of the union of opposites, elaborated in Chapter 14 of the *Biographia Literaria* and elsewhere, had, no doubt, a similar source. His copy of Taylor's *Proclus* was heavily annotated.

Moreover, both in Pausanias and in Maurice's *History of Hindostan*, Coleridge would have found Bacchus associated with India as well as Greece. Pausanias writes:

This Bacchus, too, in my opinion, was the same with the one who first led an army to the Indies, and first raised bridges over the

---

[1] Coleridge, *Shakespearean Criticism*, ii, 263. [2] Wind, pp. 161–2.
[3] ibid., p. 162. [4] ibid., p. 163.

Euphrates, in that part of the city which is called Zeugma, and where even at present a rope is preserved, made of vine and twigs, which Bacchus is said to have used when he built the bridges. . . .[1]

Maurice's *History of Hindostan* is no ordinary travel book; his real theme is the common roots in mythology between the Eastern and Western world. This is a subject after Coleridge's own heart and his notebooks show that he had read Maurice with great care. The *History of Hindostan* describes the history and origin of Bacchus in India in considerable detail, but not until the second volume which was published in October 1798, when *Kubla Khan* was, probably, already written. Nevertheless, the poem was not published until 1816, and Maurice himself explains that he got his information from Herodotus and Plutarch and other sources with which Coleridge was certainly familiar. His own description of Bacchus, in the lecture on drama already quoted, as 'the conqueror and civiliser of India',[2] seems almost to echo the description given by Maurice:

> We shall first, however, summarily state a few general observations concerning the ancient Bacchus himself . . . whom all the classical writers of antiquity have, with one consent, joined in asserting to have been the first conqueror, and not merely the conqueror, but the reformer and legislator, of India.[3]

Coleridge connects him chiefly with the awful and mysterious power which forces man to surrender to passionate emotion so that he loses all conscious control, becomes intoxicated with the divine madness, or, as the Greeks said, possessed by the god. Like the river, Bacchus was for Coleridge an image of the power of the unconscious, the ideas and impulses which rise unbidden from the depths and can be both a terror and an inspiration. He might easily have got some of his information about Bacchus from *A Dissertation on the Eleusinian and Bacchic Mysteries*, published by his favourite, Thomas Taylor, in 1791. Taylor connects the descent of Aeneas to the underworld in Virgil's *Aeneid*, Book 6, with the Mysteries, and notes in Virgil also the images of the

[1] Pausanias, iii, 184.
[2] Coleridge, *Shakespearean Criticism*, i, 184.
[3] T. Maurice, *History of Hindostan*, London, 1798, ii, 121.

black lake, the caves and the dark woods. He interprets Hades as the irrational part of man:

> A representation of the descent of the soul must certainly form no inconsiderable part of these mystic shews . . . he who in this present life is in subjection to his irrational part is truly in Hades.[1]

Coleridge would have met in Taylor also an account of a partly subterranean river, with a Neoplatonic commentary very close to his own interpretation of Bacchus. Here Taylor is writing about Virgil's description of the abodes of the blessed:

> Nor is it without reason that the river Eridanus is represented as flowing through these delightful abodes; and it is at the same time denoted 'plurimus', because a great part of it was absorbed in the earth without emerging from thence: for a river is the symbol of life, and consequently signifies in this place the nature of an intellectual life, proceeding from on high, that is from divinity itself, and gliding with prolific energy through the occult and profound recesses of the soul.[2]

This suggests that Virgil's river on the surface in the 'abodes of the blessed' is the symbol of consciousness, but, when flowing underground in Hades, represents the unconscious mind. The wording is close, in places, to Coleridge's account of Bacchus, and it seems highly probable that it merged with another reference to the Eridanus in Maurice, this time from the first volume of *The History of Hindostan*, published in 1795. Maurice is pointing out the connection between constellations and rivers, in the context of a more general discussion of the identity of Indian and Greek fables:

> The Indians, after borrowing the Chaldean sphere, converted the Euphrates into the Ganges; for it is surely not a little remarkable, that according to the Hindoo mythologists . . . the Ganges is said to flow from the foot of Veeshnu; an irrefragable proof that the Ganges is the Grecian Eridanus, and that the mythology originally belonged to the Greater, and not to the Lesser Asia.[3]

---

[1] T. Taylor, *The Bacchic Mysteries*, London, 1791, p. 53.
[2] ibid., p. 58. [3] Maurice, 1795, i, 355.

The Ganges, the sacred river of India, is thus linked with the Greek Eridanus which Taylor describes as flowing through Virgil's Elysium and descending from it to the underworld. The 'sacred river' of *Kubla Khan* may, then, have been associated in Coleridge's mind, like Bacchus, with both India and Greece. The strange power of the unconscious in both the river and the god exerted its force upon both Eastern and Western civilization.

In the West we think of Bacchus mainly as the god of Delphi where he shared with Apollo the worship of the ancient world. He and his band of Maenad women, maddened by the god, traditionally roamed the wild slopes of Parnassus, often tearing animals to pieces in their frenzy. So Teiresias, in *The Bacchae* of Euripides, cries:

> A prophet is our God, for Bacchanalism
> And madness are alike prophetical.
> . . . .
> From Dionysos springs this frenzy too,
> And him shall we behold on Delphi's crags
> Leaping, with his pine torches lighting up
> The rifts of the twin-headed rock[1]

The *Bacchae* shows the terrifying power of the god under whose influence the wretched Agave unconsciously tears her own son to pieces.

According to Maurice, however, Bacchus had come originally from Egypt, where he taught his subjects the art of cultivating the ground, and then extended his empire to the rest of the East:

> The forces of Dionysius entered India, from the Persian frontier, in a magnificent procession; and all the pomp and splendour becoming the monarch of a great and civilised empire were displayed upon this occasion. . . .[2]

Not only the crags of Delphi but the mountains of Cashmere must have echoed the shouts of his maddened devotees:

> Already exalted into a divinity by the prostrate adoration of those who beheld the wonderful effects of power . . . Dionysius retained

---

[1] Euripides, *The Bacchae*, trans. H. Milman, Rinehart, 1960, p. 251.
[2] Maurice, 1798, ii, 125.

among the attendants of his court a certain number of female devotees . . . who, by their frantic outcries and extravagant gesticulations, exhibited the appearance of divine inspiration. These, under the impulse of a holy phrenzy, rushed furiously up and down the mountains and made the forests resound with reiterated acclamations of 'Io Bacche, Io Triumphe!' Each was furnished with a *thirsus*, that is a kind of lance or spear wrapped up in vine-leaves, to amuse the unpractised Indians and induce them to believe that no hostilities were intended.[1]

This comes from the second volume of the *History of Hindostan* and, no doubt, Herodotus and Plutarch and Maurice's other sources contributed to Hellenising it.

In the hymn to Bacchus, from Thomas Taylor's translation of the Orphic hymns, his Maenad followers call him, though the frenzy is somewhat tamed by the decorous couplets of the eighteenth century:

> Triennial, whom the leaves of vine adorn,
> Of Jove and Proserpine, occultly born,
> Immortal daemon, hear my suppliant voice.[2]

Or again:

> With all thy Satyrs on our incense shine,
> Daemons wild formed and bless the rites divine,
> Our orgies shining through the night inspire . . .[3]

Miss Harrison says:

The gods whose worship Orpheus taught were two, Bacchus and Eros. . . . The religion of Orpheus *is* religious in the sense that it is the worship of the real mysteries of life, of potencies (daemons) rather than personal gods; it is the worship of life itself in its supreme mysteries of ecstasy and love.[4]

Professor Wind points out that the rites of the Orphic mysteries resembled death;[5] the orgies in which his female followers surrendered

---

[1] Maurice, 1798, ii, p. 126.
[2] T. Taylor, *Hymns of Orpheus*, trans. 1787, p. 155.
[3] ibid., p. 185.   [4] J. Harrison, p. 657.   [5] Wind, p. 132.

to the power of Dionysus were madly destructive. The Medici philosophic circle interpreted this as a dying into life which explains why Roman sarcophagi were decorated with the loves of gods for mortals. Lorenzo de Medici himself said:

> ... The beginning of the *vita amorosa* proceeds from death, because whoever lives for love, first dies to everything else. And if love has in it a certain perfection ... it is impossible to arrive at that perfection without first dying with regard to the more imperfect things.[1]

This highly Platonic explanation tends to remove the savagery from the ancient legends of the love encounters between god and mortal. The ecstasy which possessed the women who followed Bacchus was a fierce and blind desire to be lost in the daemon-god. Whether Coleridge imagined his worship at Delphi or Cashmere, both were 'savage places', 'holy and enchanted' by the presence of Dionysus. The original Crewe manuscript of *Kubla Khan* confirms this association by spelling the 'demon-lover' of the 1816 version as 'Daemon Lover'.[2] Coleridge used capitals erratically so this may not be significant, but the spelling is.

> A savage place! as holy and enchanted
> As e'er beneath a waning Moon was haunted
> By Woman wailing for her Daemon Lover!

certainly suggests a surrender to the power of the unconscious which is still a mystery.

The note of violence is continued in the next lines of *Kubla Khan* which describe the fountain where the river rises:

> And from this chasm, with ceaseless turmoil seething,
> As if this earth in fast thick pants were breathing,
> A mighty fountain momently was forced:
> Amid whose swift half-intermitted burst
> Huge fragments vaulted like rebounding hail,
> Or chaffy grain beneath the thresher's flail:
> And mid these dancing rocks at once and ever
> It flung up momently the sacred river.

[1] ibid., p. 133.
[2] A facsimile of the manuscript is conveniently reprinted in an article by J. Shelton, 'The Autograph Manuscript of *Kubla Khan* and an Interpretation', *Review of English Literature*, January 1966, VII, i, 32–3.

The rhythm itself becomes urgent and strained, especially in the strongly stressed monosyllables, 'fast thick pants', and one can feel the shaking of the earth as the fountain bursts through. One remembers that the Earth worship at Delphi was older than Apollo's or Dionysus' and the strange fumes which the Pythian priestess inhaled above the chasm seemed to come from the breathing centre of the earth itself. There was a famous fountain at Delphi too, the Castalian spring, which became synonymous with the inspiration of poetry and prophecy. Coleridge referred to it in an early poem, 'To a Friend, [Charles Lamb] who had declared his intention of writing no more poetry':

> Dear Charles! whilst yet thou wert a babe, I ween
> That Genius plung'd thee in that wizard fount
> Hight Castalie: . . . .
> Steadfast and rooted in the heavenly Muse
> And wash'd and sanctified to Poesy.[1]

and in the *Ode to Dejection* he laments the loss of the fountain from which his own poetry sprang:

> I may not hope from outward forms to win
> The passion and the life, whose fountains are within.[2]

But he also uses the image to suggest something older, the ancient wisdom which flows from the earth itself. So, in a notebook of 1795, he quotes Milton:

> Truth is compared in scripture to a streaming fountain; if her waters flow not in perpetual progression, they stagnate into a muddy pool of conformity and tradition. Milton.[3]

Or, again, he associates truth with a fountain and, significantly, an underground river in a passage which owes its origin to Jeremy Taylor:

> There is not a new or strange opinion –
> Truth returned from banishment –
> A river run underground –
> Fire beneath embers –[4]

[1] *PW*, p. 158.　　　　　[2] ibid., p. 365. See p. 202.
[3] N 1, 119 G. 113.　　　　[4] ibid., 177 G. 172 and Notes.

Miss Coburn, in her note on this passage, quotes a very interesting extract from Jeremy Taylor's *Sermons*, which suggests that the ancient sources of wisdom are never lost, and, though they die in one civilisation, reappear again in another:

> This only I desire to be observed, that when a truth returns from banishment by a *postliminium*, if it was from the first, though the holy fire hath been buried or the river ran underground, yet we do not call that new; since newness is not to be accounted of by a proportion to our short-lived memories, or to the broken records and fragments of story left after the inundation of barbarism and war, and change of kingdoms, and corruption of authors; but by its relation to the fountain of our truths . . .

The fountain of *Kubla Khan* could, then, have risen either in Cashmere or Delphi, and the sacred river which ran underground might have belonged to Greece or India. All sprang from the same ancient unconscious source of wisdom, the hiding-place of man's power, which enriched and fertilised great civilisations and poetry in different countries at different times, wherever and whenever it rose to the surface.

*   *   *

The next lines of the poem suggest the all too brief course of the river, flung up 'momently' and so soon to disappear into 'the lifeless ocean' at the sound of war which threatens Kubla's kingdom:

> Five miles meandering with a mazy motion
> Through wood and dale the sacred river ran,
> Then reached the caverns measureless to man,
> And sank in tumult to a lifeless ocean:
> And 'mid this tumult Kubla heard from far
> Ancestral voices prophesying war!

The serene dreamy movement of the river suggests the ease and harmony of the creative achievement of man before it disappears into oblivion. For, when the river returns to the underworld, great civilisations die, poetic inspiration fades; 'where there is no vision the people perish.' The Alph left his realm with a sound of confusion,

And 'mid this tumult Kubla heard from far
Ancestral voices prophesying war!

According to Maurice, Kubla had many ancestors, for *The History of Hindostan* describes the Tartar kingdoms as extending through India, Persia and even Europe. He writes of the dissensions

> ... which had shaken the foundations of the Tartarian grandeur in India.[1]

and of

> ... kingdoms whose names ... gave birth to those mighty conquerors of the Tartar race, whose arms spread terror through Asia and Europe and who, in their imperial city of Samarcand, reigned with a splendour and magnificence unequalled in the most splendid aeras of ancient Persia.[2]

Coleridge may have, half-consciously, remembered Purchas's account of the Tartar priests who could foretell the future, but, if Kubla stands in his mind for the great emperors of the East, his lineage is, indeed, ancient. It may extend as far as Bacchus himself, the conqueror of India, who later made Delphi the heart of his realm in Greece; its famous oracle prophesied and survived the fall and rising of many kingdoms.

Before the dome disappears, however, it is caught for a moment reflected in the river, as if Coleridge is saying farewell to it:

> The shadow of the dome of pleasure
> Floated midway on the waves;
> Where was heard the mingled measure
> From the fountain and the caves.
> It was a miracle of rare device,
> A sunny pleasure-dome with caves of ice!

But a reflection is only an image of the reality about to disappear, and this the poet himself seems to suggest in his quotation from a later poem, *The Picture*, in the 1816 Preface to *Kubla Khan*:

[1] Maurice, i, 4.
[2] ibid., p. 15.

> Then all the charm
> Is broken – all that phantom-world so fair
> Vanishes, and a thousand circlets spread,
> And each mis-shape[s] the other . . .

The rhythm too becomes lighter and swifter and the lines shorter, as if Coleridge is trying to catch the essence of the dream before it fades. The caves of ice come, as E. H. Coleridge and Lowes pointed out, again from Maurice's *History of Hindostan*: 'In a cave in the mountains of Cashmere an Image of Ice', to which Coleridge referred in his notebooks.[1] Since the dome too came from a Cashmere pleasure-garden, the whole picture seems to suggest the strange beauty of the Eastern mountain paradise created from this high world of ice. The poet salutes it a little wistfully as one of man's most magical achievements:

> It was a miracle of rare device
> A sunny pleasure-dome with caves of ice!

Then he turns to another mountain garden of the East, Abyssinia, with its echoes of Purchas and Milton:

> A damsel with a dulcimer
> In a vision once I saw:
> It was an Abyssinian maid,
> And on her dulcimer she played,
> Singing of Mount Abora.

The ' ". . . Damosels skilfull in Songs and Instruments of Musicke and Dancing " ', came from Mahomet's sensual Paradise in Purchas, as Lowes pointed out.[2] The comparison with Milton was also made by Lowes and has been interestingly developed by Miss Bodkin in *Archetypal Patterns in Poetry*. Both stress that in *Paradise Lost* the river of Eden 'pass'd underneath ingulf'd', through 'the shaggy hill', and, later,

> Rose a fresh fountain, and with many a rill
> Water'd the garden; thence united fell
> Down the steep glade, and met the nether flood.[3]

[1] N 1, 240 G. 236.   [2] Lowes, p. 330.
[3] Milton, *PW*, ed. H. Beeching, OUP, 1938, p. 252.

The parallel with *Kubla Khan* is close and we know from constant references in the notebooks how devoted Coleridge was to Milton. The passage describing other famous paradises in which the lines about Abyssinia occur had, however, many echoes:

> . . . Not that faire field
> Of *Enna*, where *Proserpin* gathring flours
> Her self a fairer Floure by gloomie *Dis*
> Was gather'd, which cost *Ceres* all that pain
> To seek her through the world; nor that sweet Grove
> Of *Daphne* by *Orontes*, and th' inspir'd
> *Castalian* Spring might with this Paradise
> Of *Eden* strive; nor that *Nyseian* Ile
> Girt with the River *Triton*, where old *Cham*,
> Whom Gentiles *Ammon* call and *Libyan Jove*,
> Hid *Amalthea* and her Florid Son
> Young *Bacchus* from his Stepdame *Rhea's* eye;
> Nor where *Abassin* Kings their issue Guard,
> Mount *Amara* . . .[1]

Proserpine was taken by Dis to become his queen in the dark world of Hades; the associations the Castalian spring and Bacchus had for Coleridge need no further elaboration. Indeed these memories seem more closely linked with the last lines of the poem which follow than Mount Amara or Abora:

> Could I revive within me
> Her symphony and song,
> To such a deep delight 'twould win me,
> That with music loud and long,
> I would build that dome in air,
> That sunny dome! those caves of ice!
> And all who heard should see them there,
> And all should cry, Beware! Beware!
> His flashing eyes, his floating hair!
> Weave a circle round him thrice,
> And close your eyes with holy dread,
> For he on honey-dew hath fed,
> And drunk the milk of Paradise.

[1] Milton, *PW*, ed. H. Beeching, OUP, 1938, p. 253.

Coleridge now enters his own poem and draws a picture of the inspired poet he would like to be, could he remember the music of paradise and recreate in poetry the beauty of the dome and all it stood for in his mind. H. House, in his Clark lectures on Coleridge, takes the poem to be '. . . a triumphant positive statement of the potentialities of poetry', and uses the movement of these lines to reinforce his view:

> The metre is light and fast; the paragraph moves from delight and surprise, through enthusiasm to ecstasy; no sensitive reader can read it otherwise.[1]

Other critics, including Miss Coburn[2] and Miss Schneider, think the last lines express tragic frustration, an apology for not finishing the poem. Miss Schneider denies its wholeness and thinks the last part breaks abruptly from the rest.[3] I agree with House that the last lines express ecstasy, though I feel that Coleridge here, as so often, is more intoxicated with the thought of the poetry he will one day write than with what he had just achieved in *Kubla Khan*. The music with which he hopes 'to build the dome in air', is 'loud and long', which suggests, I think, one of those epic plans which Southey said Coleridge spawned like a herring – perhaps 'The Conquest of India by Bacchus in Hexameters'. The shining dome of *Kubla Khan* came to him as 'a vision in a dream' which represented, I believe, the beauty of Eastern civilisation he had met in his recent reading of Maurice's *Hindostan* and other books. He had plans to describe it more fully in a long poem on India or Mohammed; *Kubla Khan* is merely a foretaste of what is to come and he becomes excited by his poetic projects. The lightness and speed of the last lines seem to convey, as House says, ecstasy rather than frustration, but, 'I would build that dome in air', refers to the future not the past, for, if the dome stands only for poetry, as House seems to suggest, the line would have little point. Why should he want to describe the beauty of the dome in fitting words, since he had done it so perfectly already? The rhythm certainly conveys assurance and power rather than frustration, and the lines, as I shall suggest, are closely linked with all that has gone before in the total activity of Coleridge's mind, to

---

[1] House, p. 116.
[2] K. Coburn, 'Coleridge Redivivus', in *The Major English Romantic Poets*, Illinois, 1957, p. 123.
[3] E. Schneider, p. 249.

which they form a triumphant climax. All who will hear his music or
see the visions of his future poem, who are susceptible to his rhythm
and imagery, will recognise his poetic power:

> . . . all who heard should see them there,
> And all should cry, Beware! Beware!
> His flashing eyes, his floating hair!
> Weave a circle round him thrice
> And close your eyes with holy dread,
> For he on honey-dew hath fed
> And drunk the milk of Paradise.

Behind these lines lie Bacchus who inspired men and poets with divine
madness, the rites of the Orphic mysteries and a whole world of Greek
philosophy.

Miss Schneider and others have remarked on the picture Socrates
draws in Plato's *Ion* of the divine madness of the poet:

> The composers of lyrical poetry create these admired songs of theirs
> in a state of divine insanity, like the Corybantes, who lose all control
> over their reason in the enthusiasm of the sacred dance. . . . Like the
> Bacchantes, who, when possessed by the god, draw honey and milk
> from the rivers, in which, when they come to their senses, they find
> nothing but simple water.[1]

In the *Phaedrus* too Socrates remarks with a certain irony:

> Truly there seems to be a divine presence in this spot, so that you must
> not be surprised, if, as my speech proceeds, I become as one possessed;
> already my style is not far from dithyrambic.[2]

But he goes on quite seriously to describe the different forms of divine
madness:

> . . . in reality, the greatest blessings come by way of madness, indeed
> of madness that is heaven-sent. It was when they were mad that the
> prophetess at Delphi and the priestesses at Dodona achieved so much
> for which both states and individuals in Greece are thankful . . .[3]

[1] Plato, *Ion*, trans. P. B. Shelley, Everyman, p. 6.
[2] Plato, *Phaedrus*, trans. R. Hackforth, Library of Liberal Arts, CUP, 1952, p. 43.
[3] ibid., p. 56.

and Socrates, a little later, describes the madness of the poet:

> There is a third form of possession or madness, of which the Muses
> are the source. This seizes a tender, virgin soul and stimulates it to
> rapt passionate expression, especially in lyric poetry. . . . But if any
> man comes to the gates of poetry without the madness of the Muses,
> persuaded that skill alone will make him a good poet, then shall he
> and his works of sanity with him be brought to naught by the poetry
> of madness, and behold, their place is nowhere to be found.[1]

In *The Bacchae* Pentheus mocks his grandfather for wearing his hair
loose in order to follow Bacchus, and, a few pages later, the Bacchanals

> Light scraping with their finger-ends the soil
> Had streams of exquisite milk; the ivy wands
> Distilled from all their tops rich store of honey.[2]

There is, thus, little doubt about the source of the 'floating hair', the
milk and honey, and the divine madness of the poet. Coleridge was
steeped in Plato and the Neoplatonists and refers to the *Phaedrus* in his
notebooks, while he quotes at times from Euripides too. To find

> Weave a circle round him thrice,
> And close your eyes with holy dread,

we have to return to the Orphic mysteries and to the *Phaedrus*.

Miss Harrison, in her study of Orphism, quotes from another probably Orphic tablet, found at Compagno:

> I have flown out of the sorrowful weary Wheel
> I have entered the bosom of Despoina, Queen of the
> Underworld,
> I have passed with eager feet from the Circle desired.
> Happy and blessed One, thou shalt be god instead of mortal.[3]

Another version begins:

> Out of the pure I come, Pure Queen of the Pure below,
> Eukles and Eubouleus and the other Gods and Daemons.

[1] ibid., p. 57.
[2] *The Bacchae*, trans. Milman, Rinehart, p. 263.   [3] J. Harrison, p. 585.

Miss Harrison explains that 'Eukles and Eubouleus are titles of the god of Orphism and stand equally for Hades or Dionysos'.[1] The powers of the underworld are being invoked again, those dark inscrutable forces of the unconscious which inspired both prophets and poets in the name of Dionysos. The Wheel was an image, Miss Harrison continues, of '. . . a cycle of life upon life endlessly revolving, in which the soul is caught',[2] familiar, as she says, in the *Phaedo* and the *Phaedrus*. Orpheus took the ancient idea of the transmigration of souls etc. and refined and moralised it:

> Rebirth, reincarnation, became for him *new* birth. The savage logic which said that life could only come from life, that new souls are old souls reborn in endless succession, was transformed by him into a Wheel or cycle of ceaseless purgation.[3]

Coleridge had met some of this in the *Phaedo* for, in a notebook of 1796–7 he gives a Greek quotation from it and comments:

> Plato in Phaedone: and Synesius, the hyper-Platonic Jargonist, would have waved his claims to a Bishopric than allow his *Soul to be younger* than his *Body*.[4]

This belief in the Wheel of purgation was, apparently, symbolised in Orphic ritual by a circle into which the initiate stepped and out of which he was released:

> The mystic has escaped from the Wheel of Purgation, he passes with eager feet over the Ring or circle that includes the bliss he longs for, he enters and perhaps passes out of some sort of sacred enclosure.[5]

Maurice also points out that belief in the soul's pre-existence was originally Indian and became Greek later:

> . . . the immortal spirit, Creeshna, tells Arjun, 'both I and thou have passed many births; mine are known to me, but thou knowest not of thine'. Hence it is evident that the Indians believe in the *pre-existence of souls*; and probably that doctrine, which seems to have originated among them, was, in after ages, together with many other

[1] J. Harrison, p. 587. [2] ibid., p. 588. [3] ibid., p. 589.
[4] N 1, 200 G. 196. [5] J. Harrison, p. 593.

Indian dogmas, transported by Pythagoras into the schools of Greece; for the Platonic as well as the Pythagorean philosophers inculcated it in their disciples.[1]

On that very page, 107, on which Coleridge made the special note; 'Read the whole 107ᵗʰ page of Maurice's Indostan',[2] we find not only the bubble of ice in the cave in Cashmere but a fascinating description of a circular dance. It took place on a holy day when the faithful were adjured to wash in the sacred river, Ganges, and was known as

... The RAAS JATTRA, or circular dance, which is the nineteenth festival, must by no means be passed over, as I have the strongest reasons for thinking it allusive to that of the planetary train ...[3]

Maurice then describes in some detail how Creeshna, the Indian Apollo, in the centre of the circle, divides himself (his rays) into seven parts and dances with seven virgins (the planets).

Plato, in the *Phaedrus*, also has several passages, influenced by Orphism, which describe the procession of the gods circling the heavens in their winged chariots, accompanied by such human souls as can manage the ascent:

And now there awaits the soul the extreme of her toil and struggling. For the souls that are called immortal, so soon as they are at the summit, come forth and stand upon the back of the world; and straightway the revolving heaven carries them round, and they look upon the regions without.[4]

Or a little later:

Hear now the ordinance of Necessity. Whatsoever soul has followed in the train of a god, and discerned something of truth, shall be kept from sorrow till a new revolution shall begin; and, if she can do this always, she shall remain always free from hurt ... in her first birth she shall not be planted in any brute beast, but the soul that hath seen the most of Being shall enter into the human babe that shall grow into a seeker after wisdom and beauty, a follower of the Muses and a lover.[5]

[1] Maurice, i, 396.   [2] N I, 240 G. 236.   [3] Maurice, i, 107.
[4] Plato, *Phaedrus*, p. 71.   [5] ibid., p. 79.

So those souls who had been closest to the gods and within the sacred wheel of Being became philosophers and poets on earth. In a later part of the *Phaedrus* Plato is considered to be using symbolism taken from the mysteries of Eleusis:

> But when one who is fresh from the mystery, and saw much of the vision, beholds a god-like face or bodily form that truly expresses beauty, first there comes upon him a shuddering and a measure of that awe which the vision inspired, and then reverence as at the sight of a god: and but for fear of being deemed a very madman he would offer sacrifices to his beloved as to a holy image of deity.[1]

'Three' was a mystic number in Orphic rites and stood at the heart of Pythagorean philosophy. Professor Wind stresses that the Medici circle owed their conception of a Platonic trinity to the same source:

> And since Proclus had explained in the *Theologia Platonica* that the Greek gods commune with one another and with mortals through a triple rhythm by which they unfold their power, Ficino and Pico felt no hesitation in crediting Plato himself with this trinitarian theology, which they supposed that he had derived from Orpheus and Pythagoras.[2]

Coleridge's familiarity with Proclus and also with his Renaissance interpreters leaves little doubt that he was acquainted with this tradition. Professor Wind also points to the *Phaedrus* and to a note in Taylor's commentary on Proclus, elaborated by Pico and Ficino, when discussing the rite of closing the eyes in initiation:

> The word for 'initiated' in the *Phaedrus* was derived by Proclus and Hermias from the word meaning 'to close the eyes' . . . 'for to close the eyes in initiation', Hermias explained in his commentary on the *Phaedrus*, 'is no longer to receive by sense those divine mysteries but with the pure soul itself'.[3]

Therefore one who had been closest to the mystery of the god might well have been regarded with both reverence and fear:

> Weave a circle round him thrice,
> And close your eyes with holy dread,

---

[1] Plato, *Phaedrus*, p. 96.   [2] Wind, p. 46.   [3] ibid., p. 61.

Coleridge quotes from the *Phaedrus* in his notebooks and, in a passage from *Osorio* and its parallel in *Remorse*, seems to refer to the Mysteries also. The reference occurs in a curious scene where Albert, disguised as a magician, pretends to call up his own soul from the dead in order to make Osorio confess his guilt:

> With no irreverent voice or uncouth charm
> I call up the departed. Soul of Albert!
> Hear out soft suit, and heed my milder spells;
> . . . . . .   since haply thou art one
> Of that innumerable company,
> Who in broad circle, lovelier than the rainbow,
> Girdle this round earth in a dizzy motion,
>
> . . . .
> Even now your living wheel turns o'er my head![1]

and, in the parallel passage in *Remorse*, Teresa cries:

> . . . I dare no longer
> Be present at these lawless mysteries,
> This dark provoking of the hidden Powers![2]

★   ★   ★

The exploration of *Kubla Khan* has led us a long way and into strange regions but, I hope, a little nearer to the fountain of truth. Like the sacred river, the images of the poem flow into one another and can be understood at many levels. Their richness of meaning and suggestive power are impoverished if we try to fix them too rigidly, for the conscious mind is nourished by the unconscious, as Coleridge knew and described in this poem. But the images do flow together and the course of the river can be traced, even into the darkness of the underworld where creative inspiration has its ancient source.

[1] *PW*, ii, 551.　　　　　　　　[2] ibid., p. 850.

CHAPTER V

'Christabel' and the Problem of Evil

> 'Tis the middle of night by the castle clock,
> And the owls have awakened the crowing cock;
> Tu-whit! – Tu-whoo!
> And hark, again! the crowing cock,
> How drowsily it crew.[1]

Christabel opens to the hooting of owls and the eerie sound of the cock crowing at midnight with its suggestion of innocence betrayed. Was this an attempt by the spirits of good to warn Christabel whose name 'had Christ's name in 't', against some threatening evil? Perhaps Coleridge remembered another midnight scene on the battlements of Elsinore when the ghost 'faded on the crowing of the cock', and Marcellus described the power of Christ against evil spirits:

> Some say that ever 'gainst that season comes
> Wherein our Saviour's birth is celebrated
> This bird of dawning singeth all night long,
> And then they say no spirit dare stir abroad,
> The nights are wholesome, then no planets strike,
> No fairy takes, nor witch hath power to charm,
> So hallowed and so gracious is that time.

But this cock crows only briefly and drowsily and has no power against the witch. The uneasy howling of the mastiff, the thin grey cloud covering the moon, the slow coming of Spring and the one red leaf dancing on the tree top, take us instead into the real world of Somerset in 1797 when the poem was begun. They are all recorded in Dorothy

[1] *PW*, p. 215.

Wordsworth's *Journal*, as has often been pointed out. One typical entry for March 24th, 1798, will be sufficient to recall the life the friends shared in that far off Stowey spring and the setting it provided for *Christabel*:

> Coleridge, the Chesters and Ellen Cruikshank called. We walked with them through the wood. Went in the evening into the Coombe to get eggs; returned through the wood, and walked in the park. A duller night than last night: a sort of white shade over the blue sky. The stars dim. The spring continues to advance very slowly, no green trees, the hedges leafless. .... Some brambles I observed today budding afresh, and those have shed their old leaves. The crooked arm of the old oak tree points upwards to the moon.[1]

Coleridge also recorded in his notebook:

> Behind the thin
> Grey cloud that cover'd but not hid the sky
> The round full moon look'd small. – [2]

His observation was as clear and delicate as Dorothy's, but it is her *Journal*'s atmosphere of innocent candour which seems to surround Christabel, as she makes her way through the wood to the 'huge oak tree' to pray for her lover's well being. As she kneels she hears a low moan:

> Is it the wind that moaneth bleak?[3]

But there is not enough wind to stir the last leaf on the tree, so, with beating heart, she steals to the other side of the oak:

> What sees she there?

The breathless short questions and the tense uneasy movement of the verse itself show Coleridge a master of the art of suggesting the sinister. At first it seems a relief when Christabel finds a beautiful woman, clad in shining white which glimmers in the moonlight:

> And wildly glittered here and there
> The gems entangled in her hair.

[1] D. Wordsworth, *Journals*, ed. H. Darbishire, World's Classics, p. 16.
[2] N I, 216 G. 212.   [3] *PW*, p. 217.

Most of the manuscript versions of the poem read:

> And the jewels were tumbled in her hair.

The 'wildly glittered' of the 1816 edition has more hypnotic power and recalls the haunted eyes of the Ancient Mariner. The next lines too contain a sinister hint that evil can come in the guise of beauty and grace:

> I guess, 'twas frightful there to see
> A lady so richly clad as she –
> Beautiful exceedingly!

A later notebook entry describing a thunderstorm in Sicily in 1804 shows how Coleridge linked beauty with fear and darkness:

> Vivid flashes in midday, the terror without the
> beauty. – A ghost by day time / Geraldine.[1]

Christabel invokes the Virgin to her aid as she questions the stranger. Geraldine pleads for help and tells the story of her abduction by five warriors in rather unconvincing and second-rate verse which was, no doubt, deliberately meant to sound false. Only the line, 'And once we crossed the shade of night', suggests, perhaps, the confines of the spirit world which she has broken, and has an uncanny power.

Christabel responds at once to Geraldine's appeal, touches her hand and promises her help and friendship. They cross the moat and enter the gate, Christabel supporting Geraldine whose strength ebbs and flows rather strangely. Other sinister touches are Geraldine's refusal to pray to the Virgin, the mastiff's angry moaning and the tongue of light which flames in the dying fire as she passes. The word 'tongue' may be a premonition of the snake image of Part II. They creep silently through the darkened castle so as not to waken the Baron, 'As still as death, with stifled breath!', until they reach Christabel's room. Here again there is the same feeling of innocence, extending even to the imagery:

> The lamp with twofold silver chain
> Is fastened to an angel's feet.[2]

[1] N 2, 2207 15.79.   [2] *PW*, p. 222.

As Christabel trims it, she offers the apparently exhausted Geraldine, 'this cordial wine',

> It is a wine of virtuous powers;
> My mother made it of wild flowers.

At this point the important theme of the relationship between parent and child enters the poem, to be taken up and reiterated again and again. Christabel here longs for her dead mother's presence and Geraldine echoes her wish, but the next moment cries with altered voice:

> 'Off, wandering mother! Peak and pine!
> I have power to bid thee flee'.[1]

The lines recall the curse of the witch in *Macbeth* and the first part of the poem seems to be moving to a climax of struggle between the powers of good and evil, Christabel's mother and Geraldine, for Christabel's soul. Then, as Christabel lies down and with troubled mind watches Geraldine undress, the manuscript versions of the poem say:

> Behold her bosom and half her side
> Are lean and old and foul of hue.

Later, the second line was cut and the bosom merely becomes

> A sight to dream of, not to tell!
> O shield her! shield sweet Christabel![2]

But, again in the manuscripts, the last line ran:

> And she is to sleep with Christabel.

The full crudity of physical horror and touch was thus toned down in the published version and the emphasis laid again on power of suggestion, while the following lines, describing Geraldine's reluctance to exercise her evil power to the full, were not added to the poem till 1828. Coleridge seems to have been intent on making the appeal of *Christabel* progressively more subtle. But, before Part I ends, Geraldine

[1] ibid., p. 223.   [2] ibid., p. 224.

takes Christabel in her arms, in a terrible mockery of the mother and child relationship, and binds the evil spell upon her. As she does so, the metre and verse form become incantatory and strange:

> 'In the touch of this bosom there worketh a spell,
> Which is lord of thy utterance, Christabel!
> Thou knowest tonight, and wilt know tomorrow,
> This mark of my shame, this seal of my sorrow;

In his 1816 Preface to the poem Coleridge stressed the flexibility of its metre which counted the accents, not the syllables, and so could be easily varied '. . . in correspondence with some transition in the nature of the imagery or passion'. The experiment was not entirely new in English poetry, but it seems to have had a fresh and personal meaning for Coleridge. He had already referred to it in a notebook of 1801: 'Every passion, say the Physicians, hath an distinct Pulse.'[1] The spell ends with Geraldine acknowledging Christabel's unselfish goodness, even as she binds her over to evil:

> '. . . in the dim forest
> Thou heard'st a low moaning,
> And found'st a bright lady, surpassingly fair;
> And didst bring her home with thee in love and in charity,
> To shield her and shelter her from the damp air.'

The Conclusion to Part I recalls the memory of the untouched Christabel praying in the wood and contrasts it with her present plight, 'dreaming fearfully' in Geraldine's arms,

> Fearfully dreaming, yet, I wis,
> Draming that alone, which is –
> O sorrow and shame! Can this be she,
> The lady who knelt at the old oak tree?

Geraldine, on the other hand, who 'holds the maiden in her arms',

> Seems to slumber still and mild,
> As a mother with her child.

[1] N I, 1005 21.157.

Once again we have the ironic and terrible parody of a mother's love for her child, and the whole description is so close a foretaste of a passage in Coleridge's notebooks of 1805 that we cannot escape the conclusion Miss Coburn draws: 'Geraldine is a malignity out of Coleridge's own dreams.'[1] The poet gives an account of one of the terrifying visions which so often haunted his sleep:

> ... dreams interfused with struggle and fear tho' till the very last not Victors – and the very last which awoke me, & which was a completed Night-mair, as it gave the *idea* and *sensation* of actual grasp or touch contrary to *my* will, & in apparent consequence of the malignant will of the external Form, actually appearing or (as sometimes happens) believed to exist / in which latter case tho' I have two or three times felt a horrid *touch* of Hatred, a *grasp* or a *weight*, of Hate and Horror abstracted from all (Conscious) form or supposal of Form / an *abstract touch* / an *abstract* grasp – an *abstract* weight!
> ... The last that awoke me, I was saying, tho' a true Night-mair was however a mild one. I cried out early, like a scarcely-hurt Child who knows himself within hearing of his Mother.[2]

Coleridge's underlining of 'touch' and 'grasp', his emphasis on the 'malignant will of the external form' which overcame his own, and the simile of the child crying out for his mother, all recall *Christabel* very closely. E. Bostetter, though he does not use the above notebook passage, relates other dream experiences to the poem in his interesting article, '*Christabel*: The Vision of Fear',[3] and comments on the close parallel with *The Pains of Sleep*, also published in 1816. Lines like the following, though more violent than anything in *Christabel*, also emphasise the paralysis of the will which even prayer cannot save from the invasion of evil:

> But yester-night I prayed aloud
> In anguish and in agony,
> Up-starting from the fiendish crowd
> Of shapes and thoughts that tortured me:
>
> . . . .

---

[1] K. Coburn, 'Coleridge and Wordsworth and "the Supernatural"', *University of Toronto Quarterly*, 1955–6, p. 130.

[2] N 2, 2468 17.42.

[3] E. Bostetter, *Philological Quarterly*, 1957, pp. 183–94.

> Thirst of revenge, the powerless will
> Still baffled, and yet burning still![1]

It is not surprising that in the same year, 1803, Coleridge links the origin of evil with this terrifying activity of the unconscious mind:

> I will at least make the attempt to explain to myself the Origin of moral Evil from the *streamy* Nature of Association, which Thinking =Reason, curbs & rudders / how this comes to be so difficult / Do not the bad Passions in Dreams throw light & shew of proof upon this Hypothesis? – [2]

Geraldine then represents, to some extent, the evil that comes in sleep when the will is powerless. The nature of this sin and the persistency with which it haunted Coleridge will become clear later in our study of the poem. For the moment, the Conclusion to Part I ends on a happier note. Christabel wakens from her trance and, once again, Coleridge suggests her innocence in the imagery:

> And oft the while she seems to smile
> As infants at a sudden light!

The beautiful simile undoubtedly came from the poet's close and loving observation of his own children, as the notebooks of 1797–8 show:

> Infancy & Infants –
> 1. The first smile – what kind of *reason* it displays – the first smile after sickness.
> . . . .
> 9. An infant's prayer on its mother's Lap (mother directing a Baby's hand. Hartley's love to Papa – scrawls pothooks & reads what he *meant* by them –)[3]

Hartley Coleridge is indeed a presence in the background of *Christabel*, who appears more openly at the end. In the meantime Christabel smiles and weeps

[1] *PW*, p. 389.
[2] N I, 1770 16.156. See pp. 118 and 223.
[3] ibid., 330 21.32.

> Like a youthful hermitess,
> Beauteous in a wilderness,
> Who, praying always, prays in sleep.
>
> . . . .
>
> No doubt, she hath a vision sweet.
> What if her guardian spirit 'twere,
> What if she knew her mother near?
> But this she knows, in joys and woes,
> That saints will aid if men will call:
> For the blue sky bends over all!

So the first part ends on the more hopeful suggestion that the guardian spirit of Christabel's mother may be able to save her and good may overcome evil.

The reference to the 'youthful hermitess' and the saints also suggests the comment Coleridge made to Allsop about the poem. He quoted Crashaw's lines on Saint Theresa:

> Since 'tis not to be had at home
> She'l travel to a martyrdome
>
> . . . .
>
> She offers them her dearest breath
> With Christ's name in't, in change for death.
>
> . . . .
>
> Farewell whatever dear'st may be,
> Mother's arms or father's knee;
> Farewell house and farewell home,
> She's for the Moores and martyrdome.

After quoting the passage entire, Coleridge added:

> These verses were ever present in my mind whilst writing the second part of *Christabel*; if indeed, by some subtle process of the mind, they did not suggest the first thought of the whole poem.[1]

It is significant in view of the parent-child theme in *Christabel* that

---

[1] Allsop, *Recollections of S. T. Coleridge*, included in *Table Talk*, OUP, 1917, p. 441.

Coleridge remembered the description of the youthful martyr, leaving 'Mother's arms or father's knee.' House also quotes the account by Derwent Coleridge of the meaning of the poem:

'The sufferings of Christabel were to have been represented as vicarious, endured for her 'lover far away' . . . that the holy and innocent do often suffer for the faults of those they love, and are thus made the instruments to bring them back to the ways of peace, is a matter of fact, and in Coleridge's hands might have been worked up into a tale of deep and delicate pathos.'[1]

Gillman, also very close to the poet in his later years, said that ' "The story of Christabel is partly founded on the notion, that the virtuous of this world save the wicked. . . . " '.[2] It seems probable then that Coleridge originally intended Christabel's suffering to have a redemptive power; in the end her holiness and innocence were to prevail over Geraldine's evil, as the happier tone of the First Part's ending seems to suggest. But several years momentous in Coleridge's life intervened between the First part and the Second; he discovered bitterly in his own experience, as he struggled to finish the poem, that evil was not redeemed by human power. The innocent indeed suffered, but the evil which caused their pain and his remained deep-rooted in his own nature. I believe it was because he came to see this that he was unable to complete *Christabel*.

* * *

Dorothy Wordsworth's *Journal* of October 1800 records: 'Exceedingly delighted with the second part of *Christabel*',[3] and the next day: 'Coleridge read a 2nd time *Christabel*; we had increasing pleasure.'[4] But the following day she notes the surprising decision: 'Determined not to print *Christabel* with the L.B.'[5] Coleridge's letter of October 9th to Humphry Davy throws some light on this puzzle:

– The Christabel was running up to 1300 lines – and was so much admired by Wordsworth, that he thought it indelicate to print two Volumes with *his name* in which so much of another man's was in-

---

[1] House, p. 127. [2] ibid., p. 126.
[3] D. Wordsworth, *Journals*, p. 57. [4] ibid., p. 57.
[5] ibid., p. 58. Dorothy refers to the second edition of *The Lyrical Ballads*.

cluded – & which was of more consequence – the poem was in direct opposition to the very purpose for which the Lyrical Ballads were published – viz – an experiment to see how far those passions, which alone give any value to extraordinary Incidents, were capable of interesting, in & for themselves, in the incidents of common Life.[1]

Since none of the manuscript or published versions of *Christabel* ever contained more than 677 lines, no one has been able to explain how Coleridge claimed to have written twice that number or, if so, what happened to them. It is presumably possible that, in a fit of discouragement, he destroyed them or that they never existed except in his own head. An equal puzzle is his apparent concurrence with Wordsworth's verdict that the poem was opposed to the purpose of *The Lyrical Ballads*, yet, in the *Biographia Literaria*, published in 1817, a year after *Christabel*, he claims that he '. . . was preparing among other poems, *The Dark Ladie* and the *Christabel* in which I should have more nearly realised my ideal, than I had done in my first attempt.'[2] This, of course, is a retrospective account of the beginning of the poem, 'during the first year that Mr Wordsworth and I were neighbours', when Coleridge's part of the project was to be

> . . . directed to persons and characters supernatural, or at least romantic; yet so as to transfer from our inward nature a human interest and a semblance of truth sufficient to procure for these shadows of imagination that willing suspension of disbelief for the moment, which constitutes poetic faith.[3]

Why should Coleridge in 1800 have agreed with Wordsworth that the poem had little truth to nature but in 1817 have stated that it was a fuller attempt to realise the purpose of *The Lyrical Ballads* than even *The Ancient Mariner* had been? The answer may lie partly in the break with Wordsworth which occurred in 1810, so that by 1817 Coleridge was no longer suffering from what Lamb referred to as 'prostration' before Wordsworth. I believe the key may also lie in the Conclusion to Part II, obviously inspired by his son, Hartley, which Coleridge included in a letter to Southey in May 1801. Without this the poem of 1800 might well have seemed mere fantasy, for the lines reveal the deep and bitterly personal meaning of which even the author might

---

[1] Griggs, i, 631.   [2] *BL*, p. 169.   [3] ibid., p. 168.

not have been conscious at an earlier date. His letter of November 1800 to Josiah Wedgwood describes the attempt to finish *Christabel*:

> . . . I tried & tried, & nothing would come of it. I desisted with a deeper dejection than I am willing to remember.[1]

Much had happened to Coleridge since he began *Christabel* in 1797. He had left Somerset and Tom Poole for the Lake District, mainly to be near the Wordsworths, but Sara Hutchinson with whom he had fallen deeply in love during the autumn of 1799 was also an attraction to the North. The damp climate of the Lakes roused his old rheumatic tendency and the letters of 1800-1 are full of various symptoms of illness for which he began the regular taking of opium. A letter to Poole of May 1801, about the same date as the lines on Hartley, which later formed the Conclusion to Part II of *Christabel*, gives a gloomy account of his health and an ominous reference to laudanum:

> . . . but O dear Poole! the attacks on my stomach, & the nephritic pains in my back which almost alternated with the stomach fits – they were terrible! – The Disgust, the Loathing, that followed these Fits & no doubt in part too the use of the Brandy & Laudanum which they rendered necessary – this Disgust, Despondency, & utter Prostration of Strength. . .[2]

Coleridge was suffering from distress of mind as well as body; he and his wife had never been close companions but the pleasant domestic picture revealed by the 1798 notebook of Hartley sitting on his mother's lap scrawling pothooks for Papa was now entirely changed. Mrs Coleridge's very natural jealousy of her husband's devotion to Sara Hutchinson and their growing estrangement become more and more obvious in the letters of this time, while Coleridge's anxious affection for his children, especially Hartley, is intensified by his lack of sympathy with their mother. In a letter to Southey of October 1801, he complains:

> . . . Sara – alas! we are not suited to each other. . . I will go believing that it will end happily – if not, if our mutual unsuitableness continues, and (as it assuredly will do, if it continue) increases & strengthens, why then, it is better for her & my children, that I should live apart. . .[3]

[1] Griggs, i, 643.   [2] ibid., ii, 731.   [3] ibid., p. 767.

Again writing to Southey in November 1801, he describes how

> – Hartley was breeched last Sunday – & looks far better than in his petticoats. He ran to & fro in a sort of dance to the Jingle of the Load of Money, that had been put in his breeches pockets . . . . O bless him! bless him! bless him! If my wife loved me, and I my wife, half as well as we both love our children, I should be the happiest man alive – but this is not – will not be! – [1]

Most of Coleridge's letters to Sara Hutchinson have been destroyed but a surviving fragment of 1802 again describes Hartley and the close ties between him and his son:

> – Hartley's *attachments* are excessively strong – so strong, even to places, that he does not like to go into town – or on a visit / The field, garden, & river bank / his Kitchen & darling Friend – they are enough / & Play fellows are burthensome to him / excepting *me* / because I can understand & sympathize with his wild Fancies – & suggest others of my own – I am tolerably – my best Love . . . [2]

Did Coleridge realise that the happiness of the passionate little boy he was describing was already threatened by his father's feeling for the recipient of this letter?

Another, to Thomas Wedgwood of October 1802, describes a domestic situation which must have had a devastating effect on a sensitive child, and did have a debasing one on Coleridge himself, as he notes:

> – Ill tempered Speeches sent after me when I went out of the House, ill-tempered Speeches on my return, my friends received with freezing looks, the least opposition or contradiction occasioning screams of passion, & the sentiments, which I held most base, ostentatiously avowed – all this added to the utter negation of all, which a Husband expects from a Wife – especially, living in retirement – & the consciousness, that I was myself growing a worse man / O dear Sir! no one can tell what I have suffered. [3]

The self-disgust here mingles with the self-pity but one is most aware of what the silent children in the background expected of their parents.

---

[1] ibid., p. 774.   [2] ibid., p. 804.   [3] ibid., p. 876.

Another letter, to his wife, just before the birth of their third child, insists with extraordinary tactlessness at such a time:

– I hope, that Sara Hutchinson is well enough to have come in – it would be a great comfort, that one or other of the three Women at Grasmere should be with you – & Sara rather than the other two because you will hardly have another opportunity of having her by yourself & to yourself, & of learning to know her, such as she really is. How much this lies at my Heart with respect to the Wordsworths, & Sara, and how much of our common Love & Happiness depends on your loving those whom I love, – why should I repeat? – I am confident, my dear Love! that I have no occasion to repeat it.[1]

One pities Coleridge during these years for having met too late a woman who might have made him happy, for his constant ill-health and distress of mind, but one is also irritated by the weakness which drove him to opium and to a self-pity which blinded him to the needs of others. His wife, Sara Hutchinson, and most of all, his children, were also victims of a tragic situation for whose creation the last at least were not responsible. This was the background of the Second Part of *Christabel*; it is no wonder that it opens on a sombre note.

* * *

The sound of the heavy bell tolling 'knells us back to a world of death',[2] as it echoes round Langdale Pike and Witch's Lair and Dungeon-ghyll, for Part II belongs firmly to the Lake District where Coleridge was living in 1800. 'Witch's Lair' and 'Dungeon-ghyll' are names with gloomy associations anyway, and a notebook entry of 1800 makes Langdale equally so:

Bell thro' a mist in Langdale vale – the [? fable / toll] of the [? offending / self-ending Matin] what a [? simile] for a melancholy [. . . .][3]

The devil replies with a mocking 'peal from Borodale' as Geraldine rouses Christabel from sleep. She wakens perplexed and uncertain but Geraldine looks so beautiful and guileless that Christabel repents her suspicions and leads her guest to meet Sir Leoline. He welcomes her

[1] Griggs, i, p. 894.   [2] *PW*, p. 227.   [3] N I, 720 5½.2.

with courtesy but is disturbed to hear her father's name for it reminds him of a friendship of his youth which anger had broken. This passage was later described by Coleridge in a letter to Poole as ' . . . the sweetest Lines, I ever wrote',[1] and their theme of anger destroying love is central to the poem:

> And to be wroth with one we love
> Doth work like madness in the brain.[2]

Sir Leoline now welcomes the opportunity of reconciliation with his former friend by vowing to avenge his daughter and slay her captors. Here too, for the first time, the snake image enters the poem, as Sir Leoline longs for the day when he,

> . . . may dislodge their reptile souls
> From the bodies and forms of men!'

As her father turns to embrace Geraldine, the spell begins its work on Christabel who, reliving the fear and pain of the previous night,

> . . . drew in her breath with a hissing sound:[3]

This is the first indication that the snake's power has entered into her and she is unable to reply to her father's startled question;

> 'What ails then my belovéd child?'

Sir Leoline then calls Bracy, the bard, to be his emissary to Geraldine's father, tell him his beautiful daughter is safe in Langdale Hall and beg his forgiveness for the past. Bracy, however, unexpectedly demurs because he has been troubled by a dream which seemed to concern Christabel. He describes how he has had a vision of the wood (where Christabel had prayed) and the dove,

> That gentle bird, whom thou dost love,
> And call'st by thy own daughter's name –
> Sir Leoline! I saw the same
> Fluttering, and uttering fearful moan,
> Among the green herbs in the forest alone.

---

[1] Griggs, iii, 435.   [2] *PW*, p. 229.   [3] ibid., p. 230.

He could see no cause for the dove's distress,

> But yet for her dear lady's sake
> I stooped, methought, the dove to take,
> When lo! I saw a bright green snake
> Coiled around its wings and neck.
> Green as the herbs on which it couched,
> Close by the dove's its head it crouched;
> And with the dove it heaves and stirs,
> Swelling its neck as she swelled hers![1]

This is, of course, an eerie recalling of the night Christabel had spent in the arms of Geraldine but its only effect is to make Sir Leoline mistake the snake for the dove as, turning to Geraldine, he vows,

> 'Sweet maid, Lord Roland's beauteous dove,
> With arms more strong than harp or song,
> Thy sire and I will crush the snake!'

Now, with the father also in her power, Geraldine turns her full malice upon the daughter:

> A snake's small eye blinks dull and shy;
> And the lady's eyes they shrunk in her head,
> Each shrunk up to a serpent's eye,
> And with somewhat of malice, and more of dread,
> At Christabel she looked askance! –
> One moment – and the sight was fled!
> But Christabel in dizzy trance
> Stumbling on the unsteady ground
> Shuddered aloud, with a hissing sound;[2]

She seems, in fact, compelled almost to take on the snake's identity:

> The maid, devoid of guile and sin,
> I know not how, in fearful wise,
> So deeply had she drunken in
> That look, those shrunken serpent eyes,

[1] *PW*, p. 232. [2] ibid., p. 233.

158

> That all her features were resigned
> To this sole image in her mind:
> And passively did imitate
> That look of dull and treacherous hate![1]

When the trance passes, Christabel makes a desperate appeal to her father to send Geraldine away but cannot tell him why. Sir Leoline stands for a moment torn between love for his daughter and angry pride:

> Dishonoured thus in his old age;
> Dishonoured by his only child,
> And all his hospitality
> To the wronged daughter of his friend
> By more than woman's jealousy
> Brought thus to a disgraceful end – [2]

The anger and pride prove stronger; he turns away with Geraldine, leaving his own 'wronged daughter' abandoned and rejected.

What, then, was the truth of 'our inward nature'[3] which Coleridge in the *Biographia Literaria* thought he had realised more fully in *Christabel* than in *The Ancient Mariner*? His power to create the supernatural shadows of the imagination, the poem's sinister atmosphere of suggestion, has never been questioned. The vision of evil here is more terrible than in the earlier poem, for the Ancient Mariner did commit a sin against the bird who trusted him, even though his suffering seemed out of all proportion to his crime. But Christabel violated no law of hospitality; on the contrary, she opened her father's gates to one who seemed in distress and received the stranger 'in love and in charity'. In return, an insidious evil creeps upon her and she is left, alone and helpless, estranged from her father, in an isolation more terrible even than the Mariner's since she cannot communicate it. Innocence has rarely been more completely and terribly betrayed.

Miss Coburn tells us that, in a notebook as late as 1823/4, Coleridge wrote:

> Were I free to do so I feel as if I could compose the third part of *Christabel*, or the song of her desolation.[4]

[1] ibid., pp. 233–4.   [2] ibid., p. 235.   [3] *BL*, p. 168.
[4] K. Coburn, 'Coleridge, Wordsworth and "the Supernatural" ', *University of Toronto Quarterly*, 1955–6, p. 127.

There is no suggestion here that Christabel's suffering was to have any redemptive power. Perhaps Coleridge saw more and more clearly that no human being could ever save another, for, in *Aids to Reflection*, published in 1825, soon after his notebook comment, he writes of the mystery of evil, a subject which continued to haunt him:

> . . . the existence of EVIL – evil essentially such, not by accident or outward circumstances, not derived from its physical consequences, nor from any cause, out of itself. . . . There is nothing, the absolute ground of which is not a Mystery.[1]

He goes on to maintain, ' . . . in direct opposition to the Necessitarians . . . that man was and is a *fallen* creature . . . diseased in his *Will*.' Absolute evil, the very existence of Geraldine, remains a mystery, which is one reason why *Christabel* is so frightening, but the method by which sin can enter a human soul is more understandable and this also fascinated Coleridge.

Man is a creature whose will is diseased, he says, or, once again, in a letter to Sara Hutchinson describing a dangerous descent in the Lake District:

> . . . if this Reality were a Dream, if I were asleep, what agonies had I suffered! what screams! – When the Reason & the Will are away, what remain to us but Darkness & Dimness & a bewildering Shame . . . [2]

It was not only in dreams that Coleridge's will power was in abeyance. His inability to make decisions, to complete projects he had begun, even to open letters if he feared their contents, are all too well known, while his slavery to opium both illustrated and intensified this weakness. Drink was another refuge, as he confesses in a notebook of 1804 which is both sad and disarming, since it shows how well he understood himself:

> – I verily am a stout-headed, weak-bowelled, and O! most pitiably weak-*hearted* Animal! But I leave it, ⟨as I wrote it⟩ – & likewise have refused to destroy the stupid drunken Letter to Southey, which I wrote in the sprawling characters of Drunkenness / & If I should

[1] *Aids to Reflection*, Bell, 1904, p. 91. [2] Griggs, ii, 842.

perish without having the power of destroying these & my other pocket books, the history of my own mind for my own improvement. O friend! Truth! Truth! but yet Charity! Charity! I have never loved Evil for its own sake; ⟨no! nor⟩ ever sought pleasure for its own sake, but only as the means of escaping from pains that coiled round my mental powers, as a serpent around the body & wings of an Eagle! ⟨My sole sensuality was *not* to be in pain! – ⟩[1]

The pains were both mental and physical and the coils of the serpent were only temporarily loosened by his various anodynes.

He uses the snake image in other places in the notebooks – not always in the same way. In 1799 it is employed to suggest genius and he includes a quotation from *Paradise Lost* on the serpent's beauty:

The Serpent by which the ancients emblem'd the Inventive faculty appears to me, in its mode of motion most exactly to emblem a writer of Genius. He varies his course yet still glides onwards – all lines of motion are his – all beautiful, & all propulsive – [2]

Geraldine too was beautiful at the beginning of *Christabel*. Bard Bracy wanted to rid the wood of evil by playing on his harp, and a notebook entry of December 1801 says:

Draw out the secrets from men's Hearts, as the Egyptian Enchanters, by particular Strains of Music draw out serpents from their lurking places – [3]

Wordsworth's lack of understanding on their Scottish tour of 1803 is referred to in the same image:

My words & actions imaged on his mind, distorted & snaky as the Boatman's Oar reflected in the Lake / – [4]

All these suggest insidious movement – one the distortion of truth, one the gradual weakening of the will, one the subtle beauty of the mind and one the strange secrets which it holds. It is not, perhaps, an accident that the most harmless of the snake images are the earliest. Those on the beauty, fascination and strangeness of the mind belong to 1799 and

---

[1] N 2, 2368 21.548. [2] N 1, 609 4.25.
[3] ibid., 1079 21.204. [4] ibid., 1473 7.26.

1801; the image of distortion and the definite association with evil were made in 1803 and 1804.

Whether Coleridge was conscious of all the snake could mean when he wrote *Christabel* we cannot be sure. His commentators have tended to stress the climax of the Second Part of the poem, when Christabel seems to be assuming the serpent's characteristics. Nethercot in *The Road to Tryermaine* says:

> Whatever Geraldine may be, Christabel is already being transformed into a similar being – likewise through no fault or willingness of her own. Those who have been infected by a vampire become vampires themselves.[1]

Yet, even when the last vampire or lamia has been hunted to its lair, I do not feel that Nethercot brings us much closer to the meaning of *Christabel*. C. Tomlinson, in his interesting article on the poem, comes nearer:

> One has in *Christabel*, in allegorical form, that same concern which tormented the self-analyst of the notebooks . . . 'the mind's failure to guide the Will.' For Christabel, bewitched, suffers simultaneously with the disintegration of personality the disintegration of the will.[2]

D. G. James, discussing the tragedy of Coleridge's life in *The Romantic Comedy*, uses a very similar phrase to apply to the poet himself:

> It was apparently necessary that this, the most richly endowed man of his time, should come near to a dissolution of his personality (in the first decade of the century) in order that he, and therewith, in large measure, his times and generation, should come to perceive the riches and strength which are contained in Christianity.[3]

The slow disintegration of the will and, with it, the whole personality may then contain part of the meaning of *Christabel*. Evil may so corrupt what had been innocent that, in the end, the two are indistinguishable, as Sir Leoline mistook the snake for the dove and *Christabel* took on the identity of the snake. Perhaps this was what Coleridge meant when he

[1] A. N. Nethercot, *The Road to Tryermaine*, Chicago, 1939, p. 69.
[2] C. Tomlinson, 'Christabel', in *Interpretations*, ed. J. Wain, 1955, p. 105.
[3] D. G. James, *The Romantic Comedy*, OUP, 1948, p. 161.

told his nephew that, though he had always had the plan of *Christabel* in his mind, he 'could not carry on with equal success the execution of the idea, an extremely subtle and difficult one.'[1]

The plan or story of the poem somehow became separated in Coleridge's mind from the idea or inner meaning and we experience the same difficulty when trying to analyse *Christabel*. It may be intellectually satisfying to say that it is about the corruption of the will, so that, in the end, evil is indistinguishable from good, but it means that we lose the humanity of the poem. Christabel has become a symbol and ceased to be a person, but, as we read the poem, no evil really seems to touch her inner essence. Far from feeling her to be sinful, we are tormented with sympathy for her, as her creator surely was when he qualified the snake expression on her face by adding,

> As far as such a look could be
> In eyes so innocent and blue!

Perhaps it was because he wished to link the essential idea of the poem more firmly with human feeling that Coleridge wrote the Conclusion to Part II. It was included in a letter to Southey of May 1801 in the middle of an anxiously affectionate account of Hartley:

> – Dear Hartley! – we are at times alarmed by the state of his Health – but at present he is well – if I were to lose him, I am afraid, it would exceedingly deaden my affection for any other children I may have –

> A little child, a limber Elf
> Singing, dancing to itself . . . etc.[2]

The lines do not exist in any other manuscript version nor do we know at what date between 1801 and 1816 Coleridge decided to add them to *Christabel*. It is quite probable that they were from the first intended to form part of the poem. Most of Coleridge's critics (E. Bostetter is a notable exception) have considered the ending of *Christabel* a sort of irrelevant postscript added by the poet to lengthen out an unfinished work. This seems to me an insult to Coleridge's critical faculty. In a letter to Joseph Cottle of March 1815, a year before *Christabel's*

---

[1] *Table Talk*, OUP, 1917, p. 259. [2] Griggs, ii, 728.

publication, he insists strongly, as always, upon the wholeness and shape of poetry:

> The common end of all *narrative*, nay, of *all* Poems is to convert a *series* into a *Whole*: to make those events, which in real or imagined History move on in a *strait* Line, assume to our Understandings, a *circular* motion – the snake with its Tail in its Mouth.[1]

It is true that *Christabel* was unfinished but, nevertheless, unlikely that Coleridge would have added a mere twenty lines unless in an attempt to give wholeness to the poem on publication. The use of the snake-image again for poetic activity is interesting and, moreover, the lines on Hartley do give a 'circular motion' to the poem, for their subject is the relationship between parent and child which is an important theme in *Christabel* and had been emphasised in the imagery of the Conclusion to Part I:

> What if her guardian spirit 'twere,
> What if she knew her mother near?

Part II had ended with Christabel abandoned by her father and its Conclusion is also about a father's feeling for his child, though this time the father is Coleridge himself. That the lines were an accurate description of Hartley is obvious from a letter to John Thelwall in January 1801, even without Coleridge's definite reference:

> Hartley is quite the contrary – a fairy elf – all life, all motion – indefatigable in joy – a spirit of Joy dancing on an Aspen Leaf. From morning to night he whirls about and about, whisks, whirls, and eddies, like a blossom in a May-breeze. – [2]

In the letter to Southey, four months later, and in *Christabel* this became:

> A little child, a limber elf,
> Singing, dancing to itself,
> A fairy thing with red round cheeks,
> That always finds, and never seeks,
> Makes such a vision to the sight
> As fills a father's eyes with light;[3]

[1] Griggs, iv, 545.   [2] Griggs, ii, 668.   [3] *PW*, p. 235.

But the lines that follow are strange and sad:

> And pleasures flow in so thick and fast
> Upon his heart, that he at last
> Must needs express his love's excess
> With words of unmeant bitterness.

Was the bitterness a reaction from the too intense weight of emotion which Coleridge gave to his children, especially Hartley, because by 1801 he had ceased to love their mother? Even the syntax of the lines that follow becomes tormented like the feeling:

> Perhaps 'tis pretty to force together
> Thoughts so all unlike each other;
> To mutter and mock a broken charm,
> To dally with wrong that does no harm.
> Perhaps 'tis tender too and pretty
> At each wild word to feel within
> A sweet recoil of love and pity.

The unlike thoughts that Coleridge is forcing together are love and bitterness, pity and anger, while the very inadequacy of the language – 'tender too and pretty' – conveys the mood of ironic self mockery. The father had tried to deceive himself:

> To mutter and mock a broken charm,
> To dally with wrong that does no harm.

Now, in one of those stark flashes of self-revelation common to the notebooks also, he realises the truth. Even love itself can become corrupted by unhappiness and those who suffer from our sin and angry reactions are often the most innocent:

> And what, if in a world of sin
> (O sorrow and shame should this be true!)
> Such giddiness of heart and brain
> Comes seldom save from rage and pain,
> So talks as it's most used to do.

165

Just as he suffered, Just as his son suffered

The 'sorrow and shame' recall Christabel in Geraldine's evil embrace in the Conclusion to Part I:

> Fearfully dreaming, yet, I wis,
> Dreaming that alone, which is –
> O sorrow and shame! Can this be she,
> The lady who knelt at the old oak tree?

The 'rage and pain' were also Sir Leoline's as he cast off his daughter in angry pride, thinking more of himself than of her:

> Within the Baron's heart and brain
> If thoughts, like these, had any share,
> They only swelled his rage and pain,
> And did but work confusion there.[1]

The whole poem is about the corruption of the good, of love itself, through sin, and the suffering this brings to the innocent; the snake has its tail in its mouth and the Conclusion to Part II is the key to *Christabel*.

Several of the entries in the notebooks of 1807 show that this situation persisted and that there was no solution to the poem or to the problem in Coleridge's own life. They were made in cipher, possibly to hide them from his wife or, more likely in view of the second entry, to conceal their harsh reality even from himself. The first, as Miss Coburn deciphers it in her notes, refers again to Hartley:

> As usual even the epoch of a po[c]ket book must be marked with agitati[–]on Mrs Coleridge this morning first planted in Hartley's mind the pang of divided duty / & left me stormy and miserable. – The same day received the second letter from Sara.[2]

The next, even more difficult to read, is, as Miss Coburn says, 'one of Coleridge's clearest indications of self-awareness and revulsion at his own deceptions and self-deceptions.':

> Thought becomes a thing when it acts at once on your more [? conscious / consciousness] i.e. [? conscience / conscientiousness] therefore I dread to tell my whole & true case it seems to make a

[1] *PW*, p. 234. [2] N 2 3041 19.2 (Notes).

substantial reality / I want it to remain a thought in which I may be deceived whole [? wholly][1]

'I dread to tell my whole and true case' reveals his reluctance to face the harsh truth of his situation; his inability to finish *Christabel* shows how near it lay to his own life. Another entry at this time closely resembles the tormented feeling of the Conclusion to Part II:

> The anger with a beloved object mingling with a yearning after & anticipation of a deeper love from reconciliation & the angry struggles of the head at its own duplicity.[2]

The imagery of the Asra poems, written during these years to Sara Hutchinson, also shows a close correspondence with *Christabel*. His verse *Letter to Asra* of April 1802, later revised as the *Ode to Dejection*, twice uses the image of the dove for Sara. The first time, like Christabel, she is in a wood by moonlight:

> O Sara! in the weather-fended Wood,
> Thy lov'd haunt! where the Stock-doves coo at Noon,
> I guess, that thou hast stood
> And watch'd yon Crescent, & it's [sic] ghost-like Moon.[3]

and, again at the end of the poem, Coleridge rejoices in Sara's happiness with the Wordsworths, though it was one from which he felt excluded:

> And feeling in thy Soul, Heart, Lips, & Arms
> Even what the conjugal and mother Dove
> That borrows genial Warmth from those, she warms,
> Feels in her thrill'd wings, blessedly outspread – [4]

But earlier lines show that he had deeply distressed her by writing of his own pain, and his self-reproach again recalls the end of *Christabel*:

> . . . the fretting Hour
> Then when I wrote thee that complaining Scroll
> Which even to bodily Sickness bruis'd thy Soul!

[1] ibid., 3045 19.6 (Notes). [2] ibid., 3052 19.13 (Notes).
[3] Griggs, ii, 792. See p. 203. [4] ibid., p. 798. See p. 203.

> And yet thou blam'st thyself alone! And yet
>   Forbidd'st me all Regret!
> And must I not regret that I distress'd
> Thee, best belov'd! who lovest me the best?
> My better mind had fled, I know not whither,[1]

As House points out, the ' "dark distressful Dream" from which he turns, is the thought of his misery if Sara were ill in body or in mind and he, necessarily absent, were unable to comfort her.'[2] But, in the later version of the poem, the cutting of the personal references means that

> Hence, viper thoughts, that coil around my mind,
>   Reality's dark dream![3]

apply to his sorrowful self-analysis of the loss of his creative power where they seem awkward and inappropriate. I agree with House that, especially in view of the use of the snake image, 'the viper thoughts' that coiled around his mind were much more likely to have been connected with Sara's illness and his own responsibility for it:

> That thou art weak & pale with Sickness, Grief, & Pain –
> And I – I made thee so![4]

For this love too was tainted with corruption, as all frustrated love tends to be, and in the same poem Coleridge links it with his feeling for his children who, he wishes, were the children of *this* Sara and not of his wife:

> My little Children are a Joy, a Love,
>   A good Gift from above!
> But what is Bliss, that still calls up a Woe,
>   And makes it doubly keen
> Compelling me to *feel*, as well as KNOW,
> What a most blessed Lot mine might have been.
> Those little Angel Children (woe is me!)
> There have been hours, when feeling how they bind
> And pluck out the Wing-feathers of my Mind,
> Turning my Error to Necessity,

[1] Griggs, ii, 793.   [2] House, p. 134.
[3] *PW*, p. 367. See p. 204.   [4] Griggs, ii, 793.

I have half-wish'd, they never had been born!
That seldom! But sad Thoughts they always bring[1]

It would not have been surprising if he had sometimes reacted against the children with 'words of unmeant bitterness'. The last verse of *The Day-Dream*, written 1801–2, describes the same situation. He had been imagining himself married to Sara Hutchinson and was awakened from the day-dream to reality by a little boy called 'Frederic' whose 'bright eyes' and 'elfin laugh' belonged surely to Hartley, the child of the other Sara:

> And now, when I seemed sure thy face to see,
> Thy own dear self in our own quiet home;
> There came an elfish laugh, and wakened me:
> 'Twas Frederic, who behind my chair had clomb,
> And with his bright eyes at my face was peeping.
> I blessed him, tried to laugh, and fell a-weeping![2]

A notebook entry of about the same date says:

> Wordsworth & [? M] – S & Coler. – Little Boy seeking me – N.B. poems – [3]

which once again links Coleridge and Sara and the little boy, contrasted in his mind probably with Wordsworth, now happily married to Sara's sister.

Coleridge's translation of a sonnet of Marini which Professor Whalley puts among the Asra poems may also be significant. During his stay in Malta he had already transcribed several of Marini's sonnets in his notebooks, accompanied by some searching critical commentary. This sonnet, however, is not among them and it is in poetic quality far less good, in fact rather crude. It seems odd, therefore, that Coleridge should have bothered to translate it, had it not had some personal meaning for him. E. H. Coleridge dates it tentatively 1805 and, if it was written with Sara Hutchinson in mind, it certainly describes a mood of revulsion, when love had turned to lust:

---

[1] ibid., p. 797. See p. 204.
[2] *PW*, p. 387. See p. 200.
[3] N I, 1144 6.82.

> Lady, to Death we're doom'd, our crime the same!
> Thou, that in me thou kindled'st such fierce heat;
> I, that my heart did of a Sun so sweet
> The rays concentre to so hot a flame.

It is, however, the next quatrain which is most startling:

> I, fascinated by an Adder's eye –
> Deaf as an Adder thou to all my pain;
> Thou obstinate in Scorn, in Passion I –
> I lov'd too much, too much didst thou disdain.[1]

because, in the original, there is no mention of an adder. Marini compares the lady to a wild beast who was deaf and unresponsive to his pain:

> Io che una fiera rigida adorai,
> Tu che fosti sord' aspra a' miei dolori;[2]

after that, the quatrain is very closely translated by Coleridge:

> Tu nell' ire ostinata, io negli amori:
> Tu pur troppo sdegnasti, io troppo amai.

The last six lines are, again, a faithful translation, though Coleridge gives the final vision of Hell a rather more sardonic twist:

> Hell for us both fit places too supplies –
> In my heart *thou* wilt burn, I *roast* before thine eyes.[3]

The 'Adder's eye' is thus Coleridge's alteration, and it is a startling reminder of Geraldine, suggesting with the dove image of the *Letter to Asra* that Sara Hutchinson may lie behind *Christabel* also. If so, his love for her has become debased at moments into a hell of desire – the dove has become the snake. J. Beer, in *Coleridge, the Visionary*, quotes from a late notebook a passage which is similar in feeling. Coleridge was interpreting *The Book of Tobit* as an allegory of love and lust – (and Tobias' wife was called Sarah):

[1] *PW*, p. 393.   [2] *PW*, ii, 1132. See p. 212.   [3] *PW*, p. 393.

'More than happy that Man who has never had occasion or an opportunity for noticing in himself a transition of pure and tender affection for a lovely object into a movement of concupiscence'.[1]

Finally, in the sombre little poem, *Psyche*, also listed by Professor Whalley among the Asra poems, Coleridge uses the reptile image again, though, this time, with the caterpillar in mind. He remembers that the Greeks used the same word for the butterfly and the soul, the free and winged thing which eventually escapes the evil of mortal life, but only by the death of the caterpillar on which it has fed. The complex reptile image at the end seems to suggest the same experience as *Christabel*, that we are doomed in this life to hurt and destroy others in the name of love:

> The butterfly the ancient Grecians made
> The soul's fair emblem, and its only name –
> But of the soul, escaped the slavish trade
> Of mortal life! – For in this earthly frame
> Ours is the reptile's lot, much toil, much blame,
> Manifold motions making little speed,
> And to deform and kill the things whereon we feed.[2]

We can understand why Coleridge could not bring himself to write the third part of *Christabel*, because, in her desolation, he would too clearly have seen his own.

[1] J. Beer, *Coleridge the Visionary*, p. 126. [2] *PW*, p. 412. See p. 213.

CHAPTER VI

'The Asra Poems': Realities and Shadows

COLERIDGE first met and fell in love with Sara Hutchinson in the autumn of 1799 when he went North on receiving news of Wordsworth's illness. Their final parting in 1810 inevitably followed his break with Wordsworth, for Sara had by then become an indispensable member of her sister's home. How far Sara returned his love is never entirely clear for all her letters to Coleridge have been destroyed. She was always in a difficult position for he was already married when he met her; this was a love doomed to unfulfilment from the start. Coleridge, however, records in his notebooks every mood of his love, his dreams, his joy, his anguish and bitterness; the poems that he wrote for Sara during this decade, under the name of 'Asra', are almost as intimate as the notebook entries and form a very close parallel to them. Their sources are not obscure or to be found in books but spring directly from Coleridge's feeling, thus providing us with a rare opportunity to watch the very genesis of poetry itself. Since the Wordsworths, his dearest friends, were, through their relationship with Sara, already deeply involved, Coleridge could confide his fears, ecstasy and jealousy only to his notebooks. There they become mingled with his philosophy and his whole response to life, but he himself stresses the importance of emotion as a unifying factor. So he writes to Southey in August 1803 that ideas seldom recall ideas, '. . . any more than Leaves in a forest create each other's motion – The Breeze it is that runs thro' them – it is the Soul, the state of Feeling – '[1] House considers that: 'In some recent uses or adaptations of parts of Coleridge's theory, I think this emotional element has been given inadequate weight . . . ' He quotes the well-known notebook entry of 1803 which describes in retrospect Coleridge's first love for Sara, already discussed in relation to *Kubla Khan*:

[1] Griggs, ii, 961.

172

O Heaven when I think how perishable Things, how imperishable Thoughts seem to be! – For what is Forgetfulness?† Renew the state of affection or bodily Feeling, same or similar – sometimes dimly similar / and instantly the trains of forgotten Thought rise from their living catacombs![1]

House comments:

This statement that 'affection and bodily feeling' become a focus-point for selective associating memory, must be seen in connection with the statement to Humphry Davy, in February 1801, that the book of poetry which should 'supersede all the books of metaphysics and all the books of morals too' grew from the contemplation of 'the affinities of the feelings with words and ideas' . . .[2]

Coleridge himself says in the *Ode to Dejection* of 1802, which grew from the more intimate *Letter to Asra*, that it is his loss of Joy which has suspended his 'shaping spirit of Imagination'. Much later, in 1817, when discussing Shakespeare's *Venus and Adonis* in the *Biographia Literaria*, he makes the same connection between imagination and feeling:

It has been before observed that images, however beautiful, though faithfully copied from nature, and as accurately represented in words, do not of themselves characterize the poet. They become proofs of original genius only as far as they are modified by a predominant passion; or by associated thoughts or images awakened by that passion; . . .[3]

On the next page he quotes a favourite Shakespeare sonnet:

'From you have I been absent in the spring',

and italicises the last line:

'Yet seemed it winter still, and you away,
As with your shadow I with these did play!'[4]

Professor T. M. Raysor, in 'Coleridge and "Asra"', quotes a notebook

---

[1] N I, 1575 21.296(a) See p. 119.   [2] House, p. 148.
[3] *BL*, p. 177.   [4] ibid., p. 179.

entry of 1810, written after the quarrel with Wordsworth and estrangement from Sara, which clearly shows Coleridge's anguished association of this image with his love for her:

> Ο Σαρα! Σαρα [Sara]! what have you done in *deceiving* him who for 10 years did so love you as never woman was beloved! in body, in soul, in brain, in heart, in hope, in fear, in prospect, in retrospect! . . . Every single thought, every image, every perception was no sooner itself than it became *you* by some wish that you saw it and felt it or had – or by some recollection that it suggested – some way or other it always became a symbol of *you*. I played with them as with *your shadow*, Shakespeare has so profoundly expressed it in his Sonnet.[1]

Sara thus remained the centre and unifying power of his imaginative and critical life years after he had ceased to see her.

The feeling of the Asra poems, however, changed considerably from the sentimental unreality of the earliest, *Love*, through the dream-like tenderness of *A Day-Dream* and the sad self-knowledge of *Dejection* to the sombre bitterness of *Psyche*. Uncertainty of dating makes it difficult to determine the relative order of the poems exactly but, within this decade, an alteration and development of tone can be clearly seen. The notebooks can, I believe, help us to fix some dates more firmly, and they also act as a critical touchstone, for the Asra poems are very uneven in quality. The best have a delicate and wistful beauty which springs from real experience of however dream-like and spiritual a kind; this is a note new in Coleridge's poetry and it belongs to Asra alone. But several of the less successful poems, especially the earlier, are marred by self-consciousness and a kind of sentimental fantasy which the notebooks can help us to detect. It becomes obvious that the best parts of these uneven poems are those based on authentic experience, while the worst and most patently false belong to that unreal world of wish-fulfilment into which Coleridge all too easily retreated.

The notebooks are most valuable in helping us to watch the growth of the individual poems themselves from the first jottings, through the development of imagery and feeling, to their final form. We can look over Coleridge's shoulder and see the creative process at work. Professor Whalley whose study, *Coleridge and Sara Hutchinson and the Asra Poems*,

[1] T. M. Raysor, 'Coleridge and "Asra"', *Studies in Philology*, 1929, p. 321. See p. 178.

has put us all in his debt, describes the way the poems emerge in a more recent article, 'Coleridge Unlabyrinthed':

> Coleridge sees IMAGINATION as a process rather than a faculty: a state we get into rather than a faculty we *have*. . . . His view of Imagination . . . moves in a single arc from rudimentary perceptual experience, through the development of responsive feeling, to poetry and art; the only theory that is, that is able to show how the symbolising activity is radically different from the describing activity, and how items in the actual phenomenal world move into the symbolic field and achieve an energetic existence there. The notebooks (usually without deliberately intending to do so) actually show this process occurring.[1]

This is what Coleridge himself was later to describe as the movement from the world of the primary imagination, creative in perception, to that of the secondary or poetic imagination, where the images which had been visual take on a new life in the realm of ideas. It is a very complex process which Coleridge did not develop in the *Biographia Literaria* much beyond the famous definition which he leaves hanging in the air at the end of Chapter 13. Fortunately, the earlier notebooks can help us see the act of creation at work, which is much more fascinating than any theory produced long after it. There is an interesting example from an early notebook of November 1799; Coleridge had recently met Sara Hutchinson for the first time and is now with Wordsworth, exploring the Lake District:

> Now as we return the fog begins to clear off from the Lake, still however leaving straggling Detachments on it –, . . . The reflection of the huge pyramidal Crag is still hidden, & the image in the water still brighter / / but the Lyulph's Tower gleams like a Ghost, dim & shadowy – & the bright Shadow thereof how beautiful it is cut across by that Tongue of *breezy* water – now the Shadow is suddenly gone – and the Tower itself rises emerging out of the mist, two-thirds wholly hidden, the turrets quite clear – & a moment all is snatched away – Realities & Shadows – [2]

[1] G. Whalley, 'Coleridge Unlabyrinthed', *University of Toronto Quarterly*, 1962–3, p. 340.
[2] N I, 553 5.125.

A few pages earlier we find another short entry on mist:

Mist as from volcano –
Waterfall rolled after long looking at like a segment of a Wheel –
the rock gleaming thro' it – . . . [1]

The entry immediately preceding this one is:

The sunny mist, the luminous gloom of Plato – [2]

It seems clear that, in this scene or similar ones, the mist and reflections which he watched temporarily blotting out the real world suggested to Coleridge one of the great myths of Plato, as I shall discuss later. The phrase, 'Realities and Shadows', which recalls that myth and others, acts as the bridge between the world of perception and the world of ideas, as, by a swift leap of imagination, he applies to Plato this strange mingling of illumination and obscurity in the scene before his eyes. Another short entry of September 1801 about a stream and a well with shadows seems emotionally connected with Sara, but also provides an example of the real world merging into the ideal:

Item – Murmur of a stream – Item – *well** *with* Shadows. Item – Why aren't you here? –
* images & realities in the eye & memory – fantasticaly, [sic] soul going into the heart of the survivor, & abiding there with its Image.[3]

Here, the first 'image' without the capital seems to be the visual reflection and the second, capitalised, suggests the memory in the mind. A later notebook entry, written in Malta in April 1805, takes up this image again and develops it much further:

Thought and Reality two distinct corresponding Sounds, of which no man can say positively which is the Voice and which the Echo. O the beautiful Fountain or natural Well at Upper Stowey. . . . The images of the weeds which hung down from its sides, appeared as plants growing up, straight and upright, among the water weeds that really grew from the Bottom / & so vivid was the Image, that for some moments & not till after I had disturbed the water, did I

[1] N 1, 529 5.37.　　[2] ibid., 528 5.36.　　[3] ibid., 981 21.133. See p. 119.

perceive that their roots were not neighbours, & they side-by-side companions. So – even then I said – so are the happy man's *Thoughts* and *Things* – (in the language of the modern Philosophers, Ideas and Impressions) – . . . [1]

The imaginative process by which the visual perception merges with the idea is beautifully and clearly conveyed through the reflection image with all its strong emotional associations with his happiness at Stowey.

The phrasing of this passage also seems to anticipate the definition of the primary and secondary imagination in the *Biographia Literaria*:

> The primary imagination I hold to be the living power and prime agent of all human perception, and as a repetition in the finite mind of the eternal act of creation in the infinite I AM. The secondary I consider as an echo of the former, co-existing with the conscious will, yet still as identical with the primary in the kind of its agency, and differing only in degree, and in the mode of its operation.[2]

At the end of the next chapter, when describing how imagination reconciles opposite or discordant qualities, two that he mentions are:

> ' . . . the general, with the concrete; the idea, with the image . . . '[3]

which shows how his earlier notebooks anticipate his later theory. Nor was Coleridge, at this earlier date, unaware of the significance of these entries. A note of February 1801 on Christian von Wolff's *Psychologia rationalis* shows that he was:

> Imaginatio quoque in actum perceptionis influit –
> Wolff. Annot. in Psych. rat. . . . [4]

As Miss Coburn points out, he translated this, probably unconsciously, in a later entry of November 1803, altering 'imaginatio' to 'memory':

> – Mountains scarcely perceivable except by eyes long used to them, & supported by the images of Memory flowing in on the impulses of immediate Impression – [5]

---

[1] N 2, 2557 17.115. See p. 96 and p. 202.   [2] *BL*, p. 167.
[3] ibid., p. 174.   [4] N 1, 905 21.105.   [5] ibid., 1648 21.394. See p. 118.

An entry of November 1803 shows how keenly alive he was to the link between perception and metaphor:

> 4. The effect ought not to be forgotten, that from the distance in mountain Countries being so distinct, you have a continual Inducement to look forward to the distance – whereas in flat Countries you look just before you. . . . Now there certainly is an intellectual movement connected with looking forward / a feeling of Hope, a stirring & inquietude of Fancy. – To look down upon, to comprehend, to be above, to look forward to, are all metaphors that shew in the original feeling a resemblance to the moral meaning christened thereafter.[1]

Coleridge was always aware of the philosophic implications of language and behind many of these extracts, as has often been pointed out, lie the ideas of Plotinus and the Neoplatonists as well as of Plato himself. J. V. Baker, in *The Sacred River*, considers that Coleridge got the idea of the mind creative in perception, so vital to his repudiation of Hartley and passive association, from Plotinus who fathered the '. . . theory of divine interchange or creative communion between the perceiving subject – the conscious I – and the perceived object, nature, in which divinity is immanent or transcendent.'[2] A. E. Powell, in *The Romantic Theory of Poetry*, also stresses strongly Coleridge's debt to Plotinus:

> He continued to conceive of the Ideal Reality as the transcendent, self-existent ground of both Man and Nature. Nature must always be regarded as sacred because derived from that source and therefore a means of approach to the highest. . . . [3]

But, while his love for Sara was at its height, she was for him transcendental reality. Love lived in that world of pure essences and forms in whose light the real world was a pale reflection –

> As with your shadow I with these did play.

A notebook entry, quoted by Professor Whalley from Professor Raysor's article, makes this clear. It was written at Allan Bank in 1808,

---

[1] N 1, 1675 3½.49.
[2] J. V. Baker, *The Sacred River*, Louisiana University Press, 1957, p. 69.
[3] A. E. Powell, *The Romantic Theory of Poetry*, Arnold, 1926, p. 101.

the period of Coleridge's brief reunion with the Wordsworths and Sara and all whom he most loved:

> ... Love, passionate in its deepest tranquillity, Love unutterable, fills my whole Spirit – so that every fibre of my Heart, nay, of my whole frame seems to tremble under its perpetual touch and sweet pressure, like the string of a Lute – with a sense of vibratory Pain, distinct from all other sensations, a Pain that seems to shiver and tremble on the threshold of some Joy that cannot be entered into while I am embodied – a Pain of yearning which all the Pleasure on earth could not induce me to relinquish, even were it in my power ... yea, even when the Beloved is present, seeming to look thro' her and asking for her very Self within or even beyond her Apparent Form – [1]

This longing for the absolute, for a Love which could transcend the limitations of mortal life, was very deep in Coleridge. Professor Suther comments upon it in *The Dark Night of Samuel Taylor Coleridge*:

> The great fact of his love experience is precisely that he had a way of looking right through 'realities' towards something like 'Reality'; and when he failed to attain it, the realities themselves became phantoms, even phantoms of the kind that excite fear.[2]

A little later Professor Suther suggests that Coleridge

> ... was looking for the same thing from love and from poetic experience, namely, a religious, a mystical experience of the absolute, and that he failed to find it in both for the same reason, because it is not there to find.[3]

He interprets Coleridge's *Ode to Dejection* in the light of this failure, but, though there is much truth in what he says, I believe he overstates the case. Coleridge's vision of love was certainly rarefied and spiritual and, inevitably, transitory; he himself recognised that he 'trembled on the threshold of some Joy that cannot be entered into while I am embodied',

---

[1] G. Whalley, *Coleridge, Sara Hutchinson and the Asra Poems*, Routledge & Kegan Paul, 1955, p. 76.
[2] M. Suther, *The Dark Night of Samuel Taylor Coleridge*, Columbia University Press, 1960, p. 31.
[3] ibid., p. 44.

but this does not invalidate its reality, unless we deny that term to all but physical experience. For a short time Sara glorified the world for him and brought him close to the transcendental and the eternal. It was almost a religious feeling, as he himself tells us in 1805:

Real + symbolical. – Motion + Rest at the Goal. Love – and the grandeur of loving the Supreme in her – the real & symbolical united / – and the more because I love her as being capable of being glorified by me & as the means & instrument of my own glorification / In loving her thus I love two Souls as one . . . [1]

and again:

The best, the truly lovely, in each & all is God. Therefore the truly Beloved is the symbol of God to whomever it is truly beloved by! . . . The Lover worships in his Beloved that final consummation ⟨of itself which is⟩ produced in his own soul by the action of the Soul of the Beloved upon it . . . [2]

Since he held this view of love as 'a means of approach to the highest', it is not surprising that we find Plato and Plotinus everywhere behind the notebook entries, nor that their imagery becomes, as we shall see, the dominant imagery of many of the Asra poems. We have already seen how the metaphors of the river, the fountain, reflections and shadows became for Coleridge the means of fusing the seen and the unseen, the image and the idea. Plotinus lies behind the following extracts and his metaphor of the fire and the sun is also an important one in the Asra poems; Coleridge is meditating again on the philosophic implications of language:

. . . impossible to conceive that an omniscient Being should not have a distinct Idea of finite Beings, or that distinct Ideas in the mind of God should be without the perfection of real Existence – i.e. imperfect. . . . Admit for a moment, that 'to conceive' is = with creation in the divine nature, synonimous [sic] with 'to beget'. . . . Admit this, and all difficulty ceases – all Tumult is hushed – all is clear & beautiful – / We sit in the Dark, but each by the side of his little Fire in his own group, & lo! the summit of the distant mountain is

[1] N 2, 2530 17.88.   [2] ibid., 2540 17.98.

smitten with Light . . . we look at it, & know that the Sun is not extinguished . . . that he is coming to us to make our fires needless . . .[1]

The divine and intellectual Sun illumines this passage and in the comment on 'to conceive' and 'to beget' the realms of Essence and Existence become one. A slightly later entry makes the origin in Plotinus apparent:

In Plotinus the system of the Quakers is most beautifully expressed, in the 5th Book of the fifth Ennead: speaking of 'the inward Light' . . . to abide in Quiet, till it suddenly shines upon us; preparing ourselves for the blessed Spectacle, like the eye waiting patiently for the rising Sun.[2]

It was again Plotinus, A. E. Powell reminds us, who said that if man

. . . draws back into the deep places of his consciousness, he has the power to live again in the divine ground of his existence, to become one with it and so, being it, to know it. . . .[3]

This Coleridge found expressed in Smith's *Select Discourses*, a commentary on Plotinus, from which he jots down a passage in the original Greek, translated by Miss Coburn as follows:

Discourse Concerning the Existence and Nature of God: . . . not so much *That he is* as What he is. Both which we may best learn from a *Reflexion upon our own Souls*, as *Plotinus* hath well taught us, [Greek]. *He which reflects upon himself reflects upon his own Originall*, and finds the clearest impression of some Eternall Nature and Perfect Being stamp'd upon his own Soul . . .[4]

Here the metaphor of reflection, with its double meaning, demonstrates the power of imagination to fuse the divine with the human; Coleridge is to use it many times in the Asra poems.

To find the origin of these images which run like a thread through

[1] N 1, 1619 21.377, f. 76. See p. 196.
[2] ibid., 1678 21.406.
[3] A. E. Powell, *The Romantic Theory of Poetry*, p. 82.
[4] N 2, 2167 K. 22 (Notes).

the notebooks and poems of this decade we have, I think, to return to Plato himself. It was not an accident that Washington Allston, the American painter who knew Coleridge in Rome, wrote to a friend describing the pupil in terms of the master:

> And when I recall some of our walks under the pines of the Villa Borghese, I am almost tempted to dream that I once listened to Plato, in the groves of the Academy.[1]

Coleridge, in *The Destiny of Nations*, had already seen the world of the senses as an image of transcendental reality:

> For all that meets the bodily sense I deem
> Symbolical, one mighty alphabet
> For infant minds; and we in this low world
> Placed with our backs to bright Reality,
> That we may learn with young unwounded ken
> The substance from its shadow . . .[2]

He is, of course, referring obliquely to the great myth of the Cave in the *Republic* where Socrates discusses with Glaucon the nature of the ideal and the real:

> 'Imagine the condition of men living in a sort of cavernous chamber underground, with an entrance open to the light and a long passage all down the cave. Here they have been from childhood, chained by the leg and also by the neck, so that they cannot move and can see only what is in front of them, because the chains will not let them turn their heads. At some distance higher up is the light of a fire burning behind them; and between the prisoners and the fire is a track with a parapet built along it, like the screen at a puppet-show, which hides the performers while they show their puppets over the top . . . prisoners so confined would have seen nothing of themselves or of one another, except the shadows thrown by the fire-light on the walls of the Cave facing them, would they?'

When he has demonstrated the illusory nature of the prisoners' vision,

---

[1] Quoted by Miss Coburn in ibid., 2794 16.339 (Notes).
[2] *PW*, p. 132.

Socrates imagines one of them released from his bonds and forcibly dragged out of the cave up the steep ascent to the light:

'Now consider what would happen if their release from the chains and the healing of their unwisdom should come about in this way. Suppose one of them set free and forced suddenly to stand up, turn his head, and walk with eyes lifted to the light; all these movements would be painful, and he would be too dazzled to make out the objects whose shadows he had been used to see. What do you think he would say if someone told him that what he had formerly seen was meaningless illusion, but now, being somewhat nearer to reality and turned towards more real objects, he was getting a truer view? . . .
And suppose someone were to drag him away forcibly up the steep and rugged ascent and not let him go until he had hauled him out into the sunlight . . . he would then need to grow accustomed before he could see things in that upper world. At first it would be easiest to make out shadows, and then the images of men and things reflected in water, and later on the things themselves. After that, it would be easier to watch the heavenly bodies and the sky itself by night, looking at the light of the moon and stars rather than the Sun and the Sun's light in the day-time. . . . Last of all, he would be able to look at the Sun and contemplate its nature, not as it appears when reflected in water or any alien medium, but as it is itself in its own domain.'

Finally Socrates explains the meaning of his simile:

'The prison dwelling corresponds to the region revealed to us through the sense of sight, and the firelight within it to the power of the Sun. The ascent to see the things in the upper world you may take as standing for the upward journey of the soul into the region of the intelligible. . . . In the world of knowledge, the last thing to be perceived and only with great difficulty is the essential Form of Goodness . . . in the visible world it gives birth to light and the lord of light, while it is itself sovereign in the intelligible world and the parent of intelligence and truth.'[1]

[1] Plato, *Republic*, trans. F. Cornford, OUP, 1941, pp. 222–6.

This has affinities also with the *Symposium* and the *Phaedrus* for Plato, like Coleridge, certainly included Love in 'the essential Form of Goodness'. So the images of the ascent to true Reality lead away from the visible world – shadows, reflections in water, moonlight, starlight, the fire, and, finally, the light of the Sun itself. We have met them already in Coleridge's notebooks and will meet them again in the Asra poems, for they convey a great part of his philosophy of life and love.

* * *

Now, at last, we are ready to turn to the Asra poems themselves. The earliest seems to be *Love*, written in the autumn of 1799 after his first meeting with Sara. E. H. Coleridge long ago pointed out that its setting is Sockburn on the banks of the Tees where the Hutchinsons had a farm. In the church there, he tells us, '. . . there is a recumbent statue of an "arméd knight" . . . and in a field near the farm-house there is a "Grey-Stone" which is said to commemorate the slaying of a monstrous "worme" by the knight who is buried in the church.'[1] The grey stone belonged to the first version of the poem, the *Introduction to the Tale of the Dark Ladie*, but the arméd knight's statue is mentioned in *Love*. It is also sadly interesting to note that the knight wooed the 'Lady of the Land' (unsuccessfully) for 'ten long years', an ironically unconscious prophecy of the duration of Coleridge's own love. The lover meets his Genevieve by moonlight and the first verse may recall faintly Plato's vision of the absolute:

> All thoughts, all passions, all delights,
> Whatever stirs this mortal frame,
> All are but ministers of Love,
> And feed his sacred flame.

But the piteous tale of the knight driven crazy by his lady's scorn, saving her from 'outrage worse than death', and tended on his death-bed by his now remorseful beloved, 'thrilled the guileless Genevieve' more than it does us. The poem has little reality, transcendental or otherwise; one wonders whether the sane and lively Sara Hutchinson was really sufficiently ingenuous to be moved by this pseudo-medieval tale with its rather trite phrasing. The difficulty of identifying her with

---

[1] *PW*, p. 331.

Genevieve is increased by the obvious falsity of the ending which spreads a tone of rather sickly sentiment over the whole:

> I calmed her fears, and she was calm,
> And told her love with virgin pride;
> And so I won my Genevieve,
> My bright and beauteous Bride.

Sara, Professor Whalley tells us, did not include *Love* in *Sara's Poets*, her personal manuscript selection from the poems of Wordsworth and Coleridge; one would like to consider this a tribute to her natural taste.

It is unfortunate that Coleridge is represented by *Love* in so many anthologies. The next of the Asra poems, *The Keepsake*, is a far better one in every way. Professor Whalley dates it tentatively as belonging to late 1800, but some parts of it are very close in feeling to notebook entries which Miss Coburn places in October and November 1799 when Coleridge first met Sara. The first of these certainly records this meeting:

> – Few moments in life so interesting as those of an affectionate reception from those who have heard of you yet are strangers to your person.[1]

and the next entry was later elaborated twice till it became an image of the lost paradise of their love:

> – Shadow of the Tree in the ruffled water scarce distinguished from the Breeze but by its stationariness – [2]

The following entry firmly establishes the setting of the poem:

> – Oct. 28th. / We all ascended the Bank of the Tees, the high sylvan cottaged bank . . . The curve of the River . . . The rocky sylvan Bank is a single Hill, the water deep & smooth in its shadow, then rushes down at once in a rapid . . . the left finely wooded – the right a green meadow – . . . & again over the other wall of the Bridge the same scene in a long visto [sic] except that here instead of rapid a deep – solemn pool of still water, which ends in a rapid only in the far distance. – [3]

[1] N I, 493 5.104.
[2] ibid., 494 5.105, 106, f.57ᵛ. See p. 208.
[3] ibid., 495 5.107.

Professor Whalley, commenting on the poem, says:

> Whether the piece of embroidery ever existed is not known; and the
> setting of the bower and River-pool is difficult to identify.[1]

The above entry seems to me to identify it satisfactorily as the Tees near
Sara's home. The woods, shadowy reflections and smooth river-pool
are all described again in the poem:

> Softly she rose, and lightly stole along,
> Down the slope coppice to the woodbine bower,
> Whose rich flowers, swinging in the morning breeze,
> Over their dim fast-moving shadows hung,
> Making a quiet image of disquiet
> In the smooth, scarcely moving river-pool.[2]

An entry of November 1799 describes, 'The long Entrancement of a
True-love's Kiss',[3] which became in *The Keepsake*:

> Nor yet the entrancement of that maiden kiss

and in a long list of flowers which Sara copied out into Coleridge's notebook of December 1800 occurs 'Mouse-ear (= Forget me
not) . . .'[4] which shows that she had not forgotten a line of the poem
written for her:

> Hope's gentle gem, the sweet Forget-me-not!

All this helps to give *The Keepsake* a local habitation and a name, and
may point to a somewhat earlier date than Professor Whalley suggests.
The poem opens not with the river but with a harvest scene:

> The tedded hay, the first fruits of the soil,
> The tedded hay and corn-sheaves in one field,
> Show summer gone, ere come.

The foxgloves have shed 'their loose purple bells' and the rose stands,

> The thorns remaining, and the flowers all gone.

---

[1] Whalley, p. 118. [2] *PW*, p. 346.
[3] N I, 578 5.73. [4] ibid., 863 21.77, f. 15ᵛ.

The gentle melancholy of the autumn field seems a delicate evocation of this love which was doomed to unfulfilment from the start – 'summer gone ere come.' The light is 'the cool morning twilight' and the shadowy reflections of the flowers in the river-pool,

> Making a quiet image of disquiet

all suggest that, though the poem arose from authentic experience, it had moved away from it into a dream-like world of its own, slightly troubled and aware of imperfection; perhaps there is a half-conscious memory of Plato's imagery. The gently flowing, meditative rhythm contributes to this effect, and a later note of October 1803 shows us Coleridge aware of poetry as a fusion between the real and the imaginary world:

> Mix up Truth & Imagination, so that the Imag. may spread its own indefiniteness over that which really happened, & Reality its sense of substance & distinctness to Imagination / For the Soother of Absence.[1]

The delicate and dream-like melancholy of the poem is, to my mind, spoilt by the ending where the lovers meet. I very much doubt whether the embroidery ever existed; it seems a curious occupation for the 'cool morning twilight', nor is it easy to visualise Sara Hutchinson in this flowery context working her name

> Between the Moss-Rose and Forget-me-not –
> Her own dear name, with her own auburn hair!

The kiss seems real and was corroborated in the notebook, but, as in *Love*, the poem ends on a false note:

> ... she promised, that when spring returned,
> She would resign one half of that dear name,
> And own thenceforth no other name but mine!

Coleridge's recurring inability to face facts marred both his poetry and his life.

The *Ode after Bathing* and the *Ode to Tranquillity* both belong to the

[1] ibid., 1541 16.46.

summer of 1801 when Coleridge stayed with the Hutchinsons. The first is full of his delight in bathing at Scarborough and the exultation of his love for Sara:

> God is with me, God is in me!
> I cannot die, if Life be Love.[1]

looks forward to, 'Therefore the truly Beloved is the symbol of God . . .' This dream of perfect love is once again expressed in Platonic imagery:

> Dreams (the Soul herself forsaking),
> Tearful raptures, boyish mirth;
> Silent adorations, making
> A blessed shadow of this Earth!

But the fact that bathing always agreed with him could have been expressed more effectively and less pretentiously in prose:

> Dissuading spake the mild Physician,
> 'Those briny waves for thee are Death!'
> But my soul fulfilled her mission,
> And lo! I breathe untroubled breath!

The *Ode to Tranquillity* is a riot of personification and highly elaborate, artificial and Latinised in style; perhaps Coleridge was aware how much he needed peace:

> Who late and lingering seeks thy shrine,
> On him but seldom, Power divine
> Thy spirit rests . . .[2]

Towards the end, as Professor Whalley points out, '. . . Coleridge's youthful rhetoric relaxes and his own hand appears in the manuscript, his mind has personalised "Tranquillity" until it has become identified with Sara herself.'[3] The tone then becomes one of genuine feeling:

> The feeling Heart, the searching Soul,
> To thee I dedicate the whole!

* ★ * ★ *

[1] *PW*, p. 360.   [2] ibid., p. 360.   [3] Whalley, p. 110.

The *Inscription for a Fountain on a Heath* and the sonnet *To Asra*, sent to Sara with a copy of *Christabel*, seem to have been written in September 1801. The *Inscription* has a deeply personal association with both Sara and the Wordsworths, as Professor Whalley describes:

> The spring is not definitely identified, but there is little doubt that it was at or near the rock variously called 'The Rock of Names' and 'The Place of Names'; and this is perhaps identical with the 'Sara's Rock' to which Dorothy refers in her *Journal* . . . being about half-way between Keswick and Grasmere, it was a trysting-place for Coleridge and the Wordsworths. In the MS of *The Waggoner* Words-worth describes the ROCK OF NAMES in a way that makes reason-ably clear the connection between rock and spring, and the import-ance the rock held for the group of friends and lovers . . .

> An upright mural block of stone,
> Moist with pure water trickling down.
> A slender spring; . . .
> Ah dearest Spot! dear ROCK OF NAMES
> Light is the strain but not unjust
> To Thee and Thy memorial-trust
> That once seemed only to express
> Love that was love in idleness; . . .[1]

Professor Whalley also reminds us of the extract from Dorothy's *Journal* of May 1802:

> 'We parted from Coleridge at Sara's crag, after having looked at the letters which C. carved in the morning. I kissed them all. William deepened the T with C's pen-knife. . . . C. looked well, and parted from us chearfully, hopping up upon the side stones'.[2]

Coleridge's own notebook entry of September 1801, taken with the poem itself, shows that for him the spring was the symbol of 'a comfort in the strength of love', while for Wordsworth the rock stood for this; it is an illuminating indication of the difference between the two men:

> The spring with the little tiny cone of loose sand ever rising & sinking

[1] ibid., p. 120.   [2] ibid., quoted on p. 122.

at the bottom, but its surface without a wrinkle – W.W. M.H. D.W. S.H.[1]

The initials, of course, are those of Mary and Sara Hutchinson and William and Dorothy Wordsworth, the friends who were dearer to Coleridge than his own life. In the notebooks he often plays with their initials but, as Miss Coburn points out in her note on this entry, '. . . his own were usually included, as they were on the Rock of Names'. She therefore interprets the entry to mean that he felt himself excluded from the tranquil calm of the Grasmere circle and doomed to the 'Indifference or Strife' he describes in *The Letter to Asra* as his own domestic lot. This may well be so; on the other hand, Coleridge's own initials were not apparently added to the Rock of Names until May 1802, as Dorothy describes, that is eight months after he had made the notebook entry. He may merely have been describing the Rock as it then stood, recording the initials of his dearest friends as a source of comfort and strength. The calm and happy tone of the poem itself seems to fit this interpretation better. It opens once again with a tree overhanging the water:

> This Sycamore, oft musical with bees, –
> Such tents the Patriarchs loved! O long unharmed
> May all its agéd boughs o'er-canopy
> The small round basin, which this jutting stone
> Keeps pure from falling leaves![2]

The image of the stone which was, presumably, the Rock of Names, jutting out to protect the spring from the falling leaves, seems to suggest that love is more powerful than time. The importance of the notebook entries, Wordsworth's *Waggoner* and Dorothy's *Journal*, now become clear, for, without them, we could never know the full emotional implications of the poem. Another notebook entry of November 1801 clearly connects the image of the pulse with feeling: 'Every passion, say the Physicians, hath an distinct Pulse',[3] while, much later, discussing metre in the *Biographia Literaria*, Coleridge says, 'And as every passion hath its proper pulse, so will it likewise have its characteristic modes of expression.'[4] It is another example of imagina-

---

[1] N I, 980 21.132.   [2] *PW*, p. 381.   [3] N I, 1005 21.157.   [4] *BL*, p. 211.

tion connecting personal feeling with the world of art. The pulse of this spring is 'soft and even' and rises, fresh and pure, from the hidden depths:

> Long may the Spring,
> Quietly as a sleeping infant's breath,
> Send up cold waters to the traveller
> With soft and even pulse! Nor ever cease
> Yon tiny cone of sand its soundless dance,

The surface remains unwrinkled – perhaps, as Professor Whalley suggests, 'an image of permanence in the midst of change'.[1] The cool twilight is a refuge for the innocent heart and the poem ends, as it began, with the murmur of bees. The easy gentle flow of the verse with its run-on lines beautifully fits the subject which has indeed found 'its proper pulse'. What might, at first, have seemed merely a pleasant descriptive poem has a wealth of emotion behind it, but so delicately controlled and suggested that the feeling cannot be divided from the form; beneath the surface the meaning maintains its soundless dance.

The sonnet, *To Asra*, explicitly likens his love for her to a living fountain:

> Dear Asra, woman beyond utterance dear!
> This love which ever welling at my heart,
> Now in its living fount doth heave and fall,
> Now overflowing pours thro' every part
> Of all my frame, and fills and changes all,[2]

Though the poem is very clearly and smoothly developed, the thought is not quite concentrated enough for the sonnet form which gives the lines a slight rigidity less suited to the subject than the flexible rhythm of the *Inscription*. The fountain, though not technically a simile for Love, is very nearly one, for the two are set so closely side by side; yet, by this very act of definition, something of the evocative power of the image is lost. We can understand what Coleridge meant in his letter to Sotheby:

A Poet's *Heart* & *Intellect* should be *combined*, *intimately* combined &

---

[1] Whalley, p. 121. [2] *PW*, p. 361.

unified, with the great appearances in Nature, – & not merely held in solution & loose mixture with them, in the shape of formal Similies [sic][1]

The sonnet, *To Asra*, though a sincere and moving expression of love, suffers by comparison with the *Inscription for a Fountain*, perhaps because it is so much more obvious. A notebook entry made three years later in Malta shows how strongly Coleridge continued to associate the fountain with love and joy, and has a relevance also to *Dejection*:

> . . . I feel a pleasure upon me, & I am to the outward view of all cheerful, & have myself no distinct consciousness of the contrary / for I use my faculties, not indeed as once, but yet freely – but oh [Sara]! I am never happy, never deeply gladdened – I know not, I have forgotten what the *Joy* is of which the Heart is full as of a deep & quiet fountain overflowing insensibly, or the gladness of Joy, when the fountain overflows ebullient – S.T.C.[2]

*　　　*　　　*

The poems of 1802, *The Picture, A Day-Dream, The Day Dream* and the *Letter to Asra*, later revised as the *Ode to Dejection*, are all closely linked together; their relative order is more difficult to determine. E. H. Coleridge puts the two *Day-Dream* poems after *Dejection* and *The Picture*, but Professor Whalley argues, convincingly I think, that it is unsatisfactory to regard them as merely re-working material rejected from the *Letter*. He places them definitely earlier than *Dejection*. The date of *The Picture* seems to me more debatable; Professor Whalley suggests it is August 1802, four months after *Dejection*, but without any very convincing evidence. Notebook entries of March and April 1802, according to Miss Coburn's dating, seem to be linked very closely with the poem; its feeling is also, in my opinion, nearer to the *Day-Dream* poems. I, therefore, propose to consider them in the order first mentioned, since there seems to me no doubt that *Dejection*, which differs in imagery and tone from the others, was the last written; it marks a crisis in Coleridge's personal and creative life to which the earlier poems lead.

---

[1] Griggs, ii, 864.
[2] N 2, 2279 21.473.

An entry which Miss Coburn dates February–March 1802 is very like the world of *The Picture*:

> A River, so translucent as not to be seen – and yet murmuring – shadowy world – & these a Dream / Inchanted River – [1]

Another of March–April 1802 echoes Plato again not only in imagery but in phrasing:

> Quiet stream, with all its eddies, & the moonlight playing on them, quiet as if they were Ideas in the divine mind anterior to the Creation – [2]

Miss Coburn says in her Notes that the entry previous to this refers to *The Picture*:

> A Poem on the endeavor [sic] to emancipate the soul from day-dreams & note the different attempts & the vain ones – [3]

The *Day-Dream* poems themselves were, presumably, not an attempt at emancipation but rather an indulgence in this kind of escape. *The Picture* begins with the lover rejoicing in release:

> The master-passion quelled,
> I feel that I am free.[4]

and mocks the god of Love with a rather forced playfulness which perhaps protests too much:

> Chase, chase him, all ye Fays, and elfin Gnomes!
> With prickles sharper than his darts bemock
> His little Godship, . . .

For, following upon this, is the setting of tree and river, shadows and reflections, familiar to us in the Platonic notebook entries, in *The Keepsake* and the *Inscription for a Fountain*:

> Here will I seat myself, beside this old,
> Hollow, and weedy oak . . .
> Close by this river, in this silent shade,

[1] N I, 1124 6.132. [2] ibid., 1154 6.145.
[3] ibid., 1153 6.144. [4] *PW*, p. 369.

and, while proclaiming that this river never reflected his love's face, suddenly, as in a dream, he sees her:

> Behold! her open palm
> Presses her cheek and brow! her elbow rests
> On the bare branch of half-uprooted tree
> That leans towards its mirror![1]

The cheek and brow resting on the hand seem to identify the lady of the poem as Sara Hutchinson, for a notebook entry of 1804 reads:

> Artificial Brow by the hand arched over the eye / quiet vision.[2]

and a much later one, quoted by House and related chiefly to *A Day-Dream*, describes Sara at Gallow Hill in the company of Mary and Coleridge and

> . . . a dog – that dog whose restless eyes oft catching the light of the fire used to watch your face, as you leaned with your head on your hand and arm, & your feet on the *fender* / . . .[3]

Perhaps this was the same dog who suddenly appears in the sketch painted by the lady at the end of *The Picture*. In the poem itself, the lover whom we cannot now fail to recognise as Coleridge worships the lady's reflection in the stream, though aware that this is the shadow and not the substance:

> With steadfast gaze and unoffending eye,
> Worships the watery idol, dreaming hopes
> Delicious to the soul, but fleeting, vain,
> E'en as that phantom-world on which he gazed,

The lady, aware of the watcher, teases him and plucks

> The heads of tall flowers that behind her grow,
> Lychnis, and willow-herb, and foxglove bells:
> And suddenly, as one that toys with time,
> Scatters them on the pool! Then all the charm
> Is broken – all that phantom world so fair

[1] *PW*, p. 371.   [2] N 2, 1957 9.66.   [3] House, p. 147. See p. 198.

> Vanishes, and a thousand circlets spread,
> And each mis-shape the other.[1]

The foxgloves grew also in *The Keepsake*, and these are the lines which Coleridge later quoted in the Preface to *Kubla Khan* to describe the vanishing of the dream. Does this teasing gesture symbolically suggest the impatience of the real Sara, her reluctance to be worshipped as an idol, her destruction of Coleridge's fantasy image of her? It seems probable in view of two notebook entries of later years which Professor Whalley quotes. The first, originally used by Professor Raysor, was written in 1810 amid the anguish of the quarrel with Wordsworth and subsequent estrangement from Sara:

> ... for ten Years, in health and sickness, in Joy and in sorrow, in presence and absence ... I have *loved* so as I should feel no shame to describe to an Angel, and [which] as my experience makes me suspect – to an Angel alone would be intelligible.[2]

But an earlier note of 1808 gives us a vivid glimpse of Sara's reaction:

> 'My Angel'! – Nay, I am no Angel / have no wings, no glory / but flesh & Blood – The Lover's Answer, from playful to tender & from tender to grave / ⟨Sara⟩.[3]

So, once again, we see Coleridge's longing for the Platonic ideal of Love, conveyed here through the imagery of shadows and watery reflections, and in the dream-like haunting rhythm of the lines. But this was a love which could never be realised in the everyday world, as Sara obviously knew, so, when once more 'the pool becomes a mirror', the flowers and tree are reflected there but the lady has gone. The lover then turns from his fantasy to the real stream, claiming again, not very convincingly, to be: 'emancipate from Passion's dreams, a freeman, and alone', since he immediately sees the waves, separated by an island, and meeting again as an image of love:

> ... the river, whose disparted waves
> Dart off asunder with an angry sound,
> How soon to re-unite! And see! they meet,
> Each in the other lost and found ...[4]

[1] *PW*, p. 372.   [2] Whalley, p. 86.   [3] ibid., p. 137.   [4] *PW*, p. 373.

He leaves the shadows to 'pass forth into light', as in Plato's myth the light of the sun makes the shadows unreal. The poem, however, ends with what seems yet another fantasy – the lover's discovery of the picture of a child and dog, sketched with a master's haste in whortleberry juice upon a peeled birchen bark. The artist is hailed as

> Daughter of genius! stateliest of our maids!
> More beautiful than whom Alcaeus wooed,
> The Lesbian woman of immortal song!

It seems unlikely that the sketching of masterpieces on birchen bark was among Sara Hutchinson's accomplishments, and no doubt she disliked the rôle of a Sappho as much as that of an angel. The poem provides further evidence of the failure of their love, for Coleridge obstinately persisted in idealising her in one form or another; he never saw her as the flesh and blood woman she protested that she was. So he is left among the shadows and reflections, alone in the wood. One is reminded of Dante:

> Nel mezzo del cammin di nostra vita
> Mi ritrovai per una selva oscura,
> Che la diritta via era smarrita.

but Dante faced the harshest reality about himself before he reached the light of the *Paradiso* where he found Beatrice again. The best parts of *The Picture* have a dream-like haunting quality, but the structure wanders uncertainly from fantasy to a not very convincing reality and back; the least successful have a pretentiousness which betrays that the vision is not ideal but unreal.

We have already noticed the imagery of Plato and Plotinus which lies behind *A Day-Dream*:

> We sit in the Dark, but each by the side of his little Fire in his own group, & lo! the summit of the distant mountain is smitten with Light . . . we look at it, & know that the Sun is not extinguished . . . that he is coming to us, to make our fires needless . . .[1]

The Sun of absolute Good and Love will quench in its brilliance the

---

[1] N 1, 1619 21.377, f. 76. See p. 180.

small flickering light of our mortal fires but, till that day dawns, the firelight of human love can give much warmth and comfort. Coleridge describes the little fire by which he sits with 'his own group' a good many times. They are usually Sara and Mary Hutchinson or Sara alone. An entry of January 1804 records:

> A dear Room with such dear Friends, & such a dear Fire, that I seemed to love the moving Shadows on the wall, for their own sake – *das Schatten volk* – Sara & Mary – all the Time after 9 o'clock of a winter Evening, when I came down from my Study having worked hard & successfully, & surrendered myself up to Love, & innocent Sportiveness of wild fancies – [1]

Another was written, apparently, at Allan Bank in 1808, where, despite the smoky chimneys (Coleridge's room ironically was the least affected), Dorothy notes that he was

> '. . . chearful and comfortable at night. Sara and he are sitting together in his parlour, William and Mary (alas! all involved in smoke) in William's study, where she is writing for him (he dictating)' . . .[2]

Coleridge describes his side of this pleasant domestic scene:

> I fear to speak, I fear to hear you speak – so deeply do I now enjoy your presence, so totally possess you in myself, myself in you. The very sound would break the union, and separate *you-me* into you and me. We both, and this sweet Room, it's [sic] books, it's furniture, & the Shadows on the Wall slumbering with the low quiet Fire are all *our* Thought, [one dear] harmonious Imagery of Forms distinct on the still substance of one deep Feeling, Love & Joy – . . . That state, in which all the individuous nature, the distinction without Division, of a vivid Thought is united with the sense and substance of intensest Reality.[3]

It is not only the fire with its moving shadows which recalls the Cave myth but the language also – Imagery, Forms, Thought, Reality – the voice is Coleridge's voice but the terms are the terms of Plato. We can

[1] ibid., 1829 16.212.
[2] Quoted by Whalley, p. 76.
[3] ibid., p. 76.

also see more clearly now why, when he lost Sara, he felt he had lost his own identity:

> Every single thought, every image, every perception . . . some way or other it always became a symbol of *you*. I played with them, as with *your shadow*, Shakespeare has so profoundly expressed it in his Sonnet.[1]

Lastly, there is the entry, quoted by Professor Bald and later by House, with the comment that, 'The stimulus and governing principle of the whole train of association is the affection for Sara':[2]

> . . . I inevitably by some link or other return to you, or (say rather) bring some fuel of thought to the ceaseless yearning for you at my Inmost, which like a steady fire attracts constantly the air which constantly feeds it / I began strictly and as matter of fact to examine that subtle Vulcanian Spider-web Net of Steel – strong as Steel yet subtle as the Ether, in which my soul flutters inclosed with the Idea of your's – to pass rapidly as in a catalogue thro' the Images only, exclusive of the thousand Thoughts that possess the same force, which never fail instantly to awake into vivider flame the forever and ever Feeling of you – The fire / Mary, you, & I at Gallow-Hill / – or if flamy, reflected in children's round faces – ah whose children? – a dog – that dog whose restless eyes oft catching the light of the fire used to watch your face, as you leaned with your head on your hand and arm, & your feet on the *fender* . . .[3]

We see here the process by which every perception became a symbol of Sara; the fire not only flickers on the hearth at Gallow-Hill but is also 'the ceaseless yearning for you at my Inmost' so that almost any Thought can 'awake into vivider flame the forever and ever Feeling of you'. Once again, through the power of feeling, we see imagination at work; the outer and the inner, the image and the idea, the temporal and the eternal become one.

A Day-Dream, short though it is, brings together all the characteristic imagery of the Asra poems – a fountain, a willow-tree, stars and

---

[1] Raysor, 'Coleridge and Asra', *SP*, 1929, p. 321. See p. 174.
[2] House, p. 147.
[3] ibid., p. 147. See p. 194.

the crescent moon, a glowworm reflected in the water and the firelight
casting its shadow on the walls. The tree seems personal to Coleridge
and Sara but, otherwise, these are the images by which Plato suggests
the ascent from the darkness of the Cave to the light of Absolute
Reality. Yet they also hold the earthly reality of Coleridge's memories,
as a summer scene merges into a winter one with the fluid brightness
of a dream:

> 'Twas day! but now few, large and bright,
> The stars are round the crescent moon!
> And now it is a dark warm night,
> The balmiest of the month of June!
> A glow-worm fall'n, and on the marge remounting
> Shines, and its shadow shines, fit stars for our sweet fountain.
>
> . . . .
>
> The shadows dance upon the wall,
> By the still dancing fire-flames made;
> And now they slumber, moveless all!
> And now they melt to one deep shade!
> But not from me shall this mild darkness steal thee:
> I dream thee with mine eyes, and at my heart I feel thee![1]

In this poem, for once, the ideal and the real are one; through the very
perfection of the moment life achieves a measure of eternity. The
tenderness of this exquisite remembered happiness breathes through
each scene and so approaches the ideal of Love; the heart's vision is
permanent and conquers the shadows:

> Fount, tree and shed are gone, I know not whither,
> But in one quiet room we three are still together.

The stanza form is gentle yet controlled, with the couplet giving
finality and shape to each picture in the mind; the imagination has again
reconciled '. . . the idea, with the image, more than usual emotion with
more than usual order . . .' The feeling and the form have again merged
in reverie.

 Unlike *A Day-Dream*, the more personal poem which was not

---

[1] *PW*, p. 385.

published till 1828, *The Day-Dream* appeared in *The Morning Post* of October 1802. An entry in the notebook of January–February 1802:

a playful Tenderness
Touching the Heart, as with an infant's finger[1]

becomes in the poem:

A sweet and playful tenderness doth linger,
Touching my heart as with an infant's finger.[2]

The publication may explain the subterfuge of the misleading sub-title, 'From an emigrant to his absent wife', for there is no doubt that the Sara of the poem is the wife Coleridge longed for and not the one he actually had! Despite the similarity of title, stanza form and fire-light image, *The Day-Dream* is very different in feeling from its companion poem. Coleridge dreams of the home he would have liked to have:

I saw our couch, I saw our quiet room,
Its shadows heaving by the fire-light gloom;

and 'the loving mother', 'softly bending down to kiss her babe'. One remembers the firelit scene at Gallow-Hill, '. . . reflected in children's round faces – ah whose children? . . .' But Coleridge is awakened from his dream of marriage to Sara Hutchinson by the bright-eyed little boy, Frederic, who, with his 'elfish laugh' is surely a thin disguise for Hartley:

And now, when I seemed sure thy face to see,
Thy own dear self is our own quiet home;
There came an elfish laugh and wakened me:
'Twas Frederic, who behind my chair had clomb,
And with his bright eyes at my face was peeping.
I blessed him, tried to laugh, and fell a-weeping!

Since it is false in some details, more given to self-pity and wish fulfil-ment than *A Day-Dream*, it is correspondingly less moving and rich in imagery. *The Day-Dream* is concerned not with the reality of the

[1] N I, 1105 6.59.   [2] *PW*, p. 387.

happiness he and Sara had shared and which therefore remained un-touched by time, but only with the might have been.

The similarity of feeling between Coleridge's *Ode to Dejection* and Wordsworth's *Ode on the Intimations of Immortality* has often been remarked. Wordsworth too recognises that the first brightness with which his youthful imagination had illumined the earth has gone:

> Whither is fled the visionary gleam?
> Where is it now, the glory and the dream?

But his conclusion is quite different from Coleridge's; love and the music of humanity now link him to the visible world:

> Thanks to the human heart by which we live,
> Thanks to its tenderness, its joys and fears,
> To me the meanest flower that blows can give
> Thoughts that do often lie too deep for tears.[1]

For Coleridge this marriage of the outer and the inner life is broken:

> I may not hope from outward forms to win
> The passion and the life, whose fountains are within.[2]

The reason is not far to seek – indeed Coleridge himself gives it to us in *Dejection* and more fully in the *Letter to Asra*; he has lost the joy and hope of human love, the capacity to feel, and with it his imaginative power. Wordsworth was about to be married to Mary Hutchinson; Coleridge, deeply in love with her sister but imprisoned in his own unhappy marriage, must have felt the painful contrast. The *Letter to Asra* was written in April 1802 during the short and not very happy visit of the Wordsworths to Keswick. Sara was with them and seemed already to belong to the Grasmere circle in a way Coleridge at last recognised she never could to him. For the first time he faced the truth of the situation and knew that his ideal of love could never be realised. So the *Letter to Asra* and *Dejection* are different in feeling and imagery from the earlier Asra poems because Coleridge has reached a turning-point in his personal and creative life. He has lost his Platonic vision of

---

[1] Wordsworth, *Poems of 1807*, ed. H. Darbishire, OUP, 1914, p. 332.
[2] *PW*, p. 365.

the absolute and can no longer take refuge in dreams and shadows. The firelight image flickers in the *Letter to Asra* but for the last time; in *Dejection* it has disappeared.

Both the *Letter to Asra* and *Dejection* seem, in fact, to return to the imagery of Coleridge's earlier poems. They open to the wind sobbing upon the strings of the Eolian lute which had once been for Coleridge an image of the 'One Life within us and abroad'. The 'New Moon' rises with the wind, as it had done in *The Ancient Mariner* where they perhaps suggested creative power; now the 'Old Moon in her Lap' foretells the storm which, at the end, becomes completely destructive. Coleridge watches the evening sky, as the stars and moon appear,

> And those thin clouds above, in flakes and bars,[1]

Did he consciously remember:

> And straight the Sun was fleck'd with bars,[2]

and was he, by conjuring with the old images, hoping to raise the old imaginative power? If so, the attempt is vain:

> I see them all so excellently fair!
> I see, not feel, how beautiful they are.

In his unhappiness he has lost the power of feeling which makes the outer and the inner world one – the image has become divorced from the idea. So, even when he uses the fountain image, it no longer suggests love as in the *Inscription for a Fountain on a Heath* or the vital force of creative life as in *Kubla Khan*; the loss of the one has involved the loss of the other and the spring seems to have sunk back into the earth:

> I may not hope from outward Forms to win
> The Passion and the Life, whose Fountains are within!

Three years later, April 1805 in Malta, the fountain image recurs in a passage already quoted, where the reflections of the weeds growing on the sides of the well at Stowey seemed as real as those which actually '. . . grew from the bottom'. 'So' he added, 'are the happy man's *Thoughts* and *Things* . . .'[3] But *Dejection* and the *Letter to Asra* were

[1] *PW*, p. 364.   [2] ibid., p. 193.   [3] N 2, 2557 17.115. See pp. 96 and 176.

written by an *unhappy* man for whom this unity had been broken. It is significant too that, in the Malta entry, a few lines before the description of the fountain at Stowey, Coleridge, in contemplating suicide, also recalls *The Ancient Mariner*:

> – Die, my Soul, die! – Suicide – rather than this, the worst state of Degradation! . . . I work hard, I do the duties of common Life from morn to night but verily – I raise my limbs, 'like lifeless *Tools*' . . .

The fountain image and the mood of wretchedness thus link *Dejection* with *The Ancient Mariner*.

In the *Letter to Asra* several personal passages follow which were cut out in *Dejection*. The intimacy of his direct address to Sara has a tenderness lost in the later version, and the image of the dove, twice used in connection with her, suggests her influence upon *Christabel* also, as I have discussed elsewhere:

> O Sara! in the weather-fended Wood,
> Thy lov'd haunt! where the Stock-doves coo at Noon . . .

is beautifully taken up again in his prayer for her at the end where he rejoices in her happiness with the Wordsworths:

> And nested with the Darlings of thy Love,
> And feeling in thy Soul, Heart, Lips & Arms
> Even what the conjugal and mother Dove,
> That borrows genial Warmth from those, she warms,
> Feels in the thrill'd wings, blessedly outspread – [1]

The loss of this from the published version was, as House says, '. . . perhaps the worst the poem has suffered'.[2]

The description of the firelit room with Mary and Sara, which had already appeared in *A Day-Dream* and was to emerge again in the notebooks, here comes into the Asra poems for the last time:

> It was as calm as this, that happy night
> When Mary, thou & I together were,
> The low decaying Fire our only Light,
> And listen'd to the Stillness of the Air![3]

[1] Whalley, p. 164. See p. 167.   [2] House, p. 135.   [3] Whalley, p. 158.

His remorse for distressing Sara by his complaining letters now leads
him to a more selfless desire for her content:

> To all things I prefer the Permanent.
> And better seems it for a Heart, like mine,
> Always to *know*, then sometimes to behold,
>   *Their* happiness & thine – [1]

He contrasts this with the 'indifference or strife' of his own household;
then his grief rises again at the thought that Sara may be sad or in pain
and he not there to comfort her. In the *Letter to Asra* this is 'the dark
distressful dream', in whose mood he turns to

> . . . listen to the Wind
> Which long has [howled] rav'd unnoticed! What a Scream
> Of agony by Torture lengthen'd out
> That Lute sent forth!

The tortured scream of the wind obviously echoes his own agony at
his exclusion from Sara's pain, but in *Dejection*, where the personal
passage has been cut,

> Hence, viper thoughts, that coil around my mind,
> Reality's dark dream![2]

applies, as House points out, not to Sara but to his own sorrowful self-
analysis. Harsh truth has taken the place of his dream of love; with it
the snake image enters the Asra poems for the first time though not
the last.

In the *Letter to Asra* the storm leads him on to the tempest in his own
unhappy home and to the sad passages about his children whom he
loves but can never see without wishing they were Sara Hutchinson's
and not his wife's:

> My little Children are a Joy, a Love,
>   A good gift from above!
> But what is Bliss, that still calls up a Woe,
>   And makes it doubly keen
> Compelling me to *feel*, as well as KNOW,
> What a most blessed Lot mine might have been.[3]

[1] Whalley, p. 159.   [2] *PW*, p. 367. See p. 168.   [3] Whalley, p. 162. See p. 168.

This, again, has a connection with the feeling for Hartley at the end of *Christabel*.

Before the prayer for Sara's happiness, which concludes the *Letter to Asra*, he returns to his own loss of imaginative power:

> O Sara! we receive but what we give,
> And in *our* Life alone does Nature live.
> Our's is her wedding Garment, our's her Shroud –

The image of marriage follows here more naturally than in *Dejection*, for the breaking of the imaginative union between the inner and the outer world is a direct consequence of his own domestic unhappiness which he has just been describing.

As he sees his last vision of perfect Love and Joy, upon which his creative life depends and which he now recognises as unattainable, he says farewell to it once more in the images of Plato:

> O pure of Heart! thou need'st not ask of me
> What this strong music in the Soul may be,
> > What, & wherein it doth exist,
> This Light, this Glory, this fair luminous Mist,
> This beautiful & beauty-making Power!
> J o y, innocent Sara! Joy, that ne'er was given
> Save to the pure, & in their purest Hour,
> . . . .
> A new Earth and a new Heaven
> Undreamt of by the Sensual & the Proud!
> Joy is that strong Voice, Joy that luminous Cloud –
> > We, we ourselves rejoice!
> And thence flows all that charms or ear or sight,
> All melodies the Echoes of that Voice,
> All Colors a Suffusion of that Light.[1]

The *Letter to Asra* thus reveals more fully the reasons for the loss of creative power which is the subject of *Dejection*. The *Ode* has much more restraint than the *Letter* and is also far more coherent and controlled. The loose and wandering structure of the *Letter* has become firm and, though the thought and feeling remain complex, the intricate

---

[1] ibid., pp. 163–4.

and elaborate stanza form follows them with a masterly skill. Yet against the more impersonal and universal statement of *Dejection* we have to balance the loss of the *Letter*'s tenderness. The sombre power of *Dejection* lies in the terrible clarity of its self-analysis and the lucid finality of its style; the effort it cost Coleridge to achieve both can be seen in the *Letter to Asra*. *Dejection*, however, lacks the imaginative unity of Coleridge's greatest poetry. The imagery of wind, moon, lute, wedding-garment, music etc. does not really form a whole, for 'the shaping spirit of imagination' has gone. Perhaps, too, in the images of wind and moon, dove and snake, fountain and fire, Coleridge was recalling the world of *The Ancient Mariner*, *Christabel*, *Kubla Khan* and the Asra poems. Like Prospero, he summons the attendants on his creative spirit as he says farewell to his power.

★   ★   ★

After 1802 Coleridge's poems are thin and scattered. *The Pains of Sleep* of October 1803, probably written during his attempt to leave off opium, describes the horrors of his nightmares. Apart from the last lines:

> To be beloved is all I need,
> And whom I love, I love indeed.[1]

it can hardly be said to refer to Sara.

Professor Whalley dates *The Blossoming of the Solitary Date-Tree* as 1805, but some notebook entries of 1802–3 point, possibly, to an earlier date. In September 1802 Coleridge writes:

> Mother listening for the *sound* of a still-born child – blind Arab list'ning in the wilderness.[2]

In *The Solitary Date-Tree* we find the image again:

> Like a blind Arab, that from sleep doth start
> In lonesome tent, I listen for thy voice.[3]

Miss Coburn, in her note on this passage, suggests that parts of the

[1] *PW*, p. 391.   [2] N 1, 1244 21.261.   [3] *PW*, p. 396.

poem may have been earlier than 1805. Two other entries of November 1803 are very close in feeling to *The Solitary Date-Tree*:

> My nature requires another Nature for its support, & reposes only in another from the necessary Indigence of its Being. – [1]

and the next entry:

> – But one that participating in the same Root of Soul does yet spring up with excellences that I have not, to this I am driven, by a desire of Self-completion with a restless & inextinguishable Love.[2]

The Solitary Date-Tree uses the image of the grafting of a branch from another tree before the barren one can produce fruit, and speaks of 'the ache of solitariness'. But a more interesting group of entries, ranging from 1802–3, are concerned with the theme of the lost paradise which is also the subject of *The Solitary Date-Tree*'s Preface. Here Coleridge stresses the love between Adam and Eve more than their lost innocence, and in the 'guileful, false serpent's' attempt to separate them we can perhaps see why the snake enters the later Asra poems:

> While our first parents stood before their offended Maker, and the last words of the sentence were yet sounding in Adam's ear, the guileful, false serpent . . . pretending to intercede for Adam, exclaimed: 'Nay, Lord, in thy justice, not so! for the man was the least in fault. Rather let the Woman return at once to the dust, and let Adam remain in this thy Paradise.' And the word of the Most High answered Satan: '*The tender mercies of the wicked are cruel.* Treacherous Fiend! if with guilt like thine, it had been possible for thee to have the heart of a Man, and to feel the yearning of a human soul for its counterpart, the sentence, which thou now counsellest, should have been inflicted on thyself.'[3]

Now, in a notebook entry of May–June 1802, a month or so after *Dejection*, Coleridge takes up the image of the tree leaning over the water, which had definitely been associated with Sara, but, by adding

---

[1] N I, 1679 21.407.
[2] ibid., 1680 21.408.
[3] *PW*, p. 395.

the vision of the Cherubs' Swords, makes it suggest his own lost paradise:

A Light Breeze upon the *smooth* of the River, & the Shadows of the Tree turn into two-edged Cherubs' Swords.[1]

In March–July 1803, another note is still more explicit:

Et pour moi, le Bonheur n'a commencé que lorsque je l'ai en perdue. Je mettrais volontiers sur la porte du Paradis le vers, que le Dante a mis sur celle de l'Enfer.

Lasciate ogni Speranza, voi ch'entrate.[2]

Finally, in October 1803, the image is developed further and, this time, the snake enters Paradise:

Images. Shadow of the Tree in the ruffled water distinguishable from the Breeze on the water only by its stationariness – In clear water over an uneven channel, as in the Greta behind my House, a huge *Boa* convolvulus – an enormous Adder / – at other times, the waving Sword of Fire of the Cherub over Paradise.[3]

It is probable that Coleridge meant to develop these entries into a poem but they themselves are of finer imaginative quality than *The Solitary Date-Tree* which they most closely resemble. That unsatisfactory jumble of prose and verse is of little artistic value in itself, but, taken with these notebook passages of 1802–3, seems to convey the sad finality of lost love, the angel swords which bar the gates of Paradise.

Coleridge sailed for Malta on April 6th, 1804, in the hope of regaining his health and peace of mind and, perhaps, also to leave Sara free to marry someone else. The only poem which belongs definitely to the Malta period is the short but lovely *Phantom*:

> All look and likeness caught from earth
> All accident of kin and birth,

---

[1] N 1, 1199 6.170; cf. ibid., 494 5.105. See p. 185.
[2] ibid., 1373 21.232.
[3] ibid., 1589 21.312.

> Had pass'd away. There was no trace
> Of aught on that illumined face,
> Uprais'd beneath the rifted stone
> But of one spirit all her own; –
> She, she herself, and only she,
> Shone through her body visibly.[1]

Professor Whalley assigns the poem to 1805, but there seems no doubt, as Miss Coburn points out in her note on the following entry of April 1804, that it must have been written by then:

> My Dreams *now* always connected in some way or other with Isulia, all their forms in a state of fusion with some Feeling or other, that is the distorted Reflection of my Day-Feeling respecting her . . . in one or two sweet Sleeps the Feeling has grown distinct & true, & at length has created its appropriate form, the very Isulia / or as I well described it in those Lines, 'All Look' etc.[2]

Isulia' was another of his names for Sara and the image of 'distorted reflection' in dreams recalls the earlier Asra poems. Another entry, made a month later in May 1804, is a further commentary on the poem for, this time, her spirit appears to him without any resemblance to her physical form:

> . . . in some incomprehensible manner the whole Dream seems to have been – about her? nay – perhaps, all wild – no form, no place, no incident, any way connected with her! – What then? Shall I dare say, the whole Dream seems to have been *Her – She* . . . Does not this establish the existence of *a Feeling* of a Person quite distinct at all times, & at certain times *perfectly separable* from, the Image of the Person?[3]

Another entry of the same month notes the same phenomenon:

> . . . how comes it I so very rarely see those I love / I scarcely remember the time when I *saw* Wordsworth or Dorothy or the Children & very seldom Mrs C, yet I often dream of them / –[4]

[1] *PW*, p. 393. [2] N 2, 2055 15.28.
[3] ibid., 2061 15.33. See p. 9. [4] ibid., 2078 15.45, f. 36.

Finally, in February 1805, he quotes the whole of *Phantom*, preceded by the comment:

> Of Love in Sleep, the seldomness of the Feeling, scarcely ever in short absences, or except after very long Absence / a certain indistinctness, a sort of *universal-in-particularness* of Form, seems necessary – vide the note preceding and my Lines – 'All Look or Likeness caught from Earth. . .'[1]

He goes on to quote the poem entire, though later her 'brighten'd face' was altered to 'illumined'. As the poem records, the perception of the external world drops away; the Idea of Sara has become entirely separated from her Image and she belongs to the world of Essence rather than Existence. *Phantom* has a rarefied and ethereal beauty; Sara has become pure spirit, almost translucent, her face illumined by the light of transcendent Reality. The style has the same transparent spareness and delicacy, and the short lines and light stresses beautifully convey the feeling. The poem was written in Malta where he could not see her, but the danger was that, on his return, the form might not correspond with the feeling – the real Sara might be different from the illumined vision.

Recollections of Love is usually dated 1807 because of the lines:

> Eight springs have flown, since last I lay
> On sea-ward Quantock's heathy hills,

but Miss Coburn thinks parts of the poem may have been included in Coleridge's metrical experiments in Malta. She prints the first four verses with the Malta entries of October 1804, noting that the second 'is crowded in beside the previous one, for which it is clearly a second draft'.[2] The poem is close to *Phantom* in feeling, especially in lines like:

> You stood before me like a thought,
> A dream remembered in a dream.

He associates Sara with scenes he knew before he first met her, for this is a love which transcends time:

---

[1] N 2, 2441 17.15.
[2] ibid., 2224 22.15, f. 81 (Notes).

> No voice as yet had made the air
> Be music with your name; yet why
> That asking look? that yearning sigh?
> That sense of promise every where?
> Belovéd! flew your spirit by?[1]

It is again Plato's doctrine of the soul's memory of a previous existence
which may account for this sense of recognition:

> I met, I loved you, maiden mild!
> As whom I long had loved before –

Like *Phantom*, it is a beautiful and delicate poem, while the Quantock
setting, presumably added later, gives it a frame of reality:

> Eight springs have flown, since last I lay
> On sea-ward Quantock's heathy hills,
> Where quiet sounds from hidden rills
> Float here and there, like things astray,
> And high o'er head the sky-lark shrills.

The next poem mentioned by Professor Whalley is a translation of
Marini's sonnet, *Alla Sua Amico*, probably written in Malta in 1805. I
have discussed in the *Christabel* chapter the mystery of why Coleridge
chose to translate this sonnet, since it is not among the others by
Marini which he transcribes and criticises in his Malta notebooks and
yet is inferior to them in quality. One is forced to the conclusion that
it must have had some special meaning for him. If so, it marks with
Psyche a strong revulsion of feeling from idealised spiritual love to the
violence of physical passion. The story of Cecilia Bertozzoli, the siren
of Syracuse, from whose charms he was rescued by a vision of Sara's
face, shows us that Coleridge was not free from a normal man's
desires. A notebook entry of March 1805 also uses the fountain as an
image of sexual delight:

O best reward of Virtue! to feel pleasure made more pleasurable, in
legs, knees, chests, arms, cheek – all in deep quiet, a fountain with
unwrinkled surface yet still the living motion at the bottom, that
'with soft and even pulse' keeps it full . . .[2]

[1] *PW*, p. 410. [2] N 2, 2495 17.69, f. 41.

Perhaps too long a repression of this passionate side of his nature now has its revenge. The sonnet itself is crude and commonplace both in imagery and language:

> Lady, to Death we're doom'd, our crime the same!
> Thou, that in me thou kindled'st such fierce heat;
> I, that my heart did of a Sun so sweet
> The rays concentre to so hot a flame.[1]

This, is, indeed, a debasing of the image of the sun, and the sardonic humour of the last lines is cheap:

> Hell for us both fit places too supplies –
> In my heart *thou* wilt burn, I *roast* before thine eyes.

One has only to think of any poem by Donne or Shakespeare's

> The expense of spirit in a waste of shame

to recognise that this is not Coleridge's vein. The main interest of the sonnet lies in the addition of the snake image which he altered from the original. Marini's 5th and 6th lines are:

> Io che una fiera rigida adorai,
> Tu che fosti sord' aspra a' miei dolori;[2]

which Coleridge translates:

> I fascinated by an Adder's eye –
> Deaf as an Adder thou to all my pain;

But 'fiera' means 'a wild beast', not an 'adder'. Taken with *Christabel*, *The Solitary Date-Tree*, and the lost paradise entries in the notebooks, the snake certainly suggests an evil which is corrupting and debasing love. It would not be surprising if a yearning too long unsatisfied had turned, at moments, to bitterness and lust.

Psyche, though similar in feeling, is a much better poem. It was probably written in 1806–7 during Coleridge's rather uneasy reunion with Sara and the Wordsworths. The uncertainty and jealousy of these

[1] *PW*, p. 392.
[2] *PW*, ii, 1132. See p. 170.

years are clear in the notebooks; Coleridge was sick both in body and mind and shows his awareness of it in this sombre little poem:

> The butterfly the ancient Grecians made
> The soul's fair emblem, and its only name –
> But of the soul, escaped the slavish trade
> Of mortal life! – For in this earthly frame
> Ours is the reptile's lot, much toil, much blame,
> Manifold motions making little speed,
> And to deform and kill the things whereon we feed.[1]

The notebooks show that Coleridge had been fascinated for years by the process of the caterpillar becoming the butterfly, but only in the loneliness of Malta do the bitter metaphorical implications begin. Once again we can see the development from perception to symbol, here a rather painful one like the transmutation he is describing. The first entry of February–March 1803 is purely factual and scientific:

> Ichneumon laying its eggs in the body of the Caterpillar of the Purple Emperor, hatching the young ones feed on the flesh of the Caterpillar, till they arrive at their full size; when they eat their way out thro' the Skin, leaving the Caterpillar shrunk & dying . . .[2]

Another long factual entry a few pages later describes the emergence of the butterfly in great detail and, once again, stresses the caterpillar's pain:

> – The Caterpillars generally *shift* skins, once a week – they are about 7 weeks in the Caterpillar state / at the end of which time they find out a safe hiding place, where they lie 2 or 3 days, *during which time they shrink & grow shorter*, losing the use of their feet entirely, and appear as in great Agony: . . .[3]

But it is a Malta entry of December 1804 which first introduces the metaphor of love and lust:

> I addressed a Butterfly ⟨on a Pea-blossom⟩ thus – Beautiful Psyche, Soul of a Blossom that art visiting & hovering o'er thy former

<hr>

[1] ibid., p. 412.   [2] N I, 1357 8.92.   [3] ibid., 1378 21.237.

friends whom thou hadst left – Had I forgot the Caterpillar or did I dream like a mad metaphysician the Caterpillars hunger for Plants was Self-love – recollection-feeling, & a lust that in its next state refined itself into Love? – 12 Dec. 1804.[1]

A later entry of April 1805 develops this further:

> ... Worthiness, VIRTUE consist in the mastery over the sensuous & sensual Impulses – but Love requires INNOCENCE ... This is perhaps the final cause of the *rarity* of true Love, and the efficient and immediate cause of its Difficulty. Ours is a life of Probation / .... To perform Duties absolutely from the sense of Duty is the *Ideal*, which perhaps no human Being can ever arrive at, but which every human Being ought to try to draw near unto – This is – in the only wise, & verily, in a most sublime sense – to see God face to face / which alas! it seems too true that no man can do and *live*, i.e. a *human* life. It would become incompatible with his organisation, or rather it would *transmute* it, & the process of that Transmutation to the senses of other men would be called *Death* – even as to Caterpillars in all probability the Caterpillar dies – & he either does not see, which is *most* probable, or at all events he does not see the connection between the Caterpillar and the Butterfly – the beautiful Psyche of the Greeks. – Those who in this life *love* in perfection – if such there be – as in proportion as their Love has no struggles, see God darkly and thro' a Veil.[2]

This recognition that true Love can never be achieved in the ordinary human condition is important, not only for its closeness to the thought of *Psyche*, but because it is a denial of the Platonic creed of perfectibility. 'Ours is a life of probation' – the ideal cannot be reached. What personal self-disgust underlay the entry and the poem we can only guess, but it marks the last stages of Coleridge's love. 'Psyche' meant for the Greeks both 'butterfly' and 'soul' and they depicted the soul flying from the dead man's mouth in the form of a butterfly. This free and winged state, says Coleridge, can never be achieved in human life and, in trying to reach it, we hurt and destroy others in the name of love, as the butterfly destroys the caterpillar. It is a sombre vision, made more so by the reptile image which was not

[1] N 2, 2317 21.501.   [2] ibid., 2556 17.114.

present in the first version of the poem in *Sara's Poets*. There the 4th and 5th lines are:

> . . . for in this bodily Frame
> This is out Lot, much Labor & much Blame,[1]

One wonders why Sara included this poem and if she understood it. This is the second time, therefore, that Coleridge added the snake image to a love poem originally without it. Did he consciously set the snake, with its associations of the Fall of Man, against the Greek butterfly-soul metaphor, as if to repudiate the world of Plato he had loved so long? The poem is very concentrated; in lines like, 'But of the soul escaped the slavish trade / of mortal life', even the syntax becomes tortured like the feeling. Though the last line seems in apposition to 'the reptile's lot', it applies more logically to the butterfly. Nevertheless, the power of the poem lies in the tremendous impact of

> And to deform and kill the things whereon we feed.

The meaning bursts through the bonds of language as the butterfly through the caterpillar's skin.

The love of Coleridge and Sara reached a sorrowful ending in 1810 in the sharpness of the Latin poem addressed to Wordsworth, *Ad Vilmum Axiologum*:

> Me n'Asrae perferre jubes oblivia? et Asrae
> Me aversos oculos posse videre meae?[2]

which echoes the mood of his bitter pun, 'Che Sara Sara'.[3] Behind these lie many painful and jealous notebook entries, showing how deeply Coleridge resented Sara's affection for Wordsworth, innocent though it was:

> O! what mad nonsense all this would sound to all but myself – and perhaps even She would despise me for it – no! not despise – but be alarmed – and learn from *W.* – to pity & withdraw herself from my affections.[4]

---

[1] Whalley, p. 17.   [2] N 2, 3231 24.21.
[3] ibid., 3229 23.3.   [4] ibid., 3148 12.63, f. 45.

Yet it would be both sad and untrue to conclude that bitterness was Coleridge's only memory of Sara. In the lines that he wrote in the flyleaf of Menzini's *Poesie* he acknowledged with a moving dignity and simplicity all that she had meant to him. Since the joy she gave him brought both him and us closer to the secrets of his creative life, we may share his gratitude and his pain:

> I stand alone, nor tho' my heart should break,
> Have I, to whom I may complain or speak.
> Here I stand, a hopeless man and sad,
> Who hoped to have seen my Love, my Life.
> And strange it were indeed, could I be glad
> Remembering her, my soul's betrothéd wife.
> For in this world no creature that has life
> Was e'er to me so gracious and so good.
> Her loss is to my Heart, like the Heart's blood.[1]

[1] *PW*, p. 507.

CHAPTER VII

Last Poems

HIS quarrel with Wordsworth in 1810 marked a turning-point in Coleridge's life. Whether we fasten the blame on Basil Montagu's tattling tongue, on Wordsworth's coldness and self-righteousness or on his own weakness and distressing habits, the result was disastrous for Coleridge. Even before the final break took place Dorothy Wordsworth's letters describe what almost seemed to her the disintegration of his personality through opium, and what the Grasmere circle regarded as his exploitation of Sara Hutchinson. Coleridge was at this time living with the Wordsworths at Allan Bank and writing *The Friend*, most of which Sara Hutchinson transcribed at his dictation. Sara's health was not good and, finally, the strain proved too great; she left Grasmere for Wales and *The Friend* almost immediately came to an abrupt end. Dorothy's letter to Catherine Clarkson of April 1810 describes the situation with painful honesty:

... I need not tell you how sadly we miss Sara, but I must add the truth that we are all glad she is gone. True it is she was the cause of the continuance of *The Friend* so long; but I am far from believing that it would have gone on if she had stayed. He was tired, and she had at last no power to drive him on; and now I really believe that *he* also is glad that she is not here, because he has nobody to teize him. His spirits have certainly been more equable, and much better. *Our* gladness proceeds from a different cause. He harassed and agitated her mind continually, and we saw that he was doing her health perpetual injury. I tell you this, that you may no longer lament her departure. As to Coleridge, if I thought I should distress you, I would say nothing about him; but I hope that you are sufficiently prepared for the worst. We have no hope of him. None that he will ever do anything more than he has already done. If he were not under our roof, he would be just as much the slave of stimulants as ever; and his whole time and thoughts, (except when he is reading and he reads a great deal), are employed in deceiving himself, and seeking to deceive others. He will tell me that he has been writing, that he *has* written, half a Friend; when I *know* that he has not written a single line. This Habit pervades all his words and actions, and you feel perpetually new hollowness and emptiness. Burn this letter, I entreat you. I am loath to say it, but it is the truth. He lies in bed, always till after 12 o'clock, sometimes much later; and never walks out. Even the finest spring day does not tempt him to seek the fresh air; and this beautiful valley seems a blank to him.[1]

It is clear from this letter that Basil Montagu's indiscreet revelation to Coleridge of Wordsworth's warning about his personal habits merely precipitated a break which would have come anyway. The Wordsworths and Sara loved him but were powerless to help him. Three years later, in March 1813, Dorothy writes again to Catherine Clarkson:

He will not let himself be served by others. Oh, that the day may ever come when he will serve himself! Then will his eyes be opened, and he will see clearly that we have always loved him, do still [love] him, and have ever loved – not measuring his deserts. I do not now wish him to come into the North; that is, I do not wish him to do it for the sake of any wish to gratify us. But if he should do it of himself, I should be glad as the best sign that he was endeavouring to perform his duties.[2]

She was, of course, referring to Coleridge's responsibility for his children and, in other places, sorrowfully described how frequently Hartley used to ask if there were any news of his father.

Coleridge never returned to the North. He entered now upon his darkest years of loneliness, self-reproach and homelessness. His deeply affectionate nature had for long identified himself with the Grasmere circle, as a pathetic algebraic note made in Malta reminds us:

[1] *Letters of William and Dorothy Wordsworth*, ed. E. de Selincourt, OUP, 1935–9, i (The Middle Years), 365–6.
[2] ibid., ii, 556.

$$\overline{W + D + MW} + SH + \overline{HDSC} = STC.$$
$$= \text{Ego contemplans.}[1]$$

'HDSC' stands for his children, Hartley, Derwent and Sara; the other
initials need no explanation. They were engraved upon the Rock of
Names and still more indelibly upon Coleridge's heart. After the break
with Wordsworth and the loss of Sara, it is no exaggeration to say that
he felt as if he had lost his own identity. A note of October 1810,
written just before the quarrel, shows this clearly:

> My love of, κθy [Asra] is not so much in my Soul, as my soul in
> it. . . . To bid me not love you were to bid me annihilate myself –
> for to love you is all I know of my life as far as my life is an object
> of my Consciousness or my free Will.[2]

A further cry of desolation refers to his loss of Wordsworth:

> A Friend and a Lover therefore are not impossible or superhuman
> Things. Yet – what many circumstances ought to have let me see
> long ago, the events of the last year, and emphatically of the last
> month, have now freed me to perceive – No one on earth has ever
> LOVED me. Doubtless, the fault must have been partly, perhaps
> chiefly, in myself. . . . For alas! even in Love & Friendship we gain
> only what we arrogate.[3]

In 1812, writing to Wordsworth on the death of his son, Thomas, he
cries again, 'There is a sense of the word, Love, in which I never felt
it but to you & one of your Household.'[4] It was true that much of the
fault was his own, untrue that the Wordsworths did not love him. Yet
Coleridge's feeling is the truth with which we are most concerned and
there is no doubt that we are witnessing a death of the heart. He has lost
all who have given meaning to his life. No-one ever took their place
nor did he recover the meaning again.

The years from 1810 to 1816, when he found his final refuge at
Highgate, were, perhaps, the loneliest and most hopeless of all. Unable
to face life with his wife or the proximity of the Wordsworths, he
wandered from lodging to lodging, a slave to increasing doses of

---

[1] N 2, 2389 21.594.
[3] ibid., p. 87.
[2] Quoted by Whalley, p. 85.
[4] Griggs, iii, 424.

opium, the despair of his friends and of himself. At times he found temporary harbour with the Morgans who were themselves always insecure and in debt. It is no wonder that the little poetry he wrote is an expression of despair. *The Suicide's Argument* of 1811 makes the voice of Nature say:

> Think first, what you are! Call to mind what you were!
> I gave you innocence, I gave you hope,
> Gave health, and genius, and an ample scope.
> Return you me guilt, lethargy, despair?
> Make out the invent'ry; inspect, compare!
> Then die – if die you dare![1]

Limbo, in 1817, with its memories of Dante and of the ghost of his own Mariner, is the more powerful and moving cry of a lost soul:

> The sole true Something – This! In Limbo's Den
> It frightens Ghosts, as here Ghosts frighten men.
> . . . .
> 'Tis a strange place, this Limbo! – not a Place,
> Yet name it so; – where Time and weary Space
> Fettered from flight, with night-mare sense of fleeing,
> Strive for their last crepuscular half-being; –
> Lank Space, and scytheless Time with branny hands
> Barren and soundless as the measuring sands,
> Not mark'd by flit of Shades, – unmeaning they
> As moonlight on the dial of the day![2]

The imagery of ghosts, shadows and nightmare recalls his earlier poetry but is more haunting because he himself now knew this limbo of the spirit where all meaning has been lost. Some lines have a concentrated power and strangeness:

> Fettered from flight, with night-mare sense of fleeing,

or

> Lank Space and scytheless Time with branny hands
> Barren and soundless as the measuring sands,

[1] *PW*, p. 419. [2] ibid., pp. 429–30.

This is, indeed, almost the last we are to see of the poet who wrote *The Ancient Mariner*; the sage of Highgate produced something very different.

Coleridge went to the Gillmans as a temporary measure in a desperate attempt to control his opium taking under a doctor's care. But his personality soon exerted its spell and he remained with them from 1816 till his death in 1834. Highgate provided him at last with a refuge and tranquillity and the opium habit became disciplined to a great extent – but too late both for his life and for his poetry. Resignation and moralising took the place of passion; his last years were years of prose. Occasionally a rare meeting with Sara Hutchinson or a memory of her roused a flicker of the old fire and the old pain. Then, for a moment, the poetry too has a faint echo of its earlier power and the old images recur. But, in nearly twenty years, there are only a handful of poems which rise above mediocrity and these are unequal. Miss Coburn, in an interesting recent article on the imagery of the poems and notebooks of the Highgate years, claims that '. . . Coleridge continued to the end to think and feel as a poet'.[1] This, indeed, is true but it is not the same as to write like one. *Kubla Khan* and *Work without Hope* belong to different kinds of poetry, and it seems no service to Coleridge's reputation not to distinguish between them.

Using several hitherto unpublished notebook entries, Miss Coburn traces a very fascinating pattern of imagery which appears both in them and in the later poems. The images of mirror, fountain, tree, the baby at the breast, the spider and the bee, she sees as all connected with Coleridge's long search for the self, his need to find a personal identity. The loss of his earlier loves, as I have suggested, made the search more urgent. The mirror in which the self is reflected has clear associations. The fountain and the breast are both sources from which life is drawn, and the baby gradually acquires by touch an awareness both of himself and of others. The tree has its root in the nourishing soil and the bee is another image of fertility. The spider, by contrast, is negative and predatory, just as the tree can become barren or the fountain dry up. As often in Coleridge, the imagery can be ambivalent and, if I understand Miss Coburn's argument correctly, this suggests that both nourishing sympathy and opposition or, at least, an awareness of

[1] K. Coburn, 'Reflections in a Coleridge Mirror', in *From Sensibility to Romanticism*, ed. F. W. Hilles and H. Bloom, New York, OUP, 1965, p. 415.

'otherness' are necessary for the discovery of the self. The following passage sums up a great deal of her essay:

> The mirror reflects the image of the inward self. It also distances the self from itself. The intervention of a reflecting surface, whether warm, animate, or cold and inanimate, asserts the essential severance of the self from the other, from the image even, and inspires, with whatever of fear and awe it is capable, the need to bridge the gap, whether by philosophy or by poetry, between the percipient and the perceived.[1]

This seems to me illuminating and true but surely it also points to a weakness in Coleridge's later poetry. In *The Ancient Mariner* and *Kubla Khan* and all his greatest imaginative work the poet had been merged in his creation. He had lived in his Mariner and become the inspired poet with 'flashing eyes and floating hair'; we are never conscious of his own identity as separate from theirs. It is the condition of imaginative, as of other, power that you lose life in order to find it. The gap between the percipient and the perceived Coleridge had already bridged triumphantly; it is the weakness of the later poetry that he can no longer do so.

Coleridge's greatest poetry had had the brilliance, vividness and fluidity of dreams. As we have seen, he was intensely aware of the mingling of conscious and unconscious processes in poetic creation. The fusion of the two in the act of poetry explains, as far as anything can, the miracle of the great poems. But opium and its attendant evils which had once merely made his dreams more vivid had, in his later years, loosed all the hell of the unconscious mind upon him. Like Macbeth he was afraid to go to sleep, in horror of

> . . . the affliction of these terrible dreams
> That shake us nightly: . . .

As opium acquired a greater hold upon him he had even come to link dreams and the unconscious with the origin of evil. An interesting notebook entry made in Malta shows how aware he was of the dangers of surrender to day-dreams. The sad irony is that the mingling of the

---

[1] K. Coburn, 'Reflections in a Coleridge Mirror', op. cit., p. 433.

conscious and the unconscious mind in reverie had been the source of his greatest poetic power:

> There are few Day-dreams that I dare allow myself at any time. . . .
> So akin to Reason is Reality, that what I could *do* with exulting Innocence, I can not always *imagine* with perfect innocence / for Reason and Reality can stop and stand still, ~~by~~ [sic] new Influxes from without counteracting the Impulses from within, and *poising* the Thought. But Fancy and Sleep *stream on*. . . I have ~~acted~~ [sic] done innocently what afterwards in absence I have ⟨likewise⟩ day-dreamed innocently, during the being awake; but ~~after~~ [sic] the Reality was followed in Sleep by no suspicious fancies, the ~~latter~~ [sic] Day-dream *has* been. Thank Heaven! however / Sleep has never yet desecrated the images, or supposed Presences, of those whom I love and revere. . . . All the above-going throw lights on my mind with regard to the origin of Evil.[1]

Coleridge had every reason to fear the activity of the unconscious mind. This is probably why, in the *Biographia Literaria*, he laid so much stress on the conscious will in imaginative creation and debased the power of association to the lower level of fancy. His rejection of eighteenth century materialism, of course, underlies this also, but the evidence the early notebooks reveal of the part day-dream played in his poetic creation seems partially to contradict the later philosophic position in the *Biographia*. The last poems of the Highgate years seem to have been composed entirely at the conscious level; many are even self-conscious. This may have been better for Coleridge's peace of mind but it weakened his imaginative power – the tree withers without its deep roots.

An interesting, though not very perspicuous, notebook entry, hitherto unpublished, which Miss Coburn quotes in her recent article, shows Coleridge still preoccupied with this problem of Imagination:

> The image-forming or rather re-forming power, the imagination in its passive sense, which I would rather call Fancy-Phantasy . . . may not inaptly be compared to the Gorgon Head, which *looked* death into every thing – and this not by accident, but from the

[1] N 2, 2543 17.101. See p. 150.

nature of the faculty itself, the province of which is to give consciousness to the Subject by presenting to it its conceptions *objectively* but the Soul differences itself from any other Soul for the purposes of symbolical knowledge by *form* or body only – but all form as body, i.e. as shape, & not as forma efformans, is dead . . . Here then is the error – not in the faculty itself, without which there would be no *fixation*, consequently no distinct perception or conception, but in the gross idolatry of those who abuse it, & make that the goal & end which should only be a means of arriving at it. Is it any excuse to him who treats a living thing as inanimate Body, that we cannot arrive at the knowledge of the living Being but thro' the Body which is its Symbol, & outward & visible Sign? – ★

★From the above deduce the worth & dignity of poetic Imagination, of the fusing power, that fixing unfixes & while it melts & bedims the Image, still leaves in the Soul its living meaning – [1]

Though this contains Coleridge's familiar warning against the purely passive Fancy which partook of death, he, nevertheless, implies that it is an essential part of Imaginative activity. The last part of the entry is, as Miss Coburn says, 'a caution against "dead letter" interpretations of living meanings by "fixing" the images too rigidly.'[2] It is a warning some of Coleridge's critics might have done well to heed. The true Imagination, as Coleridge said in the *Biographia*, fuses 'the idea with the image'[3] so that we cannot see any dividing line. This is the power which 'fixing unfixes & while it melts & bedims the Image, still leaves in the Soul its living meaning – .' Just because *The Ancient Mariner* and *Kubla Khan* are imaginatively alive, their meaning cannot be rigidly pinned down. In the last poems, however, the images are all too obviously fixed. Their meaning has become so confined and definite as almost to approach the method of allegory. It is another sign of the death of the imagination which we shall examine in more detail later.

Coleridge himself again issued a warning against confusing allegory with symbolism. This occurs in a well-known passage in *The Statesman's Manual* of 1817 and, though it is set in a religious context, it is relevant also to poetry:

[1] K. Coburn, 'Reflections in a Coleridge Mirror', op. cit., p. 419.
[2] ibid., p. 419.
[3] *BL*, p. 174.

It is among the miseries of the present age that it recognises no *medium* between literal and metaphorical. Faith is either to be buried in the dead letter, or its name and honours usurped by a counterfeit product of the mechanical understanding, which in the blindness of self-complacency confounds symbols with allegories. Now an allegory is but a translation of abstract notions into a picture-language, which is itself nothing but an abstraction from objects of the senses. ... On the other hand a symbol (ὁ εστω ἀει ταντηγόριχον) is characterised by a translucence of the special in the individual, or of the general in the special, or of the universal in the general; above all by the translucence of the eternal through and in the temporal. It always partakes of the reality which it renders intelligible; and while it enunciates the whole, abides itself as a living part of that unity of which it is the representative.[1]

After reading this condemnation of the abstract method of allegory, so similar to the warning against 'fixed' imagery, it is disturbing to turn to the poetry of the later years and find so many poems with the subtitle, 'An Allegory'. *Time, Real and Imaginary; The Pang more Sharp than All; Love's Apparition and Evanishment*, are all called 'allegories'. Even where this is not so, the following titles have a dismaying abstraction: *Faith, Hope and Charity; Youth and Age; Work without Hope; Constancy to an Ideal Object; Duty Surviving Self-Love; Love, Hope and Patience in Education; Love and Friendship Opposite; Self-Knowledge; Forbearance*. In many cases the content is as dismaying as the title, full of lifeless personifications or ponderous moralising, expressed frequently in flat or archaic style. These poems are all too consciously 'literary', indebted to Spenser or Boccaccio or, as Miss Coburn has shown, to Quarles' *Emblems*.[2] Coleridge seems almost to be returning to the literary imitations of his youth, but the old poet who has lost his own voice is sadder than the young poet who had still to find it. As so often, Coleridge himself has the last word. In the closing year of his life he told his nephew:

After all you can say, I still think the chronological order the best for arranging a poet's works. All your divisions are in particular

---

[1] *The Statesman's Manual*, ed. Derwent Coleridge, Moxon, 1852, pp. 32–3.
[2] K. Coburn, 'Reflections in a Coleridge Mirror', op. cit., pp. 425–7.

instances inadequate, and they destroy the interest which arises from watching the progress, maturity, and even the decay of genius.[1]

If we judge the poems of his decay harshly, it is because we set so high a value on the poems of his maturity.

*   *   *

As we turn to the later poems themselves, it is kinder to pass many of them over in silence and dwell only on those which have some poetic quality. *Youth and Age* has grace and pathos and, on the whole, a clarity of style which gives dignity to the acceptance of growing old. The imagery of bee and blossom for the creativity of youth which is now lost lends vitality to the personifications of the opening lines:

> Verse, a breeze mid blossoms straying,
> Where Hope clung feeding, like a bee –
> Both were mine! Life went a-maying
> With Nature, Hope, and Poesy,
> When I was young![2]

It is interesting to see poetry still associated with the creative wind, as the Malta notebooks seem to suggest. The directness of the following passage is also moving when we remember the many notebook accounts of Coleridge's marathon climbs and walks in the Lake District:

> When I was young? – Ah, woful When!
> Ah! for the change 'twixt Now and Then!
> This breathing house not built with hands,
> This body that does me grievous wrong,
> O'er aery cliffs and glittering sands,
> How lightly then it flashed along: –
> . . . .
> Nought cared this body for wind or weather
> When Youth and I lived in't together.

The self-pity which makes his letters painful is, however, also present in the tone – 'Ah, woful When!' and 'This body that does me grievous wrong'.

The memories of wind and flowers and lakes, all the free elemental

---

[1] *Table Talk*, OUP, 1917, p. 286.   [2] *PW*, p. 439.

things which had once filled his poetry, may explain the poverty of natural imagery in the later poems. The suburban seclusion of Highgate was no substitute for Stowey or the Lake District.

The next lines are especially significant in the light of the notebook entry on 'fixed' imagery and of *The Statesman's Manual* on allegory:

> Flowers are lovely; Love is flower-like;
> Friendship is a sheltering tree;
> O! the joys, that came down shower-like,
> Of Friendship, Love, and Liberty,
> Ere I was old!

The flat and definite equation of Love with flowers and Friendship with a tree surely shows that the images *have* become too fixed. The allegorical method has deprived them of the imaginative translucence. The meaning has become limited to one level; no other can shine through. If we look back for a moment to two of the Asra poems, we can see what has happened. *The Keepsake* uses the image of flowers for love – but how differently:

> The foxglove tall
> Sheds its loose purple bells, or in the gust,
> Or when it bends beneath the up-springing lark,
> Or mountain-finch alighting. And the rose
> (In vain the darling of successful love)
> Stands, like some boasted beauty of past years,
> The thorns remaining, and the flowers all gone.[1]

The sadness of the foxglove and rose, bereft of their petals in this autumn scene, suggests with delicate restraint that the love of Coleridge and Sara was doomed to unfulfilment from the start. 'Love is flower-like' suggests very little and is rigid by comparison.

In the *Inscription for a Fountain on a Heath* the tree was used as an image for friendship and love:

> This Sycamore, oft musical with bees, –
> Such tents the Patriarchs loved! O long unharmed
> May all its agéd boughs o'er-canopy
> The small round basin, which this jutting stone
> Keeps pure from falling leaves![2]

[1] ibid., p. 345.　　　　　　　　　[2] ibid., p. 381.

The tree which leans protectively over the welling spring of water again subtly evokes the 'comfort in the strength of love' which Coleridge shared with the Wordsworths and Sara Hutchinson. 'Friendship is a sheltering tree' has lost all this wealth of suggestive power. Moreover, the foxglove bending beneath the bird's weight, the sycamore's agéd boughs and the jutting stone which was, of course, the Rock of Names, all have a real life of their own. Just because they belong to the world of actual experience, they can also become something more and suggest 'the translucence of the eternal through and in the temporal',[1] which Coleridge himself said distinguished symbol from allegory. The tree and flowers of *Youth and Age* have become abstract and fixed and have lost the fluidity which 'while it melts and bedims the Image still leaves in the Soul its living meaning'.[2] The image and the idea are no longer fused; greater rigidity is also a sign of poetic age.

Miss Coburn, in her recent article, traces some interesting correspondences between *Work without Hope*, 1825, and an unpublished notebook entry of the same date which also contains some variants of the poem. The images of mirror and spider occur in the note and some of the revisions, though not in the final version of *Work without Hope*. Part of the entry reads:

> I have often amused my ~~fancy~~ [sic] self with the thought of a Self-conscious Looking-glass, and the various metaphorical applications of such a fancy ... there was something pleasing and emblematic (of what I did not distinctly make out) in two such Looking-glasses fronting, each seeing the other in itself, and itself in the other ...
>
> . . . .
>
> as we advance in years, the World, that *spidery* Witch, spins its threads narrower and narrower, still closing in on us, till at last it shuts us up within four walls ...

One experimental revision of the poem in the same entry reads:

> The World her spidery threads on all sides spun,
> Side answ'ring Side with narrow interspace;
> My Faith (say, I: I and my Faith are one)

---

[1] *The Statesman's Manual*, p. 33.
[2] K. Coburn ,'Reflections in a Coleridge Mirror', op. cit., p. 419.

> Hung, as a Mirror there! And face to face
> (For nothing else there was, between or near)
> One Sister Mirror hid the dreary Wall.[1]

The attempt to find himself in the looking-glass (Mrs Gillman was apparently the 'Sister Mirror'!) and the sense of life closing in upon him like a spider's web both seem clear. They contrast effectively with the vigour and movement of the poem's opening lines and might, possibly, have been a more effective ending than the one which Coleridge finally adopted. The first lines describe the busy activity of Spring in contrast with the poet's unproductiveness:

> All Nature seems at work. Slugs leave their lair –
> The bees are stirring – birds are on the wing –
> And Winter slumbering in the open air,
> Wears on his smiling face a dream of Spring!
> And I the while, the sole unbusy thing,
> Nor honey make, nor pair, not build, nor sing.[2]

The bee is, again, an image of fertility – and the poet who can no longer sing or 'honey make' undoubtedly recalls *Kubla Khan*:

> He on honey-dew hath fed,
> And drunk the milk of Paradise.

The Paradise imagery continues in the second half of the poem, as finally published, with the fountain, the amaranth and nectar, but this is no longer a creative burst whose power flings up the sacred river. The clumsy archaisms, apostrophes and rhetorical question are also stylistic evidence of poetic sterility:

> Yet well I ken the banks where amaranths blow,
> Have traced the fount whence streams of nectar flow.
> Bloom, O ye amaranths! bloom for whom ye may,
> For me ye bloom not! Glide, rich streams, away!
> With lips unbrightened, wreathless brow, I stroll:
> And would you learn the spells that drowse my soul?
> Work without Hope draws nectar in a sieve,
> And Hope without an object cannot live.

[1] ibid., pp. 423–4. [2] *PW*, p. 447.

Miss Coburn points out that the last two lines have an allegorical source in Quarles's Emblems. She prints the engraving and the poem which accompanied it, explaining:

> It will be seen that the pictured globe with four smaller circles within it, two on each side, is so engraved or cut as to seem to portray two large breasts each like a mirror and each with a mirror above it. At each of the earth-mother's breasts is a child in fool's cap and bells, one sucking with hands conspicuously grasping the full round 'milky flood', the other child-fool opposite 'straining' the 'treasure' 'into an empty sieve'.[1]

The lines which Miss Coburn quotes from Quarles's poem are:

> 'And thou, whose thriveless hands are ever straining
> Earth's fluent breasts into an empty sieve,
> That always hast, yet always art complaining,
> And whin'st for more than earth has pow'r to give;'[2]

Yet, though all this fascinating erudition throws light on the last lines of *Work without Hope*, it does not make them any better poetry. It merely confirms again the abstract allegorical tendency of Coleridge's later verse. The image of 'Work without Hope' drawing 'nectar in a sieve' comes self-consciously from a literary source and does not blend with the more natural imagery of the rest of the poem.

The Two Founts, 1826, shows how far Coleridge could debase and deaden the once living image of the fountain. Troubled by the illness of a lady who recovers 'with unblemished looks from a severe attack of pain', Coleridge dreams of a Dwarf who delivers himself of the following gnomic pronouncement:

> In every heart (quoth he) since Adam's sin
> Two Founts there are of Suffering and of Cheer!
> That to let forth, and this to keep within![3]

Constancy to an Ideal Object is a much better poem and, on internal evidence, seems to have been inspired by the memory of Sara Hutchin-

---

[1] K. Coburn, 'Reflections in a Coleridge Mirror', op. cit., p. 427.
[2] ibid., p. 426.
[3] *PW*, p. 454.

son. Professor Whalley lists it among the Asra poems. The opening lines, in their pursuit of the Absolute, have a yearning rhythm and directness of language which recall the great Coleridge:

> Since all that beat about in Nature's range,
> Or veer or vanish; why shoulds't thou remain
> The only constant in a world of change,
> O yearning Thought! that liv'st but in the brain?
> Call to the Hours, that in the distance play,
> The faery people of the future day – [1]

He soon drops into allegory, however:

> Fond Thought! not one of all that shining swarm
> Will breathe on thee with life-enkindling breath,
> Till when, like strangers shelt'ring from a storm,
> Hope and Despair meet in the porch of Death!

and even into sentimentality:

> I mourn to thee and say – 'Ah! loveliest friend!
> That this the meed of all my toils might be,
> To have a home, an English home, and thee!'

Then follows a strangely haunting reminiscence of *The Ancient Mariner*:

> The peacefull'st cot, the moon shall shine upon,
> Lulled by the thrush and wakened by the lark,
> Without thee were but a becalméd bark,
> Whose Helmsman on an ocean waste and wide
> Sits mute and pale his mouldering helm beside.

This is one more piece of evidence showing how closely 'The steersman's face by his lamp gleamed white', is associated with the poet's personal feeling.

The last lines too hold memories of the shadow imagery of the Asra poems:

> And art thou nothing? Such thou art, as when
> The woodman winding westward up the glen

[1] ibid., p. 455.

At wintry dawn, where o'er the sheep track's maze
The viewless snow-mist weaves a glist'ning haze,
Sees full before him, gliding without tread,
An image with a glory round its head;
The enamoured rustic worships its fair hues,
Nor knows he makes the shadow, he pursues!

This seems to be one of Coleridge's bitter flashes of self-knowledge.
The shadow is only a projection of the self. We seem again to hear
Dorothy Wordsworth's voice:

> With respect to Coleridge, do not think that it is his love for Sara
> which has stopped him in his work. Do not believe it: his love for
> her is no more than a fanciful dream. Otherwise he would prove it
> by a desire to make her happy. . . .[1]

The Pang more Sharp than All was probably inspired by a meeting
with Sara Hutchinson in Ramsgate in 1823. It uses the imagery of the
baby at the breast, the magic glass and the blossom blown loose from
the tree which, as Miss Coburn suggests, are probably part of the search
for the self. But the poem is an allegory, as its sub-title says, full of
personifications and memories of the style of Spenser. The third verse,
with its clumsy archaisms and allegorical characters, is fairly typical of
the whole:

> Like a loose blossom on a gusty night
> He flitted from me – and has left behind
> (As if to them his faith he ne'er did plight)
> Of either sex and answerable mind
> Two playmates, twin-births of his foster-dame: –
> The one a sturdy lad (Esteem he hight)
> And Kindness is the gentler sister's name.
> Dim likeness now, though fair she be and good,
> Of that bright Boy who hath us all forsook; –
> But in his full-eyed aspect when she stood,
> And while her face reflected every look,
> And in reflection kindled – she became
> So like Him, that almost she seem'd the same![2]

[1] *Letters of William and Dorothy Wordsworth,* ed. E. de Selincourt, i (The Middle Years), 367.   [2] *PW*, p. 458.

One can only conclude that Coleridge's awareness of the loss of Sara's love is no longer intense enough for him to speak frankly. Or, perhaps, he is again employing his old method of cipher to hide the harshness of reality even from himself. Yet there are moments when the pain breaks through the veil of allegory and can still move us:

> One pang more blighting-keen than hope betray'd!
> And this it is my woeful hap to feel,
> When, at her Brother's hest, the twin-born Maid
> With face averted and unsteady eyes,
> Her truant playmate's faded robe puts on;
> And inly shrinking from her own disguise
> Enacts the faery Boy that's lost and gone.
> O worse than all! O pang all pangs above
> Is Kindness counterfeiting absent Love!

The Garden of Boccaccio is perhaps the best of the last poems. The personal note is present but does not dominate and, in many ways, Coleridge loses himself imaginatively in Boccaccio's world. There is, however, no doubt that the description of Boccaccio's paradise stirred memories of his own. Miss Coburn again quotes a late notebook passage which contains a version of some lines of the poem, with his own comment:

> And there was young Philosophy
> Unconscious of herself-pardie,
> And now she hight: Poesy –
> And like a child, in life-ful glee
> Had newly left her Mother's knee,
> Prattles and plays with flower and Stone,
> As if with faery play-fellows
> Revealed to Innocence alone –

Exerts the powers excited in her as ~~the~~ [sic] passive or negative subject by the Mother & becoming in her turn positive acts upon her Toys, like Light, that meeting eyeless things falls back & so reflects the image of her inward self.[1]

[1] K. Coburn, 'Reflections in a Coleridge Mirror', op. cit., p. 433.

As he read Boccaccio, Coleridge did find an image of himself:

> And one by one (I know not whence) were brought
> All spirits of power that most had stirr'd my thought[1]

Once again, roused probably by the imagery of an idyllic garden, a fountain and a maiden with a lute, memories of *Kubla Khan* dimly return:

> Now wander through the Eden of thy hand;
> Praise the green arches, on the fountain clear
> See fragment shadows of the crossing deer;
> And with that serviceable nymph I stoop,
> The crystal from its restless pool to scoop.
> I see no longer! I myself am there,
> Sit on the ground-sward, and the banquet share.
> 'Tis I, that sweep the lute's love-echoing strings,
> And gaze upon the maid who gazing sings:

Later lines are a delicate evocation of the spirit of medieval Florence and have the grace and charm of a Primitive painting. One can see the brightly clad youths and maidens against the background of the Tuscan garden with its dark cypress trees:

> Or pause and listen to the tinkling bells
> From the high tower, and think that there she dwells.
> With old Boccaccio's soul I stand possest,
> And breathe an air like life, that swells my chest.
> The brightness of the world, O thou once free,
> And always fair, rare land of courtesy!
> O Florence! with the Tuscan fields and hills
> And famous Arno, fed with all their rills;
> Thou brightest star of star-bright Italy!

The poem has a literary and, perhaps, slightly mannered charm but it is delightful to find Coleridge once more able to lose himself in the world of another. The last lines are as vivid as a medieval illustration and have even a touch of mischief. He describes the 'fauns, nymphs and wingéd saints':

[1] *PW*, p. 478.

Still in thy garden let me watch their pranks,
And see in Dian's vest between the ranks
Of the trim vines, some maid that half believes
The vestal fires, of which her lover grieves,
With that sly satyr peeping through the leaves!

The forgetfulness of self was only momentary. As Miss Coburn says, 'The pathos of Coleridge's problems is that he is haunted by not being able to fix an image of himself; the image in the natural glass is always restless, changing, bedimmed, misted over by qualifications and reservations'.[1] She then quotes a last touching entry which is close to the poem *Phantom or Fact*:

One lifts up one's eyes to Heaven as if to see there what one had lost on Earth / Eyes – Whose Half-beholdings thro' unsteady tears Gave shape, hue, distance to the inward Dream /[2]

In the poem he has a vision of his 'own spirit newly come from heaven',[3] at first gentle and calm, then changing to

That weary, wandering, disavowing look!

A friend asks:

This riddling tale, to what does it belong?
Is't history? vision? or an idle song?
Or rather say at once, within what space
Of time this wild disastrous change took place?

The Author replies in another of those flashes of self-knowledge:

Call it a moment's work (and such it seems)
This tale's a fragment from the life of dreams;
But say, that years matur'd the silent strife,
And 'tis a record from the dream of life.

It is one more proof of how truth came to Coleridge in dreams, even the painful truth about himself. The saddest thing is to watch the life

---

[1] K. Coburn, 'Reflections in a Coleridge Mirror', op. cit., p. 433.
[2] ibid., p. 434.   [3] *PW*, p. 485.

of dreams, which had once been the world of his greatest poetry, turn into the dream of life.

Self-Knowledge, 1832, deals with the old Greek maxim, 'Know Thyself', but this Coleridge finds impossible:

> – What is there in thee, Man, that can be known? –
> Dark fluxion, all unfixable by thought,
> A phantom dim of past and future wrought,[1]

So he turns in his perplexity to Him Who may, perhaps, offer a solution:

> Vain sister of the worm, – life, death, soul, clod –
> Ignore thyself, and strive to know thy God!

His *Epitaph* which he wrote a few months before his death again recalls *The Ancient Mariner*. The ghost of Life-in-Death which had haunted him so long is nearly laid. The lines are not very good poetry but have that disarming quality which still makes it difficult, as it did in his life-time, to know Coleridge and not love him:

> Stop, Christian passer-by! – Stop, child of God,
> And read with gentle breast. Beneath this sod
> A poet lies, or that which once seem'd he.
> O, lift one thought in prayer for S.T.C.;
> That he who many a year with toil of breath
> Found death in life, may here find life in death!
> Mercy for praise – to be forgiven for fame
> He ask'd, and hoped, through Christ. Do thou the same![2]

[1] *PW*, p. 487. [2] ibid., pp. 491-2.

Select Bibliography

Works by S. T. Coleridge

Aids to Reflection (with *Confessions of an Inquiring Spirit*), Bell, 1904.
Anima Poetae, ed. E. H. Coleridge, 1895.
Biographia Literaria, ed. G. Watson, Everyman, 1956.
Christabel, Kubla Khan and *The Pains of Sleep*, Murray, 1816.
Christabel, ed. E. H. Coleridge (with MS. facsimiles), Royal Society of Literature, 1907.
The Friend, ed. H. N. Coleridge, 3 vols., 1837.
Inquiring Spirit (from the unpublished Notebooks), ed. K. Coburn, 1951.
Collected Letters, ed. E. L. Griggs, Vols I–II (1785–1806), OUP, 1956.
— Vols. III–IV (1807–1819), OUP, 1959.
Coleridge on Logic and Learning, ed. A. Snyder, New Haven, 1929.
Lyrical Ballads, 1798, 1800 and 1802.
Miscellaneous Criticism, ed. T. M. Raysor, Constable, 1936.
Notebooks, ed. K. Coburn, Vol. I (1794–1804), Routledge & Kegan Paul, 1957. (Text and Notes.)
— Vol. II (1804–1808), Routledge & Kegan Paul, 1962. (Text and Notes).
Poems, ed. E. H. Coleridge, 1 vol., OUP, 1912.
Poetical Works, Vol. II, ed. E. H. Coleridge, OUP, 1912.
Shakespearean Criticism, ed. T. M. Raysor, 2 vols., Constable, 1930.
Sibylline Leaves, Rest Fenner, 1817.
The Statesman's Manual, ed. Derwent Coleridge, Moxon, 1852.
Table Talk (with *Omniana*), Preface by H. N. Coleridge, OUP, 1917.
Treatise on Method, ed. A. Snyder, Constable, 1934.

Other Works

Abrams, M. H., *The Milk of Paradise*, Cambridge, Mass., 1934.
— *The Mirror and the Lamp*, OUP, 1953.

Abrams, M. H., 'Structure and Style in the Greater Romantic Lyric', *From Sensibility to Romanticism*, OUP, 1965.

Allsop, T., *Letters, Conversations and Recollections of S. T. Coleridge*, 1836.

Baker, J. V., *The Sacred River*, Louisiana Univ. Press, 1957.

Bald, R. C., 'Coleridge and "The Ancient Mariner"', *Nineteenth Century Studies*, ed. H. Davis, W. de Vane, R. C. Bald, Cornell Univ. Press, 1940.

Baxter, Andrew, *An Enquiry into the Nature of the Human Soul*, 2 vols., 1745.

Beer, J., *Coleridge the Visionary*, Chatto & Windus, 1959.

Bodkin, M., 'A Study of "The Ancient Mariner" and the Rebirth Archetype', *Archetypal Patterns in Poetry*, OUP, 1934.

Bostetter, E., *The Romantic Ventriloquists*, Univ. of Washington Press, 1963.

Bowra, C. M., ' "The Ancient Mariner" ', *The Romantic Imagination*, OUP, 1950.

Burke, K., *The Philosophy of Literary Form*, New York, 1957.

Bush, D., *Mythology and the Romantic Tradition in English Poetry*, New York, 1957.

Campbell, J. D., *Coleridge: A Narrative of the Events of his Life*, 1894.

Chambers, E. K., *Coleridge: A Biographical Study*, OUP, 1938.

Coburn, K., 'Coleridge Redivivus', *The Major English Romantic Poets*, Illinois, 1957.

— 'Reflections in a Coleridge Mirror', *From Sensibility to Romanticism*, ed. F. Hilles and H. Bloom, New York, OUP, 1965.

Cottle, J., *Early Recollections of S. T. Coleridge*, 2 vols., 1837.

Cudworth, R., *The True Intellectual System of the Universe*, 1743.

Dante, *The Divine Comedy*, trans. M. Anderson, World's Classics, 1921.

De Quincey, T., *Recollections of the Lake Poets*, 1854.

Eliot, T. S., *Selected Essays*, Faber, 1932.

— *The Family Reunion*, Faber, 1939.

Euripides, *The Bacchae*, trans. H. Milman, Rinehart, 1960.

Gillman, J., *Life of Coleridge*, Vol. I, 1838.

Guthrie, W. K., *The Greeks and their Gods*, Methuen, 1950.

Haney, J. L., *A Bibliography of S. T. Coleridge*, Philadelphia, 1903.

Hanson, L., *Life of S. T. Coleridge: The Early Years*, 1939.

Harrison, J., *Prolegomena to the Study of Greek Religion*, CUP, 1922.

House, H., *Coleridge*, Hart-Davis, 1953.

James, D. J., *The Romantic Comedy*, OUP, 1948.

— *Scepticism and Poetry*, Allen & Unwin, 1937.

Jones, J., *The Egotistical Sublime*, Chatto & Windus, 1954.

Kennedy, V. and Barton, M. N., *Samuel Taylor Coleridge: A Selected Bibliography*, Baltimore, 1935.

Kermode, F., *Romantic Image*, Routledge & Kegan Paul, 1957.

Knight, G. W., 'Coleridge's Divine Comedy', *The Starlit Dome*, Methuen, 1959.

Lamb, C., *Letters*, ed. E. V. Lucas, 3 vols., 1935.

Logan, Sister E., *A Concordance to Coleridge's Poetry*, Indiana, 1940.

Lowes, J. L., *The Road to Xanadu*, rep. Vintage Books, New York, 1959.

Maurice, T., *The History of Hindostan*, Vol. I, London, 1795.

— Vol. II, London, 1798.

Milton, J., *Poetical Works*, ed. H. Beeching, OUP, 1938.

Muirhead, J., *Coleridge as Philosopher*, Allen & Unwin, 1930.

Nethercot, A. N., *The Road to Tryermaine*, Chicago, 1939.

Pausanias, *The Description of Greece*, 3 vols., trans. T. Taylor, London, 1794.

Piper, H. W., *The Active Universe*, Athlone Press, 1962.

Plato, *Ion*, trans. P. B. Shelley, Everyman.

— *Phaedo*, trans. F. J. Church, Golden Treasury series, 1946.

— *Phaedrus*, trans. R. Hackforth, Library of Liberal Arts, CUP, 1952.

— *Republic*, trans. F. Cornford, OUP, 1941.

— *Symposium*, trans. W. Hamilton, Penguin Classics, 1951.

Powell, A. E., *The Romantic Theory of Poetry*, Arnold, 1926.

Raysor, T. M., ed., *The English Romantic Poets* (A review of research), 2nd edition, 1956.

Richards, I. A., *Coleridge on Imagination*, 1934.

Robinson, H. Crabb, *Diary, Reminiscences and Correspondence*, ed. T. Sadler, 3 vols., 1869.

Schneider, E., *Coleridge, Opium and 'Kubla Khan'*, Chicago, 1953.

Snyder, A., *The Critical Principle of the Reconciliation of Opposites as employed by Coleridge*, Ann Arbor, 1918.

Suther, M., *The Dark Night of Samuel Taylor Coleridge*, Columbia Univ. Press, 1960.

Taylor, T., *A Dissertation on the Eleusinian and Bacchic Mysteries*, London, 1791.

—, trans., *The Hymns of Orpheus*, London, 1787.

Tomlinson, C., ' "Christabel" ', *Interpretations*, ed. J. Wain, 1955.

Warren, R. P., Essay on *The Rime of the Ancient Mariner*, Reynal & Hitchcock, New York, 1946.

Whalley, G., *Coleridge, Sara Hutchinson and the Asra Poems*, Routledge & Kegan Paul, 1955.

Willey, B., 'Samuel Taylor Coleridge', *Nineteenth Century Studies*, Chatto & Windus, 1949.

Wind, E., *Pagan Mysteries in the Renaissance*, Faber, 1958.

Wordsworth, D., *Journals*, ed. H. Darbishire, World's Classics, 1958.

Wordsworth, W., *Prelude* (1805), ed. E. de Selincourt, OUP, 1933.

— *Poems of 1807*, ed. H. Darbishire, OUP, 1914.

Wordsworth, W. and D., *Letters*, ed. E. de Selincourt, 6 vols., OUP, 1935–9.

Yeats, W. B., *Collected Poems*, Macmillan, 1934.

ARTICLES IN PERIODICALS

Bostetter, E., 'The Nightmare World of "The Ancient Mariner" ', *Studies in Romanticism*, Summer 1962, I, iv.

— ' "Christabel": The Vision of Fear', *Philological Quarterly*, 1957.

Coburn, K., 'Coleridge, Wordsworth and "The Supernatural" ', *Univ. of Toronto Quarterly*, 1955–6.

Marsh, F., 'The Ocean-Desert: "The Ancient Mariner" and "The Waste Land" ', *Essays in Criticism*, 1959.

Purves, A. C., 'Formal Structure in "Kubla Khan" ', *Studies in Romanticism*, Spring 1962, I, iii.

Raysor, T. M., 'Coleridge and "Asra" ', *Studies in Philology*, 1929.

Shelton, J., 'The Autograph Manuscript of *Kubla Khan* and an Interpretation', *Review of English Literature*, January 1966, VII, i, pp. 32–3.

Watson, G., 'The Meaning of "Kubla Khan" ', *Review of English Literature*, January 1961, II, i.

Whalley, G., 'The Mariner and the Albatross', *Univ. of Toronto Quarterly*, 1947.

— 'Coleridge Unlabyrinthed', *Univ. of Toronto Quarterly*, 1963.

General Index

General Index

Index of Coleridge's Poems

244

dream' with *Dejection* version, 168; sorrowful feeling for his children compared with *Christabel's* conclusion, 168; loss of Joy in, 173, 190; marks turning point in C's personal and creative life, reflected in change of imagery, 201–2; has an intimate tenderness lost in *Dejection*, 203–5; farewell to Joy expressed in Platonic imagery, 205

Asra Poems, The, 8, 30, 231, their imagery anticipated in early poems, 30–3; their imagery related to *Christabel*, 167–71; intimate record of C's love for Sara Hutchinson, 172; importance of feeling in his creative life and critical theory, 173–4; uneven in quality, 174; parallel notebook entries show imaginative process at work, 174–8; C's search for the Absolute in Love and Platonic imagery of, 178–84; *see also* individual poems

Asra, To, 191–2

Autumnal Moon, To the, 28

Bathing, Ode after, 188

Birth of a Son, Sonnet on, 55

Boccaccio, The Garden of, 233–5

Bowles, Sonnet to, 30

Christabel, 2, 3, 7, 8, 122, 189, 203, 206, 211

144–71, opening lines suggest threatening evil, 144; links with Dorothy Wordsworth's *Journal*, 144–5; tension between good and evil reflected in style, 146–7; parent and child theme enters poem, 147; appeal of poem made more subtle in later versions, 147; end of Part I terrible mockery of mother and child relationship, 148; notebook entry suggests that Geraldine comes from C's own dreams, 149; notebooks again associate evil and dreams, 150; Crashaw's lines on Saint Theresa and theme of martyrdom, 151; C. intended

Christabel's suffering to have a redemptive power, 152; Wordsworth's refusal to include *Christabel* in second edition of *Lyrical Ballads*, 152–3; key to puzzle may be lines on Hartley, 153–4; letters of 1800–1 reveal distress in which Part II was written, 154–6; sombre opening of Part II, 156; theme of anger destroying love central to poem, 157; snake image enters poem, 157–8; Christabel rejected by her father, 159; vision of evil more frightening than in *The Ancient Mariner*, 159; late notebook refers to Christabel's 'desolation', 159; C. sees evil as disease of the will and associates it with snake image in notebooks, 160–1; other snake references in notebooks, 161; personal meaning of *Christabel*, 162; evil indistinguishable from good—the dove becomes the snake, 162; story of poem became separated from inner meaning, 163; conclusion to Part II expresses C's own bitter personal feeling, 163–4; yet it also completes parent-child theme and is key to meaning, 164–6; notebook entries in cipher reveal similar situation in C's own life, 166–7; dove and snake imagery of some *Asra* poems reinforce personal theme of *Christabel*, 167–71

Constancy to an Ideal Object, 231–2

Day-Dream, A, 9, 174, 196–9

Day-Dream, The, 169, 200

Dejection, Ode to, 9, 30, 78, ironically foreshadowed in *The Nightingale*, 105; Coleridge laments loss of poetic power in image of fountain in, 132, 192; snake image related to *Christabel*, 168; loss of Joy in, 173; sad self-knowledge in, 174; interpreted by Prof. Suther as C's failure to find the Absolute, 179; cf. with Wordsworth, *Ode on the Intimations of Immortality*, 201;

Index of Coleridge's Poems